Experience Design

Experience Design

Concepts and Case Studies

Edited by Peter Benz

Bloomsbury Academic
An imprint of Bloomsbury Publishing Plc

B L O O M S B U R Y
LONDON • NEW DELHI • NEW YORK • SYDNEY

Bloomsbury Academic

An imprint of Bloomsbury Publishing Plc

50 Bedford Square   1385 Broadway
London   New York
WC1B 3DP   NY 10018
UK   USA

www.bloomsbury.com

Bloomsbury and the Diana logo are trademarks of Bloomsbury Publishing Plc

First published 2015

© Peter Benz 2015

British Library Cataloguing-in-Publication Data
A catalogue record for this book is available from the British Library.

ISBN: HB: 978-1-4725-7114-4
PB: 978-1-4725-6939-4
ePDF: 978-1-4725-7109-0
ePub: 978-1-4725-7113-7

Library of Congress Cataloging-in-Publication Data
Experience design : concepts and case studies / [edited by] Peter Benz.
pages cm
Includes bibliographical references and index.
ISBN 978-1-4725-7114-4 (hardback)-- ISBN 978-1-4725-6939-4 (paperback) 1. Industrial design--Psychological aspects. 2. Consumers--Attitudes. I. Benz, Peter, editor.
TS171.E97 2015
745.2019--dc23

Typeset by Fakenham Prepress Solutions, Fakenham, Norfolk NR21 8NN
Printed and bound in India

Contents

List of Illustrations

List of Illustrations

Foreword and Acknowledgements

"Experience Design as a discipline is so new that its very definition is in flux," wrote Nathan Shedroff in his introduction to *Experience Design 1*. Despite the passage of more than a decade since then, remarkably little seems to have changed: Experience Design as a discipline in its own right remains underdeveloped. In the Foreword of the 2011 edition of their book, *The Experience Economy*, Joseph Pine and James Gilmore lament their similar observation: "Although the book [*Experience Economy*, 1999] has since been published in fifteen languages and purchased by more than three hundred thousand people worldwide, the book's thesis has not sufficiently penetrated the minds of enough business leaders (and policy makers) to give bloom to a truly new—and desperately needed—economic order."

One would like to add that the same is true about the penetration of the design community with concepts, principles, and methodologies for designing experience. One could therefore be tempted to dismiss the entire notion of Experience Design as a kind of "professional bubble" that didn't stand the test of time, and simply forget about it.

Nevertheless, the notion of "experience" as an economic value is well accepted today, and it is common practice in a variety of professional (design) fields to refer to some sort of "experience" as one practice outcome. Lingo such as "experiential marketing" and "brand experience" permeates the advertising business, down to the most common levels of promotional communication, producing such redundant slogans as "Feel the Experience" (the slogan of Daytona International Speedway, Kazy Music, and others). Similarly "product experience," "customer experience," but also "travel experience," "educational experience," and other similar experiential derivations are commonly accepted notions within almost any new product or service development.

Thus another picture emerges; although "experience" is clearly a design issue, Experience Design remains "stuck" in playing a poorly defined service role for other areas, and, in this sense, is merely one approach among a number of competing concepts. The full potential of Experience Design as a distinct creative discipline in its own right still needs to be articulated and recognized academically and professionally.

With this background in mind it was the intention of this book to collect "over-the-shoulder-looks" of the current state of discourse about the notions that underlie the designing of experiences: What is "experience"? How can specific "experiences" be constructed purposefully, i.e. through which means can experiences be designed, regardless of their medial articulation? What are the possible methodologies and practices to be used? What are the influences, overlaps, and relations of Experience Design with other academic/professional disciplines? And so on.

To achieve this endeavour academics and professionals from the field were invited to submit their proposals in an open call for abstracts initially circulated through relevant online forums in late 2012. From the submissions received, the final list of contributors was subsequently selected through double-blind peer review: Every proposal was vetted twice, once by an academic, once by a professional with an Experience Design background, producing ultimately a normalized score to rank the papers.

While a lot of lip service is paid to interdisciplinarity as an academic practice, for many reasons it doesn't happen as often as would be desirable. With this experience in mind I am very happy that the authors of *Experience Design: Concepts and Case Studies* represent a selection of academic and professional thinkers from four continents, with backgrounds as diverse as Architecture, Design, Fine Art, IT, Psychology, and the Social Sciences, contributing their particular disciplinary views on the making of experiences. The contributors to this book believe that only through such practice Experience Design—an area that is inherently interdisciplinary—can be adequately studied.

As a result *Experience Design: Concepts and Case Studies* attempts to strike a balance between academic rigor and validity, professional applicability, and intellectual accessibility to accommodate its readership of creative professionals and academics with backgrounds in disciplines such as (User) Experience Design, Interaction Design, Product Design and/or Architecture, as well as from Psychology, Sociology and other social sciences—many of which are represented through the contributors to the book. I hope and expect that our joint efforts will provide insight and reason for further discussion.

I would like to express at this point my gratitude to the initial reviewers of the submitted papers who spent time and effort to see through many abstracts at a stage at which this project might still have failed: Professor Matthew Turner from the School of Creative Industries, Napier University Edinburgh, United Kingdom; Professor Linda Leung of the Institute for Interactive Media & Learning, University of Technology Sydney, Australia; Professor Yang Wenqing, College of Design and Innovation, Tongji University Shanghai, China, and Director of LOE Design, Shanghai, China; Mr Kingsley Ng, recently my new colleague at the Academy of Visual Arts, Hong Kong Baptist University, Hong Kong, but then with Jack Morton Worldwide, Hong Kong; and Ms. Effie Chou, Senior Principal Designer, Pico International, Hong Kong. I'm indeed very grateful for the faith these colleagues have shown in me, despite not knowing some of them before working together on this volume.

I am similarly grateful to Ms. Rebecca Barden, Senior Commissioning Editor Design at Bloomsbury London, and her assistant Ms. Abbie Sharman, who have been as supportive as can be throughout the process of developing this book.

Finally, this book shall not go to press without my acknowledging the impact my students from the Experience Design concentration of the Academy of Visual Arts' Master of Visual Arts-program have had on me and my work in recent years. Without the challenges and fun my encounters with them have brought to me—especially with the class of 2013—I might not have gotten as involved with this area to such an extent. Among all of those students, especially Ms. Wong Mei-Yin deserves special mention in this context for all the help and support in IT-matters she provided over the last two years while producing this publication.

To all of you, and those many more who offered help and support but are not specifically mentioned:

Thank you.
Peter Benz

About the Authors

Xavier Acarin holds a MA in Museum Studies from New York University and is a MA candidate at the Center for Curatorial Studies at Bard College. He has worked as an art producer and researcher for various art institutions, among others, Centre d'Art Santa Mònica (Barcelona), SITE Santa Fe, Creative Time, International Studio and Curatorial Program, and The Kitchen. His writings on art are published regularly on A-desk and others.

Barbara Adams studies the creative practices of artists, designers, and social scientists. She has written for artists and art institutions, and recently edited the book *Design as Future-Making* with Susan Yelavich (Bloomsbury, 2014). She teaches at the New School, Eugene Lang, and Parsons.

Peter Benz currently has a position as Associate Professor at the Academy of Visual Arts of Hong Kong Baptist University, where he is responsible for the coordination of the Master of Visual Arts (Experience Design) program, in which he also teaches. With a background in architecture, he takes particular interest in the experiential aspects of spatial designs, especially of "undesigned" marginal urban spaces.

Felix Bröcker originally trained as a cook and then obtained a degree in Film Studies and Philosophy from the University of Mainz. He is now doing a master in Curatorial Studies in Frankfurt/Main to observe interrelations of art and cooking. He works as a student research assistant for Prof. Dr. Thomas Vilgis in the Food-Project at the Max-Planck-Institute Mainz, and contributes to projects of Prof. Dr. Werner Sommer, that consider the interrelations of gastronomy and psychology.

Ian Coxon, Associate Professor of Experience-based Designing at the Institute of Technology and Innovation, University of Southern Denmark, is interested in the structure and epistemology of human experience. His most current research interests in this regard focus on fostering an *Ecology of Care*—promoting a healthier, more balanced zone of care between humans and technology by better understanding what is meaningful in a person's everyday lived experience and bringing this into the intentionality that constitutes designing.

Catherine Elsen is an Associate Professor at the University of Liège (Belgium) and Research Affiliate at Massachusetts Institute of Technology (USA). Her research interests cover design processes (in architecture and industrial design), and more specifically the impact design tools have on specific cognitive processes (integration of end-users' needs; creativity; cooperation between team members).

Amy Findeiss works to uncover sparks of innovation through learning about how people see, feel, and Experience Design. Much of her work is focused on understanding human behaviors, motives, and intrinsic values to identify opportunities for participatory engagement.

Silvia Grimaldi is a researcher and lecturer at London College of Communication, University of the Arts London, where she is Course Leader of the BA (Hons) Spatial Design and in the past has run the BA (Hons) Graphic Product Innovation. Her research focuses on product experience, narratives, and emotional design, in particular on the role of surprise in eliciting product emotions, and more recently on the influence of narrative in users' interpretation of product experience.

Eulani Labay believes that complex social issues can be addressed through moments of cooperation and play. Her understanding of theatrical design and performance, media, and cities has led her to design experiences and interactions with the potential to create transformative shifts in awareness.

Pierre Leclercq is a Professor at the University of Liège. He has led various fundamental and applied research projects that all relate to a multidisciplinary approach of design engineering. His primary research interests are design computing and cognition, artificial intelligence in design, human–computer interaction in design, and sketching interfaces.

Linda Leung is an Associate Professor in the Faculty of Engineering & IT at the University of Technology Sydney, Australia. She is author of *Digital Experience Design: Ideas, Industries, Interaction* (Intellect, 2008). As director of postgraduate studies in Interactive Media at the University of Technology Sydney, she is concerned with the design of technologically mediated experiences or User Experience (UX) as it is known in the field of IT. Her research interest is in how minority groups and marginalized communities appropriate technology for their needs.

Manuel M. Loeches is a cognitive psychologist working at the Universidad Complutense, Madrid. In various constellations he has collaborated with Annekathrin Schacht, Werner Sommer, and Birgit Stürmer on questions in psycho-linguistics, emotion, and cognitive control, combining behavioral with psychophysiological measurements.

Tara Mullaney is a design researcher who employs a research-through-design approach to investigate cancer patient experiences of radiotherapy treatment, and the role that design construction can play in understanding and critiquing existing social, technological, and institutional boundaries within healthcare. She also tutors, lectures, and advises graduate thesis projects within the MFA Interaction Design program at the Umeå Institute of Design (UID), Umeå University, Sweden.

Claus Østergaard is an Assistant Professor at Aalborg University researching mobile-user experiences as well as teaching courses and facilitating workshops in Experience Design and Interactive Digital Media. As he is also interested in researching cross-cultural aspects of mobile-user experience design he stayed at the Interfaculty Initiative in Information Studies at the University of Tokyo in 2012.

Kristine Munkgård Pedersen is a lecturer at the Performance Design-program of the Department of Communication, Business, and Information Technologies of Roskilde University, Denmark. Her research is mostly on issues of space and experience, spanning from analysis of tourism to investigations in festival planning and design.

Rosie Parnell is Senior Lecturer at the School of Architecture, University of Sheffield. Her research, practice, and teaching combine interests in design participation, architecture education, and children's spaces.

Lakshmi P. Rajendran is currently a PhD student at the School of Architecture, University of Sheffield. Based on studies carried out in Sheffield, her on-going research aims towards developing a spatial-behavioral model for studying identity construction in multicultural urban spaces.

Gretchen C. Rinnert is an Assistant Professor in the School of Visual Communication Design at Kent State University. She primarily teaches interactive media and motion design. Her research focuses on the intersection of design and education as a way to improve participation and comprehension. More recently her work merged with health and wellbeing.

Annekathrin Schacht is a cognitive psychologist working at the Georg-August Universität Göttingen. In various constellations she has collaborated with Manuel Martín-Loeches, Werner Sommer, and Birgit Stürmer on questions in psycho-linguistics, emotion, and cognitive control, combining behavioral with psychophysiological measurements.

Michael Shanks is an archaeologist and Professor at Stanford University. He is a Co-Director of *The Revs Program* at Stanford, whose mission is to connect the past, present, and future of the automobile, was a Co-Director of Stanford Humanities Lab, is affiliated with the Hasso Plattner Institute of Design at Stanford (d.school), and with CARS (Center for Automotive Research at Stanford). His lab in Stanford Archaeology Center is called *Metamedia*.

Werner Sommer is a cognitive psychologist working at the Humboldt-Universität zu Berlin combining behavioral with electroencephalographic measurements. In various constellations he has collaborated with Manuel Martín-Loeches, Annekathrin Schacht, and Birgit Stürmer. His current interests are in the Psychology of meals, individual differences in face and emotion recognition, and psycho-linguistics with a special emphasis on reading.

Sara M. Strandvad is Associate Professor at the Performance Design-program of the Department of Communication, Business, and Information Technologies of Roskilde University, Denmark. She has authored various publications in the field of cultural sociology, including a study of development processes in Danish film production, based on the perspective of a socio-material sociology of art.

Birgit Stürmer is a cognitive psychologist working at the International Psychoanalytic University, Berlin. In various constellations she has collaborated with Manuel Martín-Loeches, Annekathrin Schacht, and Werner Sommer, on questions in psycho-linguistics, emotion, and cognitive control, combining behavioral with psychophysiological measurements.

Connie Svabo is Associate Professor and Head of Studies in Performance Design at Roskilde University. From 2010 to 2013 she was project leader for the innovation theme *Experiencescapes* in the Danish national innovation network on experience economy, where she contributed to two large experience design projects: one for a UNESCO heritage geological site and one for a new museum on World War I. She recently co-edited *Situated Design Methods*, with Simonsen, Strandvad, Samson, Herzum, and Hansen (MIT Press, 2004).

Kelly Tierney focuses her work on both infrastructural, and social systems, designing experiences, behaviors and measures for transformational change. She creates visions for the future for communities, objects, services, experiences, and behaviors focused on a variety of contexts including disaster preparedness, healthcare reform, public spaces, and ownership.

Matthew Turner completed his PhD. on "Ersatz Design" at the Royal College of Art, and has since published widely around the world. He has also worked with a number of museums to develop exhibitions such as "Made in Hong Kong" (1988), "Designing Identity" (1994), and "Multi-Stories" (2000). He developed the "Asian Design" syllabus at Hong Kong Polytechnic University's School of Design before returning to Scotland as Head of Design at Edinburgh Napier University, where he is now Professor Emeritus. More recently he acted as Director of the Hong Kong Art School (2006), Visiting Scholar at the Academy of Visual Arts, Hong Kong Baptist University (2010), and Thinker in Residence at HKPU's Design Institute for Social Innovation (2013).

Stephen Walker is Reader and Director of the Graduate School of Architecture, University of Sheffield. His research area broadly encompasses art, architectural, and critical theory, and examines the questions that such theoretical projects can raise about particular moments of architectural and artistic practice.

Editorial Introduction and Considerations
Matthew Turner

It is easy to see why exhilarating ideas about experience design, experiential marketing and even the experience economy should have emerged in the United States two decades ago, during the roaring 90s.

Capital poured into "invisibles" such as financial services, tourism, or design that could be experienced but not weighed. Disembodied brands escalated in value above the objects to which they were attached, while share prices of immaterial dot-coms soared above those of substantial industries. As real manufacturing was offshored, stock markets surged on thin-air futures and derivatives, as bankers were loosed from regulation and, as it transpired, from reality.

Contributors to this volume explore in more detail the sea change in corporate strategy that followed, in which user experience came to be seen as a new resource for value creation. This was not simply a product of the 1990s bubble. As several writers in this collection observe, the change may be seen as a culmination of ideas put forward decades earlier by proponents of the post-industrial society.

However we interpret the 90s ideal of a coming experience economy, it clearly offered a vision of future prosperity beyond materialistic consumption, and this may have secured its widest appeal. For here was a chiliastic vision of twenty-first century capitalism, not capitalism triumphant but transcendent, cool, purified, and sensuous: a designer utopia.

It is less easy to see why this vision should retain its appeal today, after the bursting of the dot-com bubble, the return of global insecurity and instability, and the collapse of the global economy after 2008.

Accordingly, the design scholars and practitioners assembled in this volume critically explore the substance behind the rhetoric of experience design. In the opening section they turn to fundamental questions neglected by the pioneers of experience design. Just what *is* experience, and what theories or methods help us to grasp its manifold forms? And two decades after the assertion that the experience of commodities would be transformed into the commodification of experience, they evaluate the extent to which such claims have been realized in practice.

Critical exploration can be dangerous territory, for the commodification of experience is not without a history, or critics. For centuries, intellectuals have inveighed against the metropolis, or capitalism, or the mass media, or global corporations for diminishing and corrupting human experience.

As early as the mid-eighteenth century, Rousseau saw authentic experience being dissolved in the whirlpool of spectacle and fashion that was the modern metropolis. A century later, Marx grieved that capitalism had wrested our deepest experiences of love, virtue, and conscience into the marketplace of tradable commodities. And in the last century Walter Benjamin gloomily chronicled the ways in which collective experience and shared memory had atrophied under relentless assaults of media spectacle and disconnected, individual consumption. Over the last hundred years these critiques were also dramatized, first as dystopian novels from *We* to *1984*, then as popular attacks on advertising and branding from *The Hidden Persuaders* to *No Logo*. Finally, the theme runs through a score of Hollywood blockbusters that portray dystopian futures satiated with consumer delights, but in which human experience is surveilled, manipulated, standardized, and controlled by a corporate state.

Paranoiac movies aside, there are now practical concerns about the extent to which individual experience is mediated, manipulated, and merchandized by digital technologies. The enhanced user experience offered by web-based companies and internet giants has taken a toll on personal privacy. The scale of data collected on search histories and social media use may be insidious, if not pernicious—as the scale of global online surveillance by the National Security Agency and its partners has revealed.

If the pioneers of experience design were not burdened by ethical or political concerns this was largely because, two decades ago, the web was in its infancy and the potential for gathering intimate data on entire populations was inconceivable.

Confronting contemporary ethical dilemmas in experience design is a crucial issue for contributors to this book. Each surveys the subject from a different standpoint and takes differing positions on its moral and political implications. Some question the inflated scope of experience design, others its status as a practice. For not all subjects need a formal discipline or a profession. Experience, like play, or love, offers inexhaustible scope for reflection without recourse to professional "ludics" or "amatology."

Part One: Positions

Contributors to the first part of this collection also take differing positions on the particular theoretical understanding of experience essential for design practice. This is hardly surprising. Philosophers are sharply divided in their approach to experience, while the major branches of psychology have largely neglected the subject. While psychologists intensively study cognitive and affective modes of thought, they rarely discuss the conative, although this mode promises greater insight for design. Nevertheless, the authors in Part One all draw attention to philosophers' advocacy of experience as a collaborative, communal enterprise, and implicitly agree with Donald Norman, pioneer of the term "user experience design," who later rejected the word "user" as unhelpfully isolating and alienating.

Ian Coxon opens the first section by introducing the principal philosophy of experience: phenomenology. In particular, he explores distinctions drawn by Heidegger and others between experience as shared memory and wisdom, and experience as everyday sensation, event, and spectacle. Although the latter is the normal sphere for design, Coxon considers the potential, as well as the problems of designing embodied, shared experience. The problem, in Coxon's view, is reconciling the diversity of experience with the designer's impulse to standardization. His conclusion is that philosophers and designers alike are only at the beginning of an understanding of experience.

Connie Svabo and Michael Shanks approach the nature of experience from another perspective by introducing us to the philosophy of Michel Serres. While this self-professed chaotician dismisses phenomenology and disregards pragmatism, his views on collective memory and embodied knowledge share many insights with both Heidegger and Dewey. Svabo and Shanks discuss Serres' use of weaving as a metaphor for the indivisibility of experience between the body and world, and consequently his rejection of unitary explanations for the complexity of experience. The authors advocate Serres' concept of flux, here related to the psychologist Mihaly Csikszentmihalyi's idea of "flow," as a perspective that lends support to the complexity of design practice.

Catherine Elsen and Pierre Leclercq expand this section with a discussion of time: a crucial dimension of experience for phenomenologists as well as Serres. Their case studies are studio projects used to investigate professional designers' strategies to imagine what experiences audiences may have of their product. Elsen and Leclercq are intrigued that in "staged" studio sessions designers generated as many insights into imagined audiences as in real professional projects (yet in about half the time). They suggest that shorter, more reflective ideation sessions, including tools for "disciplined creativity," might be the way to reach prolific and efficient insights about end-users.

Linda Leung concludes this section by invoking a troublesome ethical dimension of experience design. The author's premise is that, as a new refinement on "user-experience" for "target markets," Experience Design is inherently exclusive, discriminatory, and unequal. When one market segment or community is enticed to share experiences, another is excluded. Leung's subjects are refugees living in Australia whose marginal status is underscored by exclusions from web-based community programs. From Leung's perspective, experience design is "business as usual" with little scope for social innovation. This study concludes by asking what happens when marginalized groups attempt to engage experiences that were not designed for them—an intriguing enquiry with implications for all forms of Experience Design.

Part Two: Objects and Environments

The second part of this volume investigates real-life experiences of (product) design and architecture from the perspective of that essential, usually anonymous but occasionally disruptive, figure: the "user." The authors argue that shared experiences, meanings, and lasting impressions of design are created as much in the public domain as in the designer's studio. In the era of customer focus, enhanced consumer experience, and increasingly customized product, their insights appear intuitively true, and inherently encouraging.

For example, if lost in Jakarta the traveller may be directed to the Mad Pizza Waiter. This monumental statue on a traffic island, one of many dating from the Sukarno era, is a bellowing, high-stepping figure that strains to hold aloft a flaming disk. The statue once represented "Eternal Youth" but has since acquired a new identity and a new function: that of helping drivers to navigate the city. The phenomenon is universal. Ambitious new buildings such as London's "Gherkin" routinely acquire monikers that stick. Old buildings about to be torn down spontaneously focus shared memories that can lead to popular protests against demolition. At an individual level we tend to anthropomorphize or personify products such as automobiles, and we all adopt, adapt, and appropriate our possessions in particular ways to express personal and collective identities.

Of course we do, because the alternative would be an environment governed by unbending determinism. Architectural determinism is a doctrine of social control that, while it appealed to a few Modernists, would be monstrous if it were not so silly. In large part the criticisms launched against this doctrine succeeded. Philosophers such as Benjamin spoke instead of the "porous city" (in a curious travelogue sandwiched between reminiscences of smoking hashish in Morocco and buying antiques in Moscow), while Lefebvre spoke of space not as the designer's abstract void but as constituted by real social relations. Encouraged by such critiques, the architect Aldo van Eyck combined order and accident in buildings of "labyrinthine clarity" to encourage informal adoption by occupants.

Until comparatively recently, however, architects and designers tended to imagine their practice as a one-way street. The role of the professional was to prescriptively determine not only how anonymous users should behave but also how they ought to feel.

This attitude was cultivated by training. Anyone involved in design education will recall students blithely assured that projects will be involuntarily appreciated by "distal end users," the "target market," or similar dehumanizing terms.

Whether on an intimate, domestic scale, or on the public stage of institutions and cities, the case studies assembled in Part Two reveal our everyday experience of design to be a crowded two-way street. Here and there the intent of designers may coincide, or collide with the preoccupations of individuals or communities, although these case studies suggest most people harbor their own perceptions, preconceptions, and obsessions, and remain largely indifferent to the designer's intent.

Contributors to Objects and Environments take their insights a stage further: that if experiences of design are negotiated rather than imposed, the corollary would be a more collaborative, collective design practice. Indeed, in recent years designers have begun to reject the cult of egotistical originality and claim themselves to act as facilitators of participation.

In reality, collective participation in professional design process remains rare, while the scope of experiential design is often limited to short-lived spectacles intended to spur individual consumption. The utopian vision glimpsed in Part One, of a future experience economy transcending materialistic consumption, remains an elusive vision.

Theorists might be dismayed that experience design is circumscribed by marketing strategies, but this will hardly come as a surprise to practitioners. Professional designers in the events industries of expos, destination tourism, themed spectacles, cities of culture, and the like, work within a long tradition. From the Field of the Cloth of Gold to the Beijing Olympics, the income of most architects and artists has often depended on contracts to design temporary religious and state festivals, aristocratic tournaments, revels and carnivals, royal entrées and magnificences, theatrical pageants, masques, allegorical tableaux and spettacoli. Yet, being ephemeral, the visual history of this tradition since the Renaissance is now largely forgotten. It may be that attempts to define Experience Design by its newness and imagined prospects miss a much richer historical context.

In Part Two of this volume, Silvia Grimaldi opens by revealing the fragments of narrative that articulate our interactions with everyday products such as a tea kettle. Like the classic devices used in theater and film, objects play a crucial role in the presentation of the self and the domestic mise en scène. And like extras on a film set, these humble objects often play multiple roles in our personal dramas. Grimaldi's metaphor is reinforced by theories of narrative, and by reference to four films in which a kettle plays roles from a murder weapon to a masochist's delight that was certainly not intended by the designer.

Xavier Acarin and Barbara Adams focus on the museum as a site for investigating Experience Design. This is particularly appropriate now that visitor experience and community participation have become keys to justifying the museum's role. Acarin and Adams explore the tension between the museum as an institution that determines value, and as a platform for a critique of institutional authority promoted by the very artists invited to deliver creative engagement programs. With a particular focus on works by artists such as Marina Abramovic, Tino Sehgal, Carsten Höller, or Christoph Büchel, the authors trace the lineage of the white cube gallery space, and contrast this with the Situationist tradition of subverting the museum's role in defining and delimiting culture. Their conclusion on this uneasy compromise is that museums offer a rare example of experience design that stands apart from the promotion of consumption.

Peter Benz continues this section on the contested relationship between design and its users with an arresting aphorism from the architectural critic Eduard Führ: "The usage of a building relates to architecture as a football game relates to the pitch." The case study here is an international hotel group with nine hotels in the city of Hong Kong—an example that offers insight into wider debates in Experience Design. The particular dilemma faced by the group's management is how to maintain brand identity while differentiating sites, and how to standardize operations while cultivating customer focus. If the "choice of pillows program" seems a less than satisfactory solution, Benz's conclusion takes up the more challenging solution proposed by the architect and phenomenologist Juhani Pallasmaa: that Experience Design demands a re-engagement between designers and those whose lives they affect.

Finally, Lakshmi P. Rajendran, Stephen Walker, and Rosie Parnell also consider the multiple and fluid experiences of design by tracing the ways in which city-dwellers construct a sense of place and identity through elements of their urban environment—in this case the city of Sheffield in the north of England. Adopting methods drawn from phenomenology and ethnography, the authors analyze the ways in which residents narrate "spatial experience" in concrete terms of boundaries, belonging, exclusion, and even the restorative quality of nature. The abstract space of the city is presented not as a background but as a field that, together with communication technologies, enable disconnected objects to be related in ways that construct a sense of place.

Taken together, the case studies in Objects and Environments reveal experience design to be a complex rather than complicated practice. Airliners and skyscrapers are highly complicated, yet their myriad elements can be specified and the outcome predicted with accuracy.

By contrast, the complexity of experience design has proved resistant to modeling, unpredictable in outcomes, and impossible to measure. Consider, for example, a typically interdisciplinary project involving destination tourism. The project will demand coordination of architecture and design alongside digital information systems, marketing, and service design. All these elements will be, in turn, presumed to articulate external promotion and attract increased visitor numbers, if not inward investment. At the same time, such a project will have to meet civic expectations for cultural development, community engagement, urban regeneration, and perhaps social cohesion.

The lesson of complexity and chaos theory for Experience Design is that such a myriad of small, fluid elements in multiplex projects will have unexpected outcomes that defy forecasting and elude impact assessment. Yet, at the same time, the lesson of experience design for more settled branches of practice from fashion to graphics, is that in essence all design may be chaotic.

Part Three: Interactions and Performances

In the final part of this collection the authors confront a contentious issue raised in earlier sections: the opportunities for and obstacles to designing for communal experience.

As we have seen, philosophers distinguish, perhaps too sharply, the kind of experience typified by momentary, individual distraction from that of a shared experience, which passes into collective memory and wisdom. In practice, Experience Design focuses on the former, and this has led many design scholars to question its claim to be a discipline transcending established practice. For example, professional design demands sensitivity to place, occasion, and atmosphere, an emotional empathy with particular groups and communities, and a user-centered approach characterized by action research. Can experience design justify its promise of a wider public reach?

Contributors to Interactions and Performances explore the ways in which design can encourage individuals to share experience by interacting with others, if only momentarily. The public settings for these interactions range from subways to banks, restaurants to theme parks.

Sara M. Strandvad and Kristine M. Pedersen open this section by presenting communal experience as a phenomenon only partially shaped by design. The case study here is the unruly "liminality" of Denmark's Roskilde Festival. In such a setting the authors argue that design merely provides a "platform" for communal experience to be co-created by its participants. The authors propose pragmatism as the most effective philosophical approach to understanding co-creation in other, less riotous forms of experience design. In the writings of Dewey, at least, pragmatism is closer to phenomenology than might appear, but his comparative clarity makes his philosophy more amenable to practical application. Indeed Denmark has taken practical application to government level where the experience economy has been adopted as national policy. That most Danish scholars have been unable to measure the value of experience, and express skepticism that it represents a blueprint for development, lead Strandvad and Pedersen to remind us that pragmatism's model of collaborative production offers a more practical approach to designing shared experiences.

Interactions and Performances also takes a fresh methodological approach to experience design by drawing on concepts and methods developed in the field of Human Computer Interaction. Initially, this interdisciplinary subject focused on interactions with static equipment but as digital technologies have become mobile, ubiquitous and, in the case of social media, communal or even political, its scope has become increasingly wide-ranging.

Amy Findeiss, Eulani Labay, and Kelly Tierney approach the design of collaborative experiences through a mix of interaction studies, action research, and a polite form of Situationist provocations. In contrast to the troublesome issues of exclusion raised earlier by Linda Leung, the optimistic conclusion here is that spontaneous interactions can create a sense of community. The group's site is the New York subway, and its aim is to create informal participatory events that, if only momentarily, bring individuals together. Successive experiments with dance and poetic interventions such as the *The Memory Exchange* promote the intangible value of spontaneous and ephemeral interactions, and dramatize the want of communal experience in an age of atomized individualism.

A similar, if more practical, commitment to communal social need informs Gretchen Rinnert's study of patients lost within the confusing world of medical treatments in the United States. Working closely with individuals suffering from Crohn's disease and Cystic Fibrosis, she develops a "patient-centred" approach that goes beyond social research methods to engage experience design strategies, such as the use of personas and animated walk-throughs. Rinnert negotiates the precarious boundary between the aloofness of medical authority and the immediacy of quack opinion garnered through Google by building on patients' mobile, online support communities.

Claus Østergaard also discovers the limits of conventional research methods when attempting to grasp social systems in continuous flux, as well as the fluidity of individual consciousness. The particular case study considers user-oriented and context-aware mobile concepts to enrich visitor experience in a theme park. Even conventional design methods prove inadequate to the task, and Østergaard proposes a less rigid and more reflexive system of feedback loops, partly inspired by Human Computer Interaction.

In a similar way, Tara Mullaney suggests that conventional design methods imply a reductivist view of experience. Adopting experimental design concepts informed by Human Computer Interaction, her case studies of electronic banking transactions on the eve of the "cashless society" rethink the social experiences that might be possible at these financial waypoints. Like a hacker, Mullaney toys with disruptive interventions to provoke transformative experiences, concluding that approaches to digital forms of experience design are moving from problem-solving to problem-setting.

Problem-setting is an appealing tactic, yet it begs the question of evidence for claims to provide transformative experience. In a unique study, the group of design researchers Werner Sommer, Felix Bröcker, Manuel Martín-Loeches, Annekathrin Schacht, and Birgit Stürmer seek evidence for the anecdotal observation that experiences of dining are shaped by the setting as much as the cuisine. Once again, their approach reveals the limitations to more reductive design research methods. Like a culinary equivalent of the Heisenberg principle, the researchers discover that the investigation of experiences as they happen displaces the very object of their study. Sommer and colleagues reflect that communal experience may be less about momentary sensation than memory.

Experience understood as the shared recollection of an event (a meal in this case, but it may be a product or building or service) offers a fruitful direction for evidence-based Experience Design.

It is clear from the studies in this collection that Experience Design is still a developing term, and one that necessarily draws from a very mixed bag of philosophies and methods stretched across the widest range of practice from architecture and city planning to design for products, mobile interactions, performance, and events. At the same time, it is clear that the term articulates an unmistakable sea change within the profession, which has already evolved from a speculative concept to become an indispensable adjunct to practice.

As the chapters in this volume reveal, the practice of Experience Design, its scope, principles, methods, and ethics are all contested. Diversity in approach and method is inevitable in any emergent subject, and controversy is vital in every field. Without the informed critical debate represented by contributors to this volume the theory of experience design would soon become dogmatic, and its practice routine.

PART ONE

Positions

Chapter 1

Fundamental Aspects of Human Experience: A Phenomeno(logical) Explanation

Ian Coxon

The central difficulty is that experience is not an explanatory posit, but an explanandum in its own right.

(VARELA 1996: 331)

It's the same situation every time. I'm in a bar or at a dinner party. I meet someone new and the inevitable question is posed, 'So what is it that you do?' I cringe, knowing from experience that this can go one of two ways, and neither is usually very much fun for anyone. And so I begin the now familiar dance of the Experience Design explanation.

Stage one, "I am a researcher and teacher in an engineering faculty." "Oh yes," they reply (the initial naïve interest which leads to the next dangerous question). "So what is it you teach?" (A fatal question, because now I have to explain it.) "I teach engineers about human experience," (they usually look at me with total bewilderment or the intelligent ones nod as if they understand and kill the conversation there; the novices tend to plough on).

"What do you mean by experience?" they usually ask. I fire back, "You know what experience is right?" "Yeah sure." "So what is it?" I hit them with, a little aggressively. (Now is when they look like a deer caught in a car's headlights and the beginnings of that, "I wish I hadn't asked" look). I usually feel sorry for them by this stage and soften off the conversation by beginning to explain. "OK, so we are sitting here in this room right, talking and drinking, eating food, etc. We are in this place having an experience together, but what is that thing we call experience? And how would you explain that something to someone else? How would you begin to understand it in any kind of structured or organized way?" This is when the foolhardy push on and want to know more, and the less foolhardy say "thank you," and suddenly need more wine or to be somewhere else, where the "normal" people are.

This common everyday experience (of mine) points to the fundamental questions that this chapter will address. How can we more clearly understand what experience is? And, as people who are interested in the field of Experience Design, how can we use this understanding to further our field as well as to enhance the way we design, so as to more positively contribute to the experiences of others?

There is a distinct imperative—in the design world at least—for a clearer understanding of the concept of experience—what it means to people who are doing the "designing for" others and what it means to people who are receiving the benefit of the things they design. Design industry-related fields such as Experience Design, the Experience Economy, as well as an array of design occupations that incorporate experiential elements into their work (User Experience Design (UX), Experience-based Designing (EBD)), increasingly need a cohesive and consistent terminological basis for "experience" as concept; one that enables a common story to be communicated by designers to their audience and also between designers themselves.

Words are always a fluid communication device, and they take their meaning from the context of use, but if the context is ever changing and always different (individual) then how can the concept of experience be usefully communicated? Before experience became popular as a marketing tool, people were immersed in their experiences as a natural part of their everyday lives. Long after it is no longer fashionable to produce or promote products with experience "tacked-on" as a value-adding component (real or not) people will still be immersed in it. The primary purpose of this chapter is therefore to provide a starting point for understanding just what experience really is at a very fundamental level so as to help clarify some of the misconceptions that have crept into the discourse in recent years.

A key to understanding experience (philosophically speaking)

With the exception of a definite beginning (birth) and end (death), the bulk of our understanding of conscious life is constructed through our phenomenal[1] way of being in, or of experiencing, the world as we travel through it.

This concept of having a "phenomenal" understanding of experience is an important one to grasp. The term *phenomenal* essentially means "our" way of experiencing something based on all of our life experiences (of various phenomena) that have gone before, as interpreted through filters such as the social (family, friends, etc.) and cultural history (religion, ethnicity, etc.) that we bring to it. That is, all of the "baggage" that helps us to see the world in the unique way that we do.

An experience that we have is always our phenomenal experience, and the meaning we ascribe to an experiential event is always a mental construct that is uniquely ours. When we talk about our phenomenal view we understand that it (including the perceptions we develop out of it) is continually changed (shaped) by our interactions with the world through our experience of it, and so the cycle continues.

To look at this from another way, we can say that our experience of the world is colored by our perception of it, and this is a product of the phenomenal (ontological[2]) view that we have developed through our living of life in the way that we have done it, so far. This progressive absorption of life events adds to our "cumulative experience" of the world and subsequent memory structures, which in turn contribute to and continually color our ontological view—and so we go around again.

The "logical" role of phenomenology

If we are going to talk about experience, especially the human kind (let's leave monkeys out of it for this chapter), and we want to do it in a structured or organized way, we really need to consider what conceptual framework we will use to approach the task. That is, the type of scientific framework that we will apply to "filter" our philosophical, theoretical, and practical understanding of the concept.

If experience is subject to our ontological view of it, then how we understand it will also be subject to the epistemological framework we apply to understanding it. At a philosophical epistemological level, there is only one philosophy that is particularly focused on understanding human lived experience as well as providing the methodological tools we will need—and that is phenomenology. Drawn from a human science tradition (and tracing its lineage back to Socratic times), this philosophical view recognizes that experience is always phenomenal (as described above), and it naturally follows that the study (logos) of such a thing should be called *phenomenology*. It is both a philosophy (a way of thinking about how we live in the world) and a methodology (a way for us to begin to understand our experience of the world). It provides a sound framework for beginning to understand the nature of experience (ontologically), and how we might study it in some methodical way (epistemologically).

The foundations of phenomenology[3]—arguably developed by Edmund Husserl and his many predecessors, and later refined by Martin Heidegger and others—made infinitely clearer by the American pragmatist John Dewey and modernized by many current scholars since, have provided us with not only a philosophical view of experience but a practical way of understanding it—a methodology. So, without summarizing the many hundreds of years it took to develop; what is it about phenomenology that we really need to know about to help us in our search for ways to understand experience at its most fundamental level?

Language of phenomenology

A good place to start with any form of discussion of this nature is to speak the same language. In order to assist those trying to understand experience for the first time (and for some of the old hands), this section will present a few of the essential terms and concepts that have evolved over many years out of seminal works in the field. In recent times it has become fashionable, particularly in the highly competitive design world, to develop new terms for existing concepts in order to colonize a section of the market (a form of intellectual branding). This has led to an oversupply of neologisms that offer very little more than to further confuse and mislead those who are new to the field. Thus in the following paragraphs we will present and discuss some of the foundational terms that will help us to clarify what we are talking about when we say "we are working with experience."

Experience—what do we mean literally?

The original etymology of the word *experience* is vaguely dated from fourteenth-century origins but it can be loosely interpreted from the Latin *experientia*, or the French *esperience* to mean "to test," or "to try out." This tends to imply a physical interaction with or exploration of something, i.e. to physically experience something. In the eighteenth to nineteenth centuries many of the German philology scholars (Husserl, Heidegger, and Gadamer among them) used various terms to describe ways of referring to experience that provided more subtle variations of meaning and began to use words that implied more metaphysical qualities. To describe these concepts we might consider at least three ways of looking at the English term "experience":

Erlebnis: referring to conscious experiences felt deeply, lived "through," or personally felt; e.g. reading this text.

Erfahrung: everyday experience that is undergone—perhaps unremarkable or not very memorable; e.g. walking to the bus stop every day.

Erlebnisse: our cumulative set of separate experiences that have contributed to our life-experience and our phenomenal view.

The German terms themselves are not particularly important in this discussion, but they do offer an initial (traditional) way to look at experience as having different forms or natures, and this again offers a basic structure that we can explore more deeply.

If we want to understand experience we don't have to be always considering *Erlebnis*, *Erfahrung*, and *Erlebnisse* all together. We can say that in this instance we are focusing on a specific identifiable and isolated[4] experience, an *Erlebnis* or "an experience." Also, in most discussions about the meaning of experience, both the earlier and the modern phenomenologists[5] are principally concerned only with the concept *Erlebnis* (personally felt experience) as an event that fully encompasses the experiencer[6] and has a profound effect on him or her.

However, in difference to the phenomenological discourse, in the context of this chapter the first two—*Erlebnis* and *Erfahrung*—are of interest to our understanding of experience because they are the ones that a designer might directly influence through design practice. In our attempt to understand experience we might start with "an experience," whether it is a particularly poignant one (*Erlebnis*) or not (*Erfahrung*), yet it will be nearly impossible for us to understand and consider all of a person's cumulative experiences of life (*Erlebnisse*) in the process of a design.

An experience—a singular unity of experience—a natural experience

The concept of "unity" within discussions of experience can be contentious and possibly confusing, depending on the way in which the writer interprets both *experience* and the term *unity*. However, it is an important concept in developing a clear understanding of what an experience is and is not. In the following we take unity to mean "the identification of differentiating factors that help to define an experience's uniqueness." Husserl[7] and others called for us to focus our attention on the "things themselves" and so we draw parameters around an experience (its unity) from the nature of the experience itself— what factors make the experience what it is.

This sounds a little like double talk, so perhaps an example might help: What if we wanted to explore the experience of, say, shopping at Walmart? For this experience to become a unit that can be studied and understood, it must have a defined beginning and end. So, if we wanted to understand an experience of shopping at Walmart, we might adopt the unity of (or establish a boundary around) the shopping experience, such that we decide to understand it from when a customer enters the parking lot (therefore it does not include the drive there) and end it when the customer leaves the parking lot.

We realize that everyday experience is continuous, seamless, and endless, and that we are simply trying to understand one small unit of it. For example, the customer we are studying might have had three other interesting experiences on the way there and two more on the way home. A researcher wishing to understand the experience of shopping at Walmart needs to place boundaries in such a way so as to define a unit of this experience. These unitary boundaries are drawn from and so help to define the thing itself—i.e. the experience of shopping at Walmart. In research terms, defining the unity is necessary for identifying the experience we wish to understand. Researchers need to be able to say, "We want to understand the experience of […]," so they can begin to limit the scope of the project. This can also be very important for shaping the guiding phenomenological question: "What is the experience of […] like?"

Dewey appears to agree with the importance of unity when he says,

> An experience has a unity that gives it its name, […].The existence of this unity is constituted by a single quality that pervades the entire experience in spite of the variation of its constituent parts. (Dewey 1934: 38)

So human experience, as it happens and as we wish to understand it, is an experience with a beginning and an end (a unity that is defined by and takes place in its original, natural setting).

Gadamer (1975) once suggested that real, original or new experience only ever takes place once, and that all other experiences after that are repetitions of the original. This does not really bear out when we consider that a particular experience might appear to be similar to a previous experience in every way, but it will never really be the same. Time, context, and perhaps other contextual elements that constitute an experience will ensure it is never exactly the same—so in this way it is inconceivable that we can ever have the same experience twice—and so our cumulative experience builds in an experience-specific way.

This does however raise the topic of repetition—for instance, experiences that build skill and familiarity through a repeated experience of use. This line of thought takes us further into the realm of cumulative experience and memory (recalling experience). Recollection or memory enables us to internally (reflection or self-talk) and externally describe our past experiences as well as to draw on these and apply them to perform various tasks that require learned (previously experienced) skills.

Recollective experience or experience as reflected upon

When we are recalling or remembering an experience, as is the case when a researcher asks us about it, or in a more natural setting when we are simply thinking back on an event—we re-experience the event through a mediating filter, i.e. how we selectively remember it—not necessarily how it actually happened. We interpret the event (phenomenally) as it goes into our memory, and, as time passes and we have other experiences, our recollected (resurfaced) memory of the first experience can change and become distorted giving it the kind of character that Forlizzi mentions (Forlizzi and Battarbee 2004). Thus our cumulative memory of events is always phenomenally filtered by our ontological view both going in and coming back out. Experience in memory or *recollective experience* is always biased or prejudiced by the phenomenal transformation that takes place in its recording (encoding) and retrieval (decoding) in memory. This is one aspect of "the problem" of subjectivity that is often referred to as a source of unreliability in qualitative research approaches. That is not in any way to infer that such approaches are without value or are lacking in reliability—it is just so we fully appreciate how they are qualified by the phenomenal nature of experience.

An interesting variation on recollective experience that we might consider here relates to *re-enacted experience*—that is, how a person feels or experiences a reliving or reviewing of the previous experience (watching video of themselves or others during role play—i.e. during participatory or collaborative gener-ative design exercises). This experience of recollection is not a regeneration of the previous experience, but an externalized interpretation of the person's filtered recollection of the experience—perhaps a close representation of it maybe, but still quite a different thing from the actual (natural) experience when it first occurred.

Van Manen offers another perspective on this by introducing the concept of *meaning construction*. He says that an experience is not only something that is lived through but also something that I "recognise as a particular type of experience" (1997: 177). This proposition hints at another layer beyond the immediate experiencing: one that contains some quality derived through reflection or mental "value construction."

Reflection may or may not take place during or within the experiencing event, but it can add subse-quent layers of complexity, after it is processed into memory; adding what might be generically called meaning. Gadamer commented that, "if something is called or considered an Erlebnis [experience] that means it is rounded into the unity of a significant whole" (1975: 58).

We have taken the significance of the wholeness he describes to refer to the increase in complexity attributed to the experience after the event. The manner in which it "constitutes itself in memory" (Gadamer 1975: 58) that is, the way it grows in stature, develops a lasting quality, and achieves greater depth of meaning, again through the intervention of our phenomenal attitude.

The internal "processing" of experience as a rich and valuable source of information and, particularly, meaning, is an area of interest, which design and engineering have pursued as a "holy grail" for many years (Anolli 2005), but how to reliably access this meaning layer continues to allude us. The importance of the goal of making things more meaningful and therefore more desirable especially can be clearly seen in the role that "ownership" or engendering a stronger bond to an interaction with a product or service has in designing for longevity or customer loyalty (Bate and Glen 2007; Coxon 2008; Fuad-Luke 2002).

Cumulative experience—being experienced—experience

A longitudinal, collective conceptualization of experience might also be understood in terms of an anthropological view of experiences or as experiences appear to us over time—the way in which whole experiences or snippets of experience might be stored and recalled in a certain phenomenal way as they are absorbed into an individual's entire well of accumulated experience.

This is one of the ways of considering experience that is most difficult to access, as it is the subject of a lifelong experiential continuum, which is buried deeply in the human psyche. It brings in matters concerning the conscious, non-conscious and unconscious layers of mind that we have little knowledge of and in most cases little access to. It is also a way of categorizing experience in broad abstract terms such as personal experience, business experience, life-experience.

Such categorizations tell us something about a type of cumulative experience that the speaker is referring to but they tell us little about the nature of the content within them. As mentioned earlier, to even begin to understand a person's life experience we would be talking about a very big book indeed. To begin the process of understanding experience at all we really need to focus on one person's individual experience, i.e. an experience. Once we move beyond this individual phenomenal view (which is hard enough to understand) we are applying a process of abstraction that only distances us further from the truth we are trying to gain access to — the real meaning in an experience. So if we begin by attempting to understand groups of experiences, group experiences, or for that matter different forms of joint-experience, we are starting at a level of abstraction that can only be counterproductive.

In recent attempts to understand user experience as well as designing for experience there has been a considerable body of work that focuses on common experience or joint experiences. In light of the above, this might be interpreted as a generalization or normalization of experience. This can most readily be seen in recent research into *co-experience* (Battarbee 2003; Battarbee and Koskinen 2008; Forlizzi and Battarbee 2004). In these situations, instead of referring to them as a form of shared experience, it would be more accurate if they were described as an experiential event (not an experience) at which two or more people are present or participate in, at the same time. We contend (from the epistemological perspective described earlier in this chapter), that experience is always phenomenal and therefore co-experience is literally and theoretically unattainable. What we are really describing is an episode of interaction or communication between two people about or in a similar event space. That is not the same thing and really cannot be described as "co-experiencing."

In the first instance, due to the presence of the two parties, the nature of the experience is changed from that which either would have experienced had they been alone (as difficult as having a one-sided cell phone call might be). As the experience is always phenomenal, even if two people share the same event in close proximity, each of those people will always experience the event to some degree uniquely. The presence of the other is a part of the phenomenal experience of each of the experiencers and vice versa. Co-experience is not a different form of experience it is simply the separate experiences had by two or more people at the same time.

It is true that each of the parties to this experiential event will be influenced by the presence of the other in the same way that the presence of the cell phone, the café that one participant is sitting in, and the bedroom that the other is staying in will also have an impact, but the mobile conversation as locus, does not make it the same experience.

> Co-experience reveals how the experiences an individual has and the interpretations that are made of them are influenced by the physical or virtual presence of others. (Forlizzi and Battarbee 2004: 263)

The experience is only the same (the "co" part) in that it might be a similar spatial context as it is for the other person sharing the event; however, there are always phenomenal and contextual elements that make the experience subtly different for each participant. We may talk about a shared experiential event (a cell phone conversation) but not a shared experience. If we are to truly understand experience we must remember that the most fundamental aspect of its nature is that it is phenomenal. It cannot ever be known (or shared) by another—this is germane to understanding its character as an experience—and, as much as it might fit with our desire as designers to say we understand the experience of another, we must accept that we really are not able to create co-experiences or for that matter to co-create an experience.

One more way to look at experience—the authentic and inauthentic balance

In our discussion of various aspects and ways of considering experience we have so far talked about ways in which we can understand and describe experience in terms of language, unity, and its key defining quality—its phenomenal nature. These ways of looking at experience have a somewhat functional character to them as they serve to enable us in understanding how to work with experience; however, they do not describe the level of intensity in terms of how well we "attend to" or are "conscious of" the experience as it takes place.

Heidegger proposed two different terms for this, which I feel are very important in helping to understand what experience is. He used the terms[8] *authentic* (*eigentlich*) and *inauthentic* (*uneigentlich*) (Heidegger 1962; Moran 1999). Moran clarifies these two Heideggerian concepts in this way:

> Authentic moments are those in which we are most at home with ourselves ... we have a deep concrete experience of "mineness", of "togetherness". However, in our more usual, normal, everyday moments, we do not treat things as affecting us deeply in our "own-most" being. Heidegger thinks we live in an inauthentic way most of the time. (Moran 1999: 240)

These two terms are not the most elegant translations from their German origins, and they are a little difficult to grasp, but at the same time they offer a powerful way of understanding quite a different set of qualities in everyday experience.

Before we go further, it is very important to understand that both of these facets of experience, the *authentic* and *inauthentic*, *always* exist in the same experiential space simultaneously. They are never discrete or separated facets of an experience and we are always in both modes simultaneously—just the mix or balance differs according to the experiential circumstances.

Beginning with *inauthentic experience*—this aspect of experience can be understood as the ordinary, everyday, often dream like way that we encounter every day. We get up, brush our teeth, shower, and make breakfast, get the bus to work, etc., often without really thinking much about what we are doing. We have all had those moments when we stop and realize we have walked or, even worse, driven a car a certain distance along a familiar route without really being conscious of seeing or noticing anything along the way. We have "zoned out" or been simply too "lost" in thought to notice our immediate surroundings. Of course this condition can also be explained in psychological terms such as mild forms of disassociation or detachment. Other fields might refer to it as not being "present."

Let's say we change those familiar surroundings to a strange city or our first day at a new job—all of a sudden we become much more aware of everything—its difference to what is familiar and its strangeness to us. We experience new stimuli, new information inputs, we become very aware of our new-ness in this place and we might even feel slightly alien in these surroundings. We begin to feel and become more aware of ourselves, our lack of familiarity with the terrain, perhaps new feelings of vulnerability and possibly some discomfort in our awareness that we feel this way. This is an example of what an *authentic* mode of being might be like—being consciously aware of our self and who we are. The example above is a little negative sounding but of course a highly *authentic experience* is not always uncomfortable. It could just as easily be a very pleasant situation that also raises our self-awareness.

Natural (primordial) experience always contains a balance between these two facets of inauthentic and authentic experience. If we were to live in a state of inauthentic experience all the time we would not be living very well—we would be in a quiet robotic, dreamlike state. Conversely, if we were to try to be authentic all of the time we would be living in such an intense way that we would have no "down-time" or periods where our brain activity and stress levels could slow down and relax—it sounds exhausting. So our natural everyday experience of the world is always a balancing act between our inauthentic experience needs and our desire for authentic experiences. This balancing process manifests itself in lots of behaviors in our lives. We want a job with good security and a regular pay cheque but we don't want to feel that we are in a rut. We crave new and exciting clothes that make us look good, but we do not want to stand out too much from the crowd. We eat a reasonably varied diet because we could not stand to live on chocolate.

These two sides of everyday experience are fundamental to our understanding of the life-world[9] in which we live. Of course in a modern world our experiences are continuously shaped by and in the process of shaping[10] many of the things around us—our apartment, our workplaces, our relationships with others. We realize that our experiences within these parts of our life-world are also always mediated by the "things"[11] we interact with, but in this discussion of experience we would like to focus on the phenomenal experience we have naturally.

Of course we must acknowledge that our experiences are never really separated from the contextual (product, services, and systems) world in which we live. We use the term *naturally* here to refer to understanding an experience in as un-mediated a way as possible—that is, to observe or understand what the experience is like when it first occurs and particularly when a researcher is not influencing it by his or her presence. What we are trying to get at in terms of a natural experience in the life-world is to understand what it is like when we are not there trying to study or control it in any way. This is a very difficult thing to do but there are ways in which we can approach this problem that help to mediate the impact of the researcher as "observer."

In terms of close observation,

the human science researcher tries to enter the life-world of the persons whose experiences are relevant study material for his or her research project. The best way to enter a person's life-world is to participate in it. (Van Manen 1997: 69)

Embodied experience—embodying experience—embodiment and intersubjectivity

As the eminent researchers above have already indicated: in order to deeply understand experience and the life-world in which it takes place, it cannot be simply observed, it must be experienced. Putting actual experience at the center of observational techniques is the only way to understand the life-world in a "truly human way." The primacy of personal experience in this way becomes part of an epistemology of experiential understanding, enabling a researcher to understand life experiences, from within. "Getting at" or into the natural life-world of others is a difficult thing for a researcher to accomplish, but there are practical ways, inspired by phenomenological and neurological theory, by which embodied experience might be understood and also applied as a research tool.

In this section we will discuss one of the most effective ways to bring both of these perspectives together in order to increase what Gallagher (2005) refers to as *intersubjectivity*. In our research projects we broadly refer to this process as "embodiment." Gallagher offers a significant perspective on the way a researcher might gain insight through an almost osmotic effect during a carefully applied and understood embodiment exercise. This description also raises the added benefits of embodiment to the researcher as they become the object of their own subjective reflection (the researcher as instrument).

> In regard to embodiment, I want to explore to what extent and in what way an awareness of my body enters into the content of my conscious experience? To what degree and in what situations am I, as an experiencing subject, aware or unaware of my own body? Does intentional action, for example, involve an explicit or implicit awareness of the body? … Such questions, however, pertain to an important aspect of the structure of experience. If throughout conscious experience there is a constant reference to one's own body, even if this is a recessive or marginal awareness, then that reference constitutes a structural feature of the phenomenal field of consciousness, part of a framework that is likely to determine or influence all other aspects of experience. (Gallagher 2005: 2)

At the Experience-based Designing Centre at the University of Southern Denmark, researchers support or "prime" their understanding of a particular life-world by "embodying" an experience that belongs to that life-world. Essentially they approach this as a design task where they need to design a "way-into" the experience they wish to understand. This is not always achievable to the highest degree, but the point is to come as close as possible to it. The question becomes: "How close can they get?" Of course a researcher's experience like everyone else's is always phenomenal and will always be their experience of it, but it is profoundly useful in two very powerful ways. It informs their individual cumulative experience with an embodied level of meaning that enhances Gallagher's notion of intersubjectivity.[12]

> […] neural activations [of the premotor cortex and Broca's area] correspond to meaning that is intersubjective in the literal sense—it is meaning that is simultaneously shared in the modalities of observation (of others) and action capability (of my own). More generally, the brain areas respon-sible for planning my own action are the same ones activated during the observation, imaginative simulation, or imitation of the action of others.

> […] embodiment plays a central role in structuring experience, cognition, and action. […] in the phenom-enological and empirical details of experience, the body both shows and hides itself in irreducible ways, and that in these performances it has a structuring effect on experience. (Gallagher 2005: 127, 136)

Gallagher's description of the role of embodiment in shaping the way we think, underpins how a researcher, through his or her embodiment, begins to understand the experience at a profoundly physical level and a far deeper cognitive level. Next, when they enter the experiencer's world or the life-world of the other, they enter it as an experiencer not an observer. This significantly changes the social dynamic between the two people involved—the researcher and the participant. Our researchers often remark that after their embodiment they feel free to discuss topics they would otherwise not have known to discuss, they feel empowered to explore areas they would previously not have felt comfortable exploring (as an outsider) and, on the flip side, research participants tend to embrace them more readily and with greater empathy.

> In relation to communication with patients, pictures and stories from our embodiment were a great tool for sparking conversation, as we were able to elaborate from our own experiences and demonstrate our willingness to learn. It helped us break down barriers to sensitive topics, thus enabling deeper conversations to take place. When we presented our embodiment to the participants, it was received with appreciation, as they knew what we had immersed ourselves into. (Nielsen et al. 2013)

Conclusion

Our intention in this chapter is to add some logical clarity to an otherwise muddied discourse on the way that human experience is understood and referred to in many design circles. For those who are new to the field we have provided a starting point for understanding what experience really is at a fairly basic level, in an effort to correct some of the many misconceptions and misdirection that has crept into the Experience Design landscape in recent years. We also hope we have presented aspects of experience in such a way as to have some unifying effect on what students of experience at many levels might relate to.

Our experiences are a powerful and important part of everyday life and if designers can understand them well and utilize that understanding properly, we will add considerable meaning and value to people's everyday life-worlds. The key to this understanding is the fundamental phenomenal property of experience—the way we all experience life differently. Valuing and holding onto this aspect of experience poses considerable challenges to a design world which is so often predicated on standardized offerings. How do we begin to work with something that is so individual and unique (particular) as to be the very opposite to general (universal)? The parts and whole conundrum (such as an experience and our ontological view) can be seen in almost everything we do but this does not diminish the fact that it is a fundamental question for our humanness. We need to address it and not deal with it by increasing our abstraction from it.

The fundamental aspects of human experience we have described in this chapter—understanding an experience; understanding the wonder and limitations of our recollections of our experiences; the near impossibility of understanding the complexity but necessity of our cumulative experience; the harmonizing qualities of authenticity and inauthenticity and the significant but somewhat mysterious power of embodied experience are only initial steps that lead to an inescapable conclusion. We need to do much more work that will help us to understand how to understand experience as an essential part of the meaning we make in life and then to use this knowledge to benefit and not just to prosper.

Notes

1   "There is a 'phenomenal field' in which a phenomenon takes shape as the appearances of things, other
     people and so on. It is in the nature of perceptual experience to forget this phenomenal field, for phenomena
     themselves always direct us beyond themselves to the things they present, the things of which they are the
     appearances. Nonetheless, if I want to return to the beginning, the foundation, of my understanding of the
     world, I need to reawaken this 'pre-objective' experience, the phenomenal field, in order to understand how
     my familiar conception of the world, the system 'self-others-things' is manifested within experience" (Baldwin
     2004: 14).

2   The close link between our phenomenal view of the world and our ontological view of it is well established.
     See, for example, Varela (1996: 334): "The ontology of the mental is an irreducibly first-person ontology."

3   Heidegger (1962); Gadamer (1975); Dewey (1934).

4   We acknowledge the continuing nature of experience, yet for the purpose of this study we will consider "an
     experience" as if it was an isolatable part of the continuum of cumulative experience.

5   Earlier: Heidegger (1962), Gadamer (1975), and Ricoeur (1978); Modern: Moran (1999), Van Manen (1997),
     and Willis (2001).

6   The term "experiencer" draws attention to the whole person having the experience of a product, service, or
     event as well as to the experience as an entity in itself. In contrast to this, the term "user" is strongly linked
     to the interactive and functional aspects of product use, very often associated with marketing and consumer
     behavior (Redström 2006).

7   That the phrase "to the things themselves" is often attributed to Edmund Husserl (Feenberg 1999) is a source
     of on-going dispute and it has not been clearly established to whom it should be attributed—however, its
     origins are not vital to this discussion.

8   This coincides with Heidegger's concept of "inauthentic life" or being in a state of "inauthenticity" (Carmen
     2003; Heidegger 1962).

9   The term "life-world" is often used in phenomenology and the human sciences to refer to the everyday world
     in which a person lives and experiences life phenomenally. This term assumes the primary role that each
     person's phenomenal (ontological) view plays in shaping their world and how they understand it. Life-world
     refers to the actual experienced world of a person corresponding to that person's intentional awareness
     (Willis 2001: 4).

10   There is a wealth of material on the socio-technical relationship—how things shape us, and how we in turn
     shape things. See, for example, the Actor Network Theory (ANT). Seminal authors in this field include Bruno
     Latour (1994, 2004) and Donna Haraway (1991).

11   Latour (2004): on the differences between objects and things—primarily the involvement of people with an
     object making it a thing.

12   Please note that this is not an alternate form of co-experience.

Chapter 2

Experience as Excursion: A Note towards a Metaphysics of Design Thinking

Connie Svabo and Michael Shanks

A fuzzy field: Design

While we generally use the term *design* in a rather loose way to refer to purpose, intention, significance, and agency in making, it is certainly right to connect the emergence of the distinctively modern field of design with the growth from the eighteenth century of industrial manufacture associated with the increasingly radical division of labor. Design became a process most often separate from manufacture—creating a plan or specification for something, an artefact, system, service, or, now, an experience, and one that might even transform you.

While designers work with mass manufacturing processes in the industrial design of everyday objects, they have also had to deal with quite intangible issues of taste and style, functionality and desirability, safety regulation and legality, and the emotional impact of what they design. Immediately implicated are the structures and cultures of modernity, class, gender, ethnicity—horizontal and vertical distinctions at the core of individual and group identities in an everyday world that have come to revolve around manufactured goods. Market competition has thrown emphasis upon innovation—developing products that offer something new or different.

Then there are the different and sometimes competing design philosophies that have come to drive much design—notoriously, of course, modernist design where form is supposed to follow function.

Since the 1960s four factors have contributed to a growing consciousness and emphasis upon design:

1 The growth of the service economy, and not only in tourism and entertainment, but also involving a broad business focus upon customer satisfaction.

2 Information technology (IT) that has come to deal with complex interactions between people and increasingly intelligent machines, that require attention to human factors of use, function, and cognition.

3   Investment in design research, training, and education, accompanying a rationalization and formalization of design practice.

4   The expansion of design beyond the simple studio—complex goods and services delivered by global corporations that require teams of collaborating experts in many different fields.

There are different fields of design focus: design of activities and services; design of material objects; design of physical environments; and design of communication. Industrial designers create products, and architects create buildings. But modern life is permeated by design, and this design saturation brings with it an interesting challenge: not only to design singular objects, services, systems, and environments, but also to understand, imagine, connect, and choreograph all of these different designs.

A plethora of related terms have come into circulation in the last three decades as part of this challenge, this consciousness and attention to design: including human factors, ergonomics, user experience design, user-centered design, interaction design, experience-driven design, experience-centered design, experience-based design, emotional design, and empathic design. Typically the common thread is that design may be unified and improved by focusing upon the human component, however that is defined: human-centered design.

An illustration of changes from the point of view of design is the evolution of the work of designer and theorist Donald Norman. His summary of human factors design, originally published under the title *The Psychology of Everyday Things* (1988), is, as the title partly suggests, an approach to industrial design rooted in cognitive science and behavioral psychology. The argument in this book being that research and knowledge of how people interact with things were essential to good design. Donald Norman's (1988) book is full of examples of both bad and good design, with the difference lying in their psychology. By the time he wrote *Emotional Design: Why We Love (or Hate) Everyday Things* (2005), he had quite radically changed his views to emphasize that designers need to accommodate the sometimes irrational emotional relationships that people have with objects in their everyday world. This perspective is included in the revised edition of *The Design of Everyday Things* (2013), as *The Psychology of Everyday Things* was renamed, while he also notably expands discussion to include the context of business, ethics, and the pragmatics of teamwork. Such human-centered design focuses on improving wellbeing, whether through the ergonomics of a chair or a user-friendly interface for a piece of medical technology. There is usually an ethical orientation, with innovation tied to improving people's lives. With others, Norman outlines "design thinking" as the transferable process of innovation at the heart of all design—a process for imagining and realizing positive change that can be applied to anything.

With a much broader view beyond design, Joseph Pine and James Gilmore, in their book *The Experience Economy* (1999), capture changes in business in the developed economies of the West that took off in the 1990s—a shift to offering not only services to consumers but also experiences. If a service business charges for the activities you perform, an experience business charges for the feelings that customers get by engaging it, while a transformation business charges for the benefit customers (or "guests") receive by spending time there.

A fuzzy concept: Experience

What then might experience designers create? Experience designers design for experience, obviously. However, other fields of design would probably also say the same. Might there be something in

Experience Design that makes it distinctive, either through the concept of experience, or in its particular design practice? Or perhaps it is simply the case that all design is Experience Design, in which case might we improve the conception of design and its practice through reflection upon the concept of (human) experience?

References to experience may be found in various design fields. Shedroff's *Experience Design 1* (2001), for example, primarily covers the design of digital interfaces. Klingmann's *Brandscapes: Architecture in the Experience Economy* (2007) and Schmitt's *Experiential Marketing: How to Get Customers to Sense, Feel, Think, Act, and Relate to your Company and Brands* (1999) are inspired by Pine and Gilmore's advice about the experience economy. Generally, however, and as pointed out both in this volume and in earlier work (Sundbo and Sørensen 2013; Sundbo and Darmer 2008), no commonly accepted and authoritative definition of experience exists.

In *Handbook on the Experience Economy* editors Sundbo and Sørensen suggest a definition that stresses experience is a mental phenomenon (2013: 2). They also note that some authors highlight the fact that experience is triggered by sensory stimuli: that internal mental processes have a physiological basis (Jantzen 2013). Sundbo and Sørensen furthermore point to the concept of flow, developed by the psychologist Csikszentmihalyi (1991), as being one of the more precise attempts at defining experience, albeit of a particular kind. Flow is the experience one gets while being immersed in an activity. Flow covers the self-reported experiences people have while engaged in what Csikszentmihalyi calls "various play-forms": rock climbing, chess, dance, and playing ball, for example. Flow experiences are characterized by complete absorption in an activity and a transcendence of ego boundaries. The concept of flow has an inherent orientation toward the experiencing subject, but flow experience is not a purely mental phenomenon. Central to flow experience is the merger of action and awareness.

Interestingly, the picture does not become much clearer when one looks at the sectors of "the experience economy." These include tourism, art and culture, entertainment and leisure, lotteries and gambling, design, image and branding, and ICT-based experiences; the most mentioned businesses are hotels, restaurants, travel agencies, TV companies, amusement parks, museums, and producers of smart phones and applications (Sundbo and Sørensen 2013: 10). Pine and Gilmore (1999) connect all these and more with the proposition that experience is performative, that designing for experience is like staging, involving set, props, scripts—scenography and dramaturgy. This is a powerful notion that is firmly rooted in social and cultural theory.

The global design consultancy IDEO is explicitly concerned with promoting human-centered design. One of its founders, Bill Moggridge, produced two extensive treatments of design involving many interviews with designers: *Designing Interactions* (2007) and *Designing Media* (2010). While not explicitly concerned with the design of experience, it is clear that experience is a key concept at the heart of this contemporary design work. Rather than offer definitions, Moggridge explores design thinking, process, and pragmatics—how designers go about their work of designing experiences that reach beyond the artefact. His close colleague David Kelley certainly describes his work as that of designing experiences (personal communication).

In spite of such treatments, our opinion is that, for the design world, experience is something that remains fuzzy, indeterminate. Experience may be conceived to have mental and physiological features, and may involve absorption and the engaged merger of action and awareness. But there is no clear definition, and there is no clearly marked sector or business.

What, then, might be the character and value of Experience Design?

Transcending singular fields

Perhaps a central value of a field of Experience Design might lie exactly in its dispersed character and in its variegated and situated capabilities. An interesting potential of Experience Design lies in the ability to transcend singular design fields. Experience Design as research and as practice can travel: Experience Design may help draw forward the interrelations and complex combinations that emerge when people engage with multiple designs in complex physical environments and manifold social constellations. Experience Design analytically should make it possible to follow experience as a phenomenon that is enacted in relations between heterogeneous elements, for example in human interactions with a place, modes of transportation, mobile mediation as well as the potential influence exerted by, say, a pair of high-heeled shoes. All of these singular designs contribute to and shape experience.

As we have said, life in modern, economically developed countries is saturated by design. We live in designed environments, are surrounded by design objects, and in many situations have our attention, capacity, and movement negotiated by design. As design and material culture scholar Ben Highmore points out, paraphrasing Herbert Simon, we live in artificial worlds; design is everywhere (Highmore 2009: 3). This makes it a central challenge for design research and practice to be able to conceptualize and choreograph the on-going experience of combinations of designs.

In the words of IDEO chief executive Tim Brown:

> As more of our basic needs are met, we increasingly expect sophisticated experiences that are emotionally satisfying and meaningful. These experiences will not be simple products. They will be complex combinations of products, services, spaces and information. (Brown 2009: 8)

Experiences emerge in the intertwinement of varieties of objects, interactions, spaces, and information. People seldom interact with only one thing in one tidy and orderly situation. On the contrary, people interact with multiple things at the same time, in shifting environments and in various social constellations. So, as pointed out by Brown, this poses challenges that experience be designed as complex combinations of objects, services, spaces, and information. The pertinence of performance as a model of Experience Design is very clear here: with staging as the coordination of actors, props, and scenery in dynamic, kinetic association, and intimately associated with location and audience.

The experience of a museum exhibition, for example, is not an experience of a singular design. The visit consists of a service encounter, an engagement with the architecture of the building, the design of the exhibition, the specific designs of each exhibit, as well as the influence exerted by signs, folders, portable media, fellow visitors, preconceptions, and expectations, even personal memories and dispositions.

Experience Design should allow researchers and designers to cross boundaries and inquire into such interrelations, negotiations and entanglements between various elements. The central relevance of Experience Design is its potential sensitivity to the complex combinations of heterogeneous elements, which are at play in practices and situations of use. Experience Design may thus act as an umbrella term for a number of design approaches that take the point of departure in actual situations of use—and are "human-centered."

Experience Design analytically makes it possible to follow experience as it emerges in relations between heterogeneous elements. The relevance of Experience Design as an umbrella term and a central focus in contemporary design work and research is exactly that it crosses boundaries between design disciplines. Instead of taking the singular logic of one design as the point of departure, the potential starting point in Experience Design should be what science and technology scholar Jaap Jelsma calls "use logic" (2006): the complexities which emerge in situations and practices where multiple designs interrelate.

Putting experience center stage and exploring how it is enacted in various kinds of situations in complex physical environments and with the participation of various elements, make it possible to build sensitivity to all of the relations and combinations which otherwise may be located in peripheral, unfitted junctions.

But how exactly can this be done?

A central idea in Experience Design is that it is important to pay close attention to situations of use. Experience Design is site specific. It is necessary to understand the people and the situations that designers design for. Designers need to understand, imagine, and fulfill human needs and desires. This implies building empathy, watching what people do and how they interact with things, environments, and each other; engaging, ethnographically, for example with real-world users in real-world situations. Experience emerges from and is enacted in these situations. This much is covered in what has been formally parsed as design thinking, such as is taught by one of the authors at Stanford d.school, the Hasso Plattner Institute of Design. This is a pragmatic approach to the challenge. Let us, however, also consider quite how we might conceive experience in relation to the interconnectedness of the everyday.

Designing for experience as think–sense–feel

One way of attempting to design for experience is to focus on thinking, sensing, and feeling. Working in Product Design, and from the basic premise that all products are for users, and that a good way to think about these users is by focusing on experience. Experience Design scholars Desmet, Hekkert, and Schifferstein (2011) argue that experience-driven design can be used for all sorts of design: from the design of floating wheelchairs to the design of mobile car parks. Traditionally in product design, and as we have just indicated, the user–product relationship has been understood in terms of the physical and cognitive abilities of the user (which encompasses physical capability, i.e. ergonomics, as well as sensory perception, i.e. aesthetics), and cognition (which is an orientation toward the mind as information processor, as well as toward meaning making). Now these foci have been supplemented with emotions; thinking of the user–product relationship also as an emotional relationship. The central feature here is that design aims at experience through three processes: cognition, sensory perception, and emotion. A similar orientation toward sensory and emotional aspects is found in "beyond cognitivism" approaches to be found in interaction design and digital user experience design, as well as in architecture (Klingmann 2007). According to McDonagh, Hekkert, van Erp, and Gyi (2002), thinking of the user as an emotional being, as well as body and mind, calls for experience-driven design strategies and methods.

Understanding experience as sense, emotion, and cognition may well be useful in design processes. Dissolving experience into physiological, emotional, and cognitive dimensions provides a take on what experience is, and thus also provides potential points of focus in efforts to design for experience. Desmet, Hekkert, and Schifferstein, for example, suggest that thinking of experience in this way is useful in design activity, reflection and evaluation:

The value of making the distinction is that it enables us to evaluate experiential impact from multiple angles. (Desmet, Hekkert, and Schifferstein 2011: 5)

In practice, in actual experience, however, these component parts are quite difficult to keep separate.

The distinctions among the three levels of experience are theoretical; in daily product experiences the layers are closely intertwined and they may influence each other. (Desmet, Hekkert, and Schifferstein 2011: 5)

Sense, emotion, and cognition are intertwined—and not only with each other but also with the rest of the world. As pointed out by Desmet, Hekkert, and Schifferstein, the purpose of analytically breaking down experience is to help designers think about experience: the concepts of sense, cognition, and emotion are "prostheses for thinking." These propositions, that, in actual experience sense, emotion and cognition are intertwined and that the purpose of analytical concepts is to support thinking, are an invitation to account for experience in a different manner.

It may seem helpful to break experience down into constituent components such as sense, cognition, and emotion, but the key question is: how helpful such reductionist analytical acts are in understanding and designing experiences of complex combinations of objects, services, spaces and information? Breaking down experience into three constituent components may overlook the entanglements and shifting flows of movement and attention, which also constitute experience.

We suggest that an alternative to understanding experience is to unfold it as fluidity. Experience is well conceived as shifting entanglements and engagements, as vectors of movement. This honors that Experience Design, if we wish to so designate a field, may be interesting for its ability to follow engagements and entanglements across different spatial, object, and digital relations, and over time.

Nomadic metaphysics

Here, with more time and space, we would explore that long and rich philosophical tradition of phenomenology—the study of structures of consciousness as experienced from the first-person point of view.

Instead we offer a particular perspective. In contemporary social and cultural thought the examination of the fixed has been displaced by an interest in exploring the fluidities of the world. A paradigmatic orientation toward mobility, process, and fluidity is seen across various disciplines—in sociology, in Urry's call for "a sociology beyond societies"; in anthropology as studies of culture and identity, as fixed and rooted phenomena are replaced by studies of routes where identities are negotiated and performed through travel; in culture studies where lived experiences of exiles, migrants, and refugees show the need for nomadic thought in order to make sense; in geography where the permanence and stability of place, territory, and landscape are challenged, and, instead, as suggested by Thrift (1994), theorized as "stages of intensity"—as traces of movement, speed, and circulation; and in architecture, in Tschumi's (1994) vision of architecture as a "movement of vectors."

This paradigmatic reorientation implies working with and from the ontological, indeed Herakleitean, position that reality is always in dynamic change: fluid, in process, on the move. Tumult, whirl, confusion, clamor, and hubbub all precede tidiness, alignment, and composition, symmetry, pattern, and structure. Stability emerges against a background of process, change, and movement. Instead of change being perceived as something, which passes over substance and stability, the relation between change and stability are reversed. Order exists against a background of disorder. This stands in opposition to the belief that reality consists of permanent substances. Cresswell outlines that this paradigm and its nomadic metaphysics offer a radical break from what he calls "sedentarist metaphysics"—approaches which work with and from "the incessant desire to divide the world up into clearly bounded [...] units" (2006: 26).

A nomadic ontology and account of experience

Focusing on flux and flow, kinetics and dynamics make it possible to account for experience as on-going processes of becoming. In a world on the move, experience has to be conceptualized also as being on the move. This links up with our experiment with accounting for experience as fleeting and shifting entanglements and engagements. The articulations—concepts—of nomadic metaphysics, which we relate to Experience Design, are marked by two central, philosophical influences. Explicitly there is Michel Serres' philosophy of mingled bodies (2008 [1985]), which is introduced with the purpose of translocating experience from foundation to flow. Implicitly, in the background, sneaking in terms without references, is the rhizomatic thinking of Gilles Deleuze. Serres' philosophy of mediation and multiplicity (Svabo 2010) and Deleuze's related approach (see Shanks 1992 for an early exploration) support thinking about experience in terms of flow, rhythm and movement, and seeing Experience Design as an on-going and negotiated choreography of engagement.

Experience as excursion

In his book *Les Cinq Sens* (2008 [1985]), Michel Serres develops what he calls "a philosophy of mingled bodies." He argues that a central feature of sensory perception is direction, orientation. Sense is movement, wandering, and visiting. Consciousness and body are on conjoint excursion (2008 [1995]: 236ff.). To experience is to go somewhere, move to something (and from something else). To sense is to wander, to move from one location to another, from one object, one intersection, one place of meeting to another.

Movement, meeting, intersection, and exchange are central in Serres' writing. A lucid example is found where Serres lets the sense of touch "play ball" with consciousness. Try it: take your finger and put it to your mouth. Use your finger to press slightly on your lips. In that moment your lips are an object to the touch of your finger. Now remove your finger from your lips, and, instead, kiss your finger. Your finger is now an object to the kiss of your lips, and consciousness has moved.

Consciousness resides in the contact between the finger and the lips—and it may move. When the finger touches the lips, consciousness resides in the finger; the lips are the object for touch. When the lips kiss the finger, the finger becomes object for the kiss. What is central here is not the location of consciousness but the "playing ball." Consciousness flares around. It does not reside in one particular location. Consciousness is on excursion (Serres 2008 [1985]: 22ff.; Connor 2008: 5).

Serres describes sensory perception as point of exchange and extension. In sensory perception body and consciousness intertwine. This has consequences for how sense and experience are defined. Sensory perception is no longer located in the realm of the physicality of the body, while experience is the amalgam of physicality, cognition, and emotion. Experience is a mobile convulsion of energies—sense, body, mediation, consciousness, and world. Experience is on the move. Experience is a nomad.

In the example where consciousness and body play ball, the human body and consciousness are in exchange with themselves. But it is central in Serres' philosophy that sense is not limited to the human body. In the example where sense plays ball with what is consciousness and what is object, sense is the intersection between body and consciousness, but the senses mediate also between the world and the I (Serres interchangeably uses consciousness, soul and I). "I mix with the world which mixes with me" (Serres 2008 [1985]: 13). Sense is both the location where consciousness and body mix with it, and where these mix with the world. Sense is the mingling of body, consciousness and world (Serres 2008 [1985]: 26).

Sense does not belong to the body. Sense belongs to the-body-and-the-world. Sense is mediator, intermediary, point of exchange, and extension. This implies that sense is dispersed. Sense may be extended into an object; the point of connection between the person and the world may be located outside of the body, in an object, a tool, or a vehicle. It is the fusion and intertwinement, the propagation and distribution which Serres stresses.

> The hand is no longer a hand when it has taken hold of the hammer, it is the hammer itself, it is no longer a hammer, it flies transparent, between the hammer and the nail, it disappears and dissolves, my own hand has long since taken flight in writing. The hand and thought, like one's tongue, disappear in their determinations. (Serres 1995 [1982]: 30)

> So what is a hand? It is not an organ, it is a faculty, a capacity for doing, for becoming claw or paw, weapon or compendium. (ibid.: 34)

The flowing together in action is stressed by Serres. This applies to an act such as hammering, but it also applies to thought, for thinking. Again it is the fusion and intertwinement that are stressed.

> When I think this object, that subject, there is no doubt that I am this subject, that object, if I truly think them; when I think a given concept, I am entirely this concept, when I think tree, I am the tree, when I think river, I am the river, when I think number, I am through and through from head to toe, number. That is the unquestionable experience of thinking. (Serres 1995 [1982]: 30)

With Serres we here see sensory perception as prosthetic, and distributed. Human, tool, thought, body flow together. They are fused in activity. Be this thinking or hammering. Or driving an automobile. World, sense, body, and I are mingled, intertwined in activity. But this unison is temporary. And this is important, for sense wanders. Sensory perception holds the capability of being directed at something—to be fused in activity, (which is very much like what Csikszentmihalyi 1991 describes as "flow experience"), but, above all, sensing is visiting (Serres 2008 [1985]: 304ff.): Being on the move, in continuous propagation, incessant dispersion and excursion, coming and going. It is the act of being directed towards something, but it is also distraction, the flickering gaze, moving on. Sense is the continuously moving intersection between body and consciousness, between human and world.

Experience as on-going engagement

With inspiration from Serres' philosophy of mingled bodies, experience may be accounted for in a manner where nomadic and voyaging features are highlighted, and where experience is explored through terms such as intersection, kneading, friction, interference, and exchange. In this account experience is the moving intersection of sense, consciousness, body, and world. Experience is on-going engagement. This account challenges us to understand experience as a verb in movement, rather than as a noun sitting still.

It furthermore follows from this that experience has rhythm, patterns, temporality, and spacing. It includes pauses, breaks. Experience is not smooth, frictionless, always, all of the time. Experience is also (being) subjected to kneading, turbulence, disruption, and distraction. There is friction in experience. Experience is the kneading of orders.

Nomadic design

It is a central challenge for design research and practice to be able to conceptualize and orchestrate the experiences of combinations of designs and their on-going reconfiguration (Brown 2009: 8; Bjögvinsson, Ehn, and Hillgren 2012; Simonsen et al. 2014: 2). One way of doing this is to approach experience from the fluidities of such a nomadic metaphysics, where experience is multiple, continuously negotiated, and on the move (Crang and Thrift 2000: 19), and where design is an arrangement and on-going assembling activity (Highmore 2009: 4) that takes place in an active field of engagements and entanglements where established combinations themselves may combine (Highmore 2009: 3). When experience is given account as voyaging engagement, nomadic convulsions of energies, Experience Design becomes an effort to choreograph forces, engagements, and energies: to manage, maneuver or direct the interrelations and combinations of heterogeneous elements and to stage patterns of interference. This implies envisioning patterns of (inter)action and providing rhythmic possibilities for engagement. Experience Design becomes a situational choreography of heterogeneous forces.

Using this approach in design implies developing imagination and sensitivity toward shifting patterns in the interrelations between heterogeneous elements. These interrelations can be explored as patterns of interference and engagement, as connection and disconnection, an on-going making and breaking of relations. Experience Design is a gathering of engagements and distractions where various elements intersect and negotiate.

A metaphysics for design pragmatics

This nomadic and fluid metaphysics (see also Harman 2005; Bogost 2012) is completely suited to design thinking, the shorthand term for the pragmatics of a transferable creative design process (Moggridge 2007, 2010; IDEO 2011; Brown 2009; Kelley and Kelley 2013; Norman 2013). Indeed, we have portrayed what we construe as Experience Design as a manifestation of such design thinking.

"Thrown-in" media res, the designer makes no attempt to wipe the slate clean and start afresh, but attends to the flow of experience, aiming to become mindful of need and desire in the complex, inter-folded flux of bodies, intentions, artefacts, identities, meanings, in the heterogeneous and ever local assemblages that constitute the human condition. Collaborative empathic understanding accompanies constant research forays to ascertain and then try out solutions to design problems that remain always provisional in interminably iterative cycles of question, discovery, trial, and return to the design challenge, whatever it may be.

Attention to this metaphysics opens up new avenues of design research and practice because it sharpens focus on the character of human experience, offering significant elaboration of the notion of the human in human-centered design, beyond the cognitive and behavioral, beyond think–sense–feel.

Conclusion

Experiences emerge in the intertwinement of a variety of objects, interactions, spaces, and information. Experience Design can act as an umbrella term for a number of design approaches that target complexities and heterogeneity in situations of use. Experience Design can allow researchers and designers to cross boundaries and inquire into interrelations, negotiations, and entanglements. One way of attempting to design for experience is to focus on thinking, sensing, and feeling, but in actual experience these elements are intertwined. For this reason, a nomadic approach, as found in Serres' philosophy of the five senses is entirely appropriate—with its accent on the mingled, mediated, and propagating character of sensory engagement. In such an account experience is the moving intersection of sense, consciousness, body, and world. This nomadic approach is an invitation to experiment with new metaphors for experience. (Metaphor, in fact, means "transport.")

What happens if we think of and design for experience as movement, passageway, excursion, and transportation? Walk, hop, skip, jump, and dance.

Chapter 3
How Much Time Does it Take for Experience Design to Unfold?
Catherine Elsen and Pierre Leclercq

Designing "for" experiences, taking into account end-users, their explicit and tacit needs, devoting time to empathic understanding, dealing with emotions and senses are topics currently fostering interests and populating debates. Methodologies such as "Design Thinking" or "Creative Problem-Solving" (considered by some as likely to become company cultures) "extensively prone" human-centered design approaches in product design (Brown 2008). Likewise, fields such as service design, marketing and even management more and more take inspiration from human and social sciences to develop new ways to deal with contemporary challenges (Olsen and Welo 2011).

In the meantime, one has to admit that little is known theoretically and empirically speaking about the context in which such approaches can ideally unfold: contradictory statements frequently flourish in the specialized press and few fundamental researches bring light on those assertions. While von Hippel et al. (1999), for instance, underlines how users (seen as innovators) heavily impacted 3M worldwide success, Steve Jobs has been reported saying that there was no market research done at Apple (Morris 2008). There are thus tremendous opportunities for research in the area of designing for experience. This chapter will more specifically focus on one of its aspects, sometimes even picked out as one of its shortcomings: the time it takes to gain better understanding of end-users[1] in order to properly design possible real-time experience for them.

State of the art

In traditional societies, where human-made objects were conceived, made, and used by the same person (Jones 1970), the experience of using the object could be fed back directly into its design and making. The industrial revolution, however, introduced a separation between the designer (the person who conceives an object), the maker (the person who produces it), and the user (the person who experiences it). As a result, the direct feedback loop between experience, design, and making is interrupted.

Users (operators, inhabitants, customers … direct or indirect) are proactively and differently stimulated by a complex range of intrinsic and extrinsic characteristics. In this regard Crilly et al. (2008: 18) write:

"consumers approach artefacts with their own motivations, experiences and expectations, and therefore artefacts will be interpreted in different ways by different people in different contexts." Experience is shaped by particularities, inherent to each individual: personality, moods, and background; cultural values and beliefs; skills and capabilities; motivation and expectations (linked to previous experiences and memory, as well as the physical, social and economic context) (Desmet and Hekkert 2007). Law et al. (2009) share this viewpoint and show, through a 275 participant survey, that researchers and designers from 25 different countries are indeed aware of the highly dynamic, context-dependent, and subjective nature of User Experiences (or UX), similar observations being certainly valid in the field of Experience Design as well.

Although research has been conducted on tools and techniques that help in gaining insights about users' needs, there is currently indeed no single "best practice" for determining how designers should employ these various tools. Olsen and Welo (2011) did compare four of the most popular methods and discovered that web-based surveys, and to some extent interview, do not provide much more than "surface information," whereas workshops and observations provide more deep and complete information, but are also more difficult to deal with for practitioners. Oelhberg, Roschuni, and Agonino (2011) formalized a list of tools helping designers to capture, reflect, and share information about users, but did not provide a clear explanation about why those tools ought to be used.

Besides tools and techniques, the timing, and what type and quantity of information should be collected about end-users also remain open-ended questions. Depending on the viewpoint, time spent on early phases design, where more than 70 percent of the final costs are being defined (Ehrlenspiel 1995) and where considerations for experiences traditionally unfold, is either considered as beneficial, or, entirely in contrary, as detrimental.

On the one hand, some consider that time and research volume granted to preliminary design constitute the safety net that guarantees incubation processes, more informed and creative outcomes, sound critical distance towards some prescriptive (and sometimes inadequate) desires, and even serendipity. Arguments supporting this approach can be found in the area of research on design tools. Yang (2005), for instance, found statistically significant, positive correlations between the time students spend on "design" (including the research, ideation, and sketching phases) and the final grade they received for their project. Acuna and Sosa (2011) also suggest that a higher investment on sketching and model-making time tends to be linked to more original solutions. More specific insights about designing for user experiences, in this regard, are sparser.

In other research, user-centered approaches are indeed rather considered as "too time consuming" (Cain 2005; Postma et al. 2012). This viewpoint is nowadays shared by a growing number of practitioners, who operate under the assumption that spending time in a "wrong" way will lead to decreased efficiency and poor use of precious design resources during this critical phase. In terms of pure user-centric research, Lai, Honda, and Yang (2010) showed that quantity of interactions with users, and time spent with them were not necessarily linked with better design outcomes. Quality of the information gained, however, could contribute to richer understanding and validate design directions. In another study, teams that generated the most design information, notably in terms of potential end-user groups, did not have a better design outcome (Elsen et al. 2012). Moreover, even if results were not strongly statistically significant, the overall trend suggested that the smaller the number of user groups generated (and, consequently, the faster and the stronger the focus), the better the overall ranking of the teams.

Globally speaking, considering the current state of the art about Experience Design and how it unfolds, it seems that at best designers can try to design "for" an experience; that is, building a context that could lead to some kind of favorable experience. When and how they should inform themselves about users' needs in order to fulfill this goal, however, is still unclear.

Research questions

In view of these sometime conflicting viewpoints, we frame two research questions:

- How "time-framing" the design process possibly filters (positively or negatively) the awareness designers have about end-users (their explicit, tacit needs; their experiences).

- How the experimental protocols, their inherent limitations, and artificialities shape the designers' involvement in the process of designing for end-users' experiences.

The following section will present how, methodologically speaking, we defined protocols in order to gain insights about these concerns.

Methodology and data treatment

This chapter is built on the comparison of four distinct settings, including three experimental settings, that build up their protocol on a real-life design project.

The real-life setting, nurturing the whole research process and offering us the opportunity to work with a coherent and valid design brief, consisted of a six-week ethnographic observation of professional designers, conducted within one design firm (i.e. developing a critical and socially embedded understanding of experiences and phenomena through close exploration of several types of data, such as active note taking, audio-video recordings, open but targeted interviews, etc.; see Ingold 2008). Three designers (two experienced professionals and one intern) were busy answering a competition call when our research team first contacted them. They welcomed us and two of our cameras to their office. We were permitted access to all visual documents related to their project (documents they had received for the design brief, the ones they looked at for inspiration, and those they themselves generated), discuss their on-going activities, and follow the design process step by step to the final stage of printing the file for submission.

Throughout the six weeks, several dozen documents (sketches, CAD printouts, reference material, technical sheets, etc.) were systematically scanned and inventoried, and around 24 hours of video were recorded, from which a little more than six hours were selected for this analysis. These six hours constitute records of design meetings that happened in the presence of an intern freshly admitted to the team—new to the world of design as well as to the project, he was very curious and asked a lot of questions. He pushed the other two designers to speak a lot about their decisions (past and present), and he solicited explanations as to how the design process had unfolded until his arrival.

Both lead designers, being naturally inclined to include him as quickly as possible in the design process in order to make him an efficient team member, were observed providing richer and more detailed explanations during those conversations than during our interviews with them, therefore justifying our selection of sequences.

The design project was about designing a "game area" for a national lottery that would be displayed inside various outlets (libraries, gas stations, supermarkets, etc.). This game area had to have the facilities to enable gamblers to play, fill-in, or scratch lottery tickets in total confidentiality. The brief stated that it should integrate a tablet to fill-in tickets (slightly tilted for use as a writing desk only; no other objects should be able to be left standing on it); a pen attached to a chain, and its pen holder; a trash bin to collect the useless lottery tickets (minimum opening to avoid throwing anything else in other than useless tickets); a place to exhibit blank lottery tickets (with their specific sizes); and a place to display lottery results and advertising campaigns. Each game area was to be designed for individual use only, but several of them may be connected in a modular way to fit each outlet's needs. The game area should attract attention and be immediately associated with the national lottery in question, which aspires to create a modern, fresh, and dynamic identity.

Submitted designs would be evaluated for market visibility (50 percent); design (25 percent); modularity and ergonomics (25 percent); and the 15-page design brief that designers received would be their sole contact with the project holder.

The other three experimental settings were built on a simplified version of the above design brief, similar to the summary presented above, only without the technical files that were considered to be superfluous and unfit for more time-constrained experimental settings.

The first experimental setting was a 180-minute design session during which a designer was asked to sketch and write down anything that could, from his point of view, answer the brief. This young designer (with limited professional experience but having a strong background in graphic and product design) was also asked to use the think aloud method (van Someren et al. 1994) during the whole design process. This designer, who we will refer to as the "180 min" subject, drew and annotated 25 distinct ideas (in 106 drawings) on 44 sheets of paper, using mainly black and colored pencils.

The second experimental setting was built on a similar protocol (including thinking aloud), except this time another designer was asked to complete the task in 45 minutes. This "45 min" subject was a Master's student in mechanical engineering with additional background in art and design. He drew and annotated nine distinct ideas (in 37 drawings) on 15 sheets of paper, using exclusively a black sharpie.

The last experimental setting was intentionally designed quite differently. We asked another Master's student (with a similar background in mechanical engineering and product design to the 45 min student[2]) to start from the same design brief but this time to use the brainstorming technique (Osborn 1963) during a 20-minute ideation session around the specific notion of users' needs and expectations. Equipped with sticky notes and sharpies, this "20 min" subject was told to write down as many users' needs he could think of when confronted with this brief. He would stick his notes to the wall, take a few steps back to look at them and reflect aloud.

All three experimental settings were video-recorded and every document safely registered. The subsequent analysis was based on the entire corpus of data, and conducted along an iteratively defined grid. Variables for analysis were eventually fixed as follows:

- Qualitative description of the user: in what terms are the designers referring to the different types of users? Do they describe profiles, abilities, anthropomorphic information, responsibilities, tasks, etc?

- Usage scenario: are the designers simply listing users and their qualities, or are they envisioning them in action, in movement, in interaction? Do users follow explicit goals? This projected "role-playing" of users in action is, following Darses and Wolff (2006), one of the designers' most important mental representations about users.

- User experience: are the designers envisioning users having certain types of experiences? Here Medway's work on experience analysis was used to structure the possible experiences in four main levels (see Luck and McDonnell 2006), namely Functional or Structural Perception (perception of objective elements of the artefact); Perceptual Awareness (second level attributes that can be perceived, such as light, sound, heaviness, etc.); Phenomenological Experience (such as feelings, experiencing an atmosphere, etc.) and Symbolic Meaning (ideas evocation or reference to mystery, memory, cultural symbol, etc.).

Starting from there, basic counting of occurrences was performed to reach exploratory quantitative results, while qualitative analysis of natural verbatim (during the real-life setting) or artificially stimulated think-aloud (during the three others experiments) provided additional support to illustrate any phenomena.

Results

Because none of the designers had access to real end-users during their design process (the "real-life" designers simply looked at a few pictures of various outlets), they all heavily relied on introspection and previous experiences (as a designer, a user, or a gambler). While the 20 min subject was explicitly asked to use the brainstorming technique, we observed that other so-called "creative methodologies" — such as analogies and forced connections (or using metaphors to create new ideas) — were naturally conveyed by other participants.

In terms of types of users envisioned during the design process, we distinguished 11 profiles. Four of them were consistently referred to, whatever the design setting:

- The game area user, interacting consciously and directly with the furniture to fill-in or scratch a lottery ticket. The designers would further attribute this client with varying scenarios (different body morphology, social situations, props, etc.).
- The visitor of venue in general, potentially interested by the outlet, the game area and the lottery tickets, potentially impacted and attracted by the branding, but not initially entering the outlet with that purpose in mind.
- The "lambda" user, present at the venue with no projected intention toward the brand, but somehow able to interact with the game area user (by looking at what is being done, by being indiscreet, etc.).
- The outlet owner, operating the game area on behalf of the national lottery and expecting extra outcomes from its display.

Table 3.1 summarizes all additional users considered inside each of the four settings. Interestingly, the real-life designers came up with many more different profiles, although not all of them (compared to the other experimental settings, where users with limited mobility were, for instance, considered).

Table 3.1 Types of end-users considered inside each of the four settings, on top of the four general profiles systematically referred to.

20 min brainstorming	45 min setting	180 min setting	Real-life setting
Maintenance person	Maintenance person	People with limited mobility	Maintenance person
Overall project holder (the national lottery)	People with limited mobility	Salesperson (not the owner), interacting with and manipulating the game area	Overall project holder (the national lottery)
	"Gamblers" (in the widest sense of the term)		"Gamblers"
			Salesperson
			Passer-by (pedestrian or inside a car), not entering the outlet but looking inside
			Manufacturer
			User at risk (in potential hazardous situations related to falling objects, sharp objects, lack of hygiene …)

Figure 3.1 shows side by side, for each of the four settings, the total number of occurrences[3] where end-users were referred to and the total duration (in minutes), either of the experimental settings or of the real-life setting (that is in total 364 minutes of meetings selected for analysis). The curve illustrates the ratio "total number of occurrences/total duration."

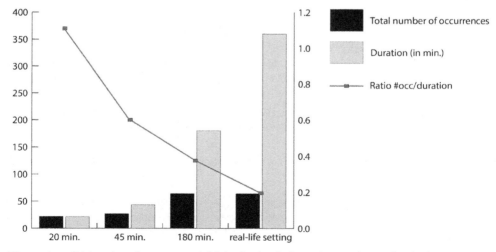

Figure 3.1 Total number of occurrences, total duration in minutes and curve of proportional ratio.

Interestingly, the 20 min brainstorming participant was significantly more prolific in terms of generating insights about end-users (proportionally to the duration of his session) than the three others settings. This can be explained, partially at least, by the fact that this participant was explicitly requested to develop as many insights as possible, whereas the other participants were not specifically told about our interest in end-users. The 20 min participant later explained that he constantly had to refrain from designing solutions, images popping-up constantly into his mind. Respecting the protocol, he did not draw them out, but referred a lot to the design prompt and made a lot of analogies to personal experiences. His work was overall highly structured as he organized his sticky notes on the wall: in "columns" of different users, with their respective characteristics and needs.

The 180 min design setting reaches the same number of occurrences as the real-life session, but in just around half the time. This participant also ideated a lot by using a wide variety of analogies (to a restaurant, to IKEA, to a forest, to an amusement park, etc.) and also reached a wider panel of situations than the 20 min or 45 min designers (for instance in terms of impact of advertisement, attractiveness, etc.). Interestingly, compared to the real-life setting, he is the participant suggesting the more eccentric physical positions for the end-user using the game area (not only standing or sitting in front of it, as suggested by anyone else, but also lying inside something, lying in a hammock, walking on a bridge like "Indiana Jones," etc.).

As for the real-life setting, it is interesting to notice that the designers made 67 references to end-users (exactly the same as the 180 min setting), but that these references were partly of quite different nature. Both expert designers, knowing very well the complete version of the design brief, made much more reference to the project holder (the national lottery), as they were obviously under real competition pressure. Experiences also reach a higher level of detail: "the tablet should be covered with a spotty, smooth surface so pens will leave less marks and it will be considered as less dirty by the users"; similarly, "footrest should be painted grey so footsteps' dirt will be less visible for users", or, later, "we could cover the tablet with colorful decor, including figures, so people could get inspired to fill-in their lottery tickets." Projected users also were considered in more hazardous situations: "We should make sure the edges of the steel sheet are not too sharp so people don't cut themselves"; later on, "what could happen if someone stumbled on the footrest? Could the whole structure fall over?" And so on.

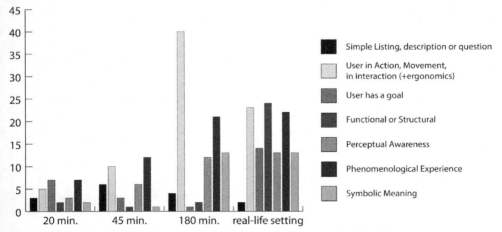

Figure 3.2 Absolute number of occurrences for each type of reference and each setting.

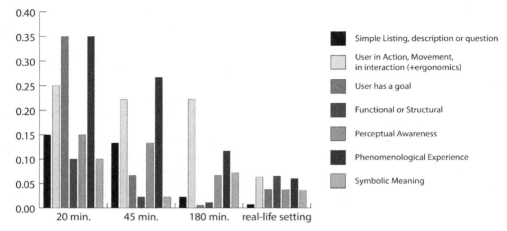

Figure 3.3   Number of occurrences per minute for each type of reference and each setting.

Interestingly, designers from the real-life situation never drew any user references. They rather merely referred verbally to end-users, and even took measures of their own bodies to make sure each part of the game area would be ergonomically fitted (but didn't draw them).

Figure 3.2 looks at how users are referred to in terms of scenario and experiences in absolute number of occurrences, while Figure 3.3 refers to the same variables but in number of occurrences per minute (to see whether intensity of generating insights evolves with total duration). Both figures show that, when it comes to listing users, to simply describe them or ask questions about their characteristics, both short settings (20 and 45 min) display similar number of occurrences or frequencies. "Users in action" seem to foster high interest from the 180 min participant (Figure 3.2), and yet we see that this approach in fact creates, in terms of frequency, similar important interests inside the three first settings (except for the real-life situation).

Looking more specifically at users experiencing something, one can observe that:

- Functional and structural levels are important, relatively, for both 20 min and real-life settings. In the first case, it can certainly be explained by the nature of those experiences, the most accessible and easy to think of in a limited amount of time. In the second case, we suggest that the competitive, realistic and constructive context creates more propensity to think of tangible solutions (in terms of human relations to shapes, materials, structures).

- Perceptual awareness is also regularly referred to, especially during the 20 min and 45 min settings.

- Interestingly, "higher level" experiences such as phenomenological experiences or references to symbolic meanings respectively decrease in frequency for longer sessions. The 180 min participant nevertheless refers a lot to symbols (as much in absolute occurrences as the real-life setting), which can be explained by his tendency to extensively rely on analogies as an idea-generator method.

Eventually, comparing the number of "experience levels" conjointly referred to when looking at a single situation, real-life setting creates the richer, complex, and intricate stories with four conjoint levels inside a single occurrence. At one point, designers indeed discussed about every type of outlet that could welcome such game areas (library, gas station, etc.) and observed that most of these spaces were really messy and full of products for sale (cigarettes, magazines, snacks, etc.). They compared these sale points to more minimalist, simple outlets fully dedicated to one product (for instance an Apple store, or a cell company) and realized that "we will never be able to reach such a level of attraction and formal simplicity ... too much mess in there to really attract people in some kind of serenity." In a handful of seconds, the designers in this way referred to functional perception (users seeing several objects side by side), to perceptual awareness (users perceiving some messy density), to phenomeno- logical experience (feeling less at ease, less welcomed), and symbolic meaning (evocation of buying, emergence of consumerist desires).

The 180 min participant, similarly, was able to produce very brief but rich references to several levels of experiences (up to three). When designing some hanging device, for instance, he said: "this would be like a sheet, hanging from the ceiling like some kind of ghost ... and you would go in there."

The 20 min and 45 min participants reached a maximum of two conjoint levels of experiences, but sometimes thought of aspects otherwise dismissed by other designers. The brainstorming participant, for instance, talked about "how people should locate updates about the jackpot to be tempted to play more" (functional awareness; symbolic meaning), while the 45 min participant's main concern was how external users (those not using the game area) could have a sense that someone was already using the furniture, but without perceiving too much of what was happening inside (sense of discretion).

Methodologically speaking, the 180 min participant, even if familiar with the think aloud procedure, had to admit being exhausted after the design session. He asked for two pauses and started repeating himself quite a lot as more time passed.

Discussion

As a short debrief of these results, several points of attention may be summarized. First, short brain- storming sessions specifically oriented toward end-users, in the context of plausible design briefs, seem to constitute valuable methods to gain insights about users' experiences and behaviors. We should also underline that too time-constrained settings as well as prevention to sketch (even quickly) might impede a complete perception of users' variabilities. People with limited mobility, for instance, were completely missed out by the 20 min participant—as well as, remarkably, by the real-life designers. Structuring sticky notes on a wall and taking a few steps back to reflect nevertheless helped the participant to reach a prolific, structured, and non-repetitive panorama of end-users' insights.

On the other end of the continuum, longer design sessions (180 minutes and more) contribute to a richer, wider perspective on end-users, nurtured with go and forth moves between reflection, ideation, and representation. If the 180 min participant reached as many occurrences as the real-life designers, although in less time, we have yet to acknowledge that the real-life designers had a more detailed, reality-focused vision of experiences. Potential end-users were put into more varied situations (some of them hazardous) and could be less proximal in their relationship with the designed artefact (for instance, some passer-by looking through a shop-window and discovering the game area). More time therefore seems to generate a more intricate set of scenarios, conjointly including more "levels of experience."

Analogies and similar strategies to reach more symbolic meanings, such as the forced connection method, were demonstrated by the 180 min participant, as other possible strategies to come to more "eccentric," "out-of-the-box" end-users' models.

Front-to-front with brainstorming and other tools for "disciplined creativity," designers should most of all be aware that each strategy has different types of insights to offer, and that a combination of several of those techniques and approaches certainly is more advisable than a one-way of doing things.

Conclusion

Even if we have to treat these results with caution (as they are issued from limited sample, and certainly have been impacted by expertise levels, "personal" style in designing, or even previous, personal experiences designers might have in relation to gambling), we would suggest pursuing investigation on how techniques such as brainstorming, analogies, or "forced connections" (seen as mediums for "disciplined creativity") could constitute powerful tools to quickly reach prolific, structured insights about end-users (their types, behaviors, goals, and experiences). A second experiment, opting for more reflective approaches to designing experiences (seen as a global mind-set rather than some additional constraints you have to check-out with at some point), and provided that they are appropriately applied on a longer perspective, could provide designers with more detailed, informed, and qualitative insights.

Insights on end-users, even if not yet universally acknowledged inside companies and institutions (because they are related to too playful, too ambiguous methods, not predictable enough, or even just incompatible with compartmentalized R&D departments), nevertheless constitute crucial assets for the whole Experience Design process and design outcomes. One should now focus on ways to develop more agile tools to support such human-centered research and design.

Acknowledgements

Our thanks go to the six designers who accepted to take part in our experiments and/or to open their doors to us, and our cameras.

Notes

1   According to Wilkie (2010), the term "user" (or, by extension, "end-user") finds its origins in cognitive sciences where it was used as a rhetorical object to distinguish the addressee from the term "operator," often used inside the human factors and ergonomic discourse. While the term has been widely impoverished during Modernism, it now regains a collective meaning translating different approaches to needs and requirements. The term "user" opens again toward the "experience" in a more broad sense of the word (Redström 2006) and will be used in that sense in this chapter, in reference to anyone getting in contact with an artefact, consciously or unconsciously. Seen as an overall term, it will thus also translate the fact that the user, the inhabitant, the customer … is most of the time nothing else than an assemblage of partial models of thoughts—a mix between what the designers know about other people, what they believe, what their future interests in the people are, and how those interests evolve through time.

2   The three subjects who took part to the experimental settings were chosen for their similar backgrounds in

engineering and design (all three majoring from the Massachusetts Institute of Technology). Among other possible participants, they were chosen because of their trusted abilities to answer a design brief of such nature, their willingness to sketch, and their voluntary interest in taking part in such experiments.

3   One occurrence was defined each time designers explicitly talked about end-users, or referred to them indirectly when saying "here you would put your arm like that on the tablet." Quick follow-ups of several occurrences came up from time to time: in those cases, occurrences were defined for each different type of user executing different type of tasks (or experiencing different facets of the artefact).

Chapter 4
Experiential Equality and Digital Discrimination
Linda Leung

This chapter attempts to interrogate the crux of Experience Design; that is, whether experiences can be designed when the outcomes can be so diverse and subjective. In particular, the consequences and inequalities that can arise when such experiences are mediated by technology will be examined.

Experience Design is inherently exclusive. Much of the industry and practitioner-oriented User Experience literature is concerned with user-centeredness and designer awareness of who they are designing for, as much as who they are *not* designing for (Leung 2008). Therefore, some experiences are designed with the intention of not being experienced by specific users or groups. This is evident in fields that are well-practiced in Experience Design such as fashion. Women's fashion is not designed for men. Designer fashion is not intended for all women.

The mediation of experiences compounds this exclusivity by requiring not only the availability of technologies that enable those experiences, but also access to the skills and knowledge to use them. In Wyatt et al. (2001), I argued that while technology can enable, it could also create inequities. Furthermore, these qualities are not inherent in any particular technology, but rather a product of how such technologies are designed. This line of thinking can also be applied to the field of Experience Design.

First, as a discipline, the field of Experience Design also demonstrates a similar kind of Utopianism in that it is premised upon fixing problems and providing solutions that will deliver idealized scenarios. Second, Experience Design is explicit about exclusiveness as part of its practice of not designing for everyone.

It follows then that experiences are inevitably unequal. What are the unintended consequences when the design of experiences is not inclusive? How can this be reconciled with principles of accessibility? What happens when excluded user groups engage in experiences that were never meant for them?

Most recently, my research has been concerned with refugees and their use of technology. As a group, they are critically affected by forced migration and displacement. They form a group of users who are characterized by their mobility, yet they are not considered a target market for cell phone use, or indeed any technologies, which might assist in sustaining connections with displaced family and friends. As a result, their access to such technologies is inequitable and their technical literacies variable. They are discriminated against because they have not experienced nor have little experience with technologies that were never designed for them.

This chapter will draw on empirical evidence (Leung 2011; Leung and Finney Lamb 2010; Leung et al. 2009) to illustrate the kinds of technological experiences that are assumed and privileged, in such a way as to marginalize the experiential differences of minorities and exclude them from vital services that are intended to be accessible to all.

Not all experiences are equal

The notion of Experience Design suggests an intended experiential outcome on behalf of the designer for the end-user. Much of the Experience Design or User Experience (UX) literature focuses on this intention (rather than the unintentional) and on instigating change.

Shedroff (2001: 4) describes good Experience Design as a process of seduction, which involves enticement and then engagement before conclusion (Khaslavsky and Shedroff 1999). Similarly, Forlizzi and Battarbee define it as follows:

> An experience has a beginning and an end, and often inspires behavioral changes in the experiencer. (2004: 263)

Norman agrees that designers can appeal to users' wants and desires through emotion, arguing that emotional responses can be designed accordingly to induce particular reactions. Positive effect can be produced by particular attributes (Norman 2004). Furthermore, experiences and objects can be designed with built-in "affordances," such that users are more predisposed to certain experiential outcomes than others. For example, a doorknob generally affords twisting rather than pushing or pulling (Norman 2002: xii). Fogg (2003) talks about the ways in which technology can be designed to "persuade" users into particular courses of action.

These affordances and persuasions can also be seen in online experiences. When comparing Facebook with LinkedIn, for example, we can see that they function in similar ways as networking sites. However, LinkedIn is intended as a professional networking site while Facebook affords a more informal, social networking experience.

Therefore, experiential inequality exists insofar as designers explicitly attempt to make interventions that privilege intended outcomes over the unintended ones. Such inequalities are also extended to the particular kinds of users that designers seek to target.

Discriminating users

The practice of user-centered design (UCD) is about designing with targeted users in mind and ignoring other users. As Kuniavsky (2003: 129) argues, defining an audience too broadly is not defining it at all. The antithesis of the "everything for everyone" approach, it requires the designer to focus on targeted users to the exclusion of others.

UCD cuts across a range of design and other disciplines. This is acknowledged in exhibition design, which Dernie (2006: 13) argues, is now explicitly audience-focused. In business, the Pareto principle states that 80 percent of sales come from 20 percent of clients. In both cases, UCD advocates knowing those key audience members/clients and designing with them in mind.

The practice of developing user profiles is precisely about personifying your target user, and solidifying an image of them. The persona is an archetype of a single person. Cooper (2004) is in favor of "narrowing the design target":

> The broader a target you aim for, the more certainty you have of missing the bull's eye. If you want to achieve a product-satisfaction level of 50%, you cannot do it by making a large population 50% happy with your product. You can only accomplish it by singling out 50% of the people and striving to make them 100% happy. It goes further than that. You can create an even bigger success by targeting 10% of your market and working to make them 100% ecstatic.

Therefore, UCD promotes the discrimination of users as part of its practice; that is, delineating between audience groups and then including or excluding them accordingly.

Deliberate exclusion

Exclusion is part and parcel of the design of experiences. While this is not done with malice, it does mean that inequality is built into the process of experiential design, unless it is explicitly intended as inclusive or universal design. Some experiences are not intended to be had by particular groups of people. For example, in the design of cars, people with vision impairments would normally be excluded from the target user group. This makes the experience of driving a car exclusive to those without vision impairments.

This process of targeting particular users while excluding others makes experiences inaccessible to those who have been excluded. While those experiences might be readily available, they often pose difficulties of access for people who are not part of the target group. Cars are readily available, but the experience of driving one is designed to be inaccessible to those with vision impairments. Furthermore, cars are designed to be inaccessible to others outside of target user groups, such as children and those without a driver's license. The point here is that availability does not equate to accessibility. Something may be available in abundance, but the way it has been designed and for whom it has been designed, may render it inaccessible.

Web pages are a case in point. The internet is saturated with web pages. However, for those who do not read well, these pages are largely inaccessible. Similarly, they are inaccessible to those who do not know how to use a computer or the internet. The World Wide Web Consortium's (W3C) Web Accessibility Initiative (WAI) has made attempts to improve accessibility through its Web Content Accessibility Guidelines (WCAG). Critics acknowledge that the guidelines help to make web experiences more accessible to those with physical disabilities; that is, those with motor or sensory impairments who require tools other than a mouse or keyboard to use the internet. Unfortunately, the guidelines do less to accommodate those who do not read well (which may include those with learning disabilities, or people from non-English backgrounds), or new or novice users of the internet. Accessibility depends on the degree of inclusiveness in the design: increasing accessibility necessitates considering more target user groups.

The design of experiences always assumes a certain level of audience literacy. Literacy, in this sense, is taken to mean knowledge and understanding of how to participate in that experience. Inclusive design can lower the literacy threshold required to participate in an experience, thereby making it more accessible. If web designers included in their target audiences those who could not read well, first, the web would look very different, and, second, it would be more accessible to those for whom English is a second language, and/or those with learning difficulties. However, it still requires users to be able to navigate those pages with an internet-enabled device. In other words, an experience can be designed to be as inclusive as possible, but is still dependent on users' literacies (such as those pertaining to technology and language) to be experienced. The variations in audience's skills and knowledge thus make experiences uneven.

Therefore, the design of experiences is inevitably unequal in that it:

- Discriminates between intended and unintended experiences
- Privileges targeted users over other users
- Does not make them inclusive or accessible just because they are available
- Relies on user literacy to participate in such experiences.

Refugees as excluded users

My research has investigated the unevenness of technology experiences with users who are largely overlooked by technology designers. In particular, I have focused on refugees, whom I have defined broadly as those that have been subject to forced migration and displacement from countries of origin due to conflict, persecution, and/ or natural disaster. This includes refugees, asylum seekers, internally displaced persons (IDPs), stateless persons, and others of concern, which the United Nations High Commissioner for Refugees (UNHCR, n.d.) estimated in 2010 to be over 43 million worldwide.

Refugees can be considered minority users or excluded users of technology for a number of reasons. First, they often (but not always) originate from countries where the availability of information and communication technologies (ICTs) is limited, either because of lack of technical infrastructure, or any existing infrastructure has been damaged or heavily controlled due to war and political instability. Second, when refugees are compelled to flee their countries of origin, their lack of experience with ICTs mean they often have difficulty accessing those technologies even when they are readily available in intermediate or transit countries. Third, during their displacement, refugees lack stable income and employment opportunities, so ICTs fall outside their realm of affordability. Therefore, refugees are excluded from ICT use through lack of availability, technical literacies that make ICTs more accessible, and financial capacity to afford such technologies.

When specific technologies are studied, such as internet or cell phone use, availability and access are assumed to be un-problematic (Preece 1998; Abdul-Rahman and Hailes 2000; Kadende-Kaiser 2000; Henderson and Gilding 2004). In other words, the use of technologies has mostly been studied with those who are advantaged in their access to such technologies. The use of mobile devices by young people has particularly been well documented (see Katz and Aakhus 2002; Wilska 2003; Leena et al. 2005; Buckingham 2008). Yet the benefits of cell phones to refugees, who are defined by their mobility, have hardly been explored.

In every respect, refugees are unintended users of ICTs, and so experiences with this technology have not been designed for them. My research investigates the unintended outcomes when refugees come into contact with ICTs. What might designers learn about refugees' exclusion from ICTs and their "undesigned" interactions with them?

Drawing from over 100 interviews and surveys with refugees, the following empirical evidence was collected from 2007 to 2010 across an Australian pilot study and subsequent funded research project. The data have been anonymized and consolidated into an online database at http://trr.digimatter.com that is possibly the most comprehensive, publicly available collection of user research on refugees' experiences of technology.

Exclusion by lack of availability

Participants from African countries of origin highlighted the lack of telecommunications infrastructure that meant communication over distances was limited to physically visiting people or using more rudimentary, analog technologies such as hand-delivered letters.

> People like me I was living without those electronics … The way that I communicate with my people in Sudan is through going to where the people is, because it was very hard there to communicate with the people … the population of the country 90 per cent living without technology use. (A27, Sudan)

> … it was a little bit difficult because we used to communicate by writing letters and then we have to possibly give it to someone to send it to communicate with the family … So sometime if there's anyone going who you trust to take the letter directly to your person or your family, you can send the letter easily, you could still send sort of letters in couple of days depending on who would take the letter. (A7, Sudan)

> Just letter. That time, just not too much mobile phone. When I want to write a letter I just call my friend who knew how to write, to write for me. (A11, Togo)

> Well, at that time we never have anything like a cell-phone … Through letter, mail letter, write, send it by someone to take it to the person. (A10, Liberia)

> If we want to communicate with each other, if you go to my family place, I just say to you what I want to say to my family. You just—I talk to you and then you just go to them … no calling, we used the letter … For old people they don't even use the letter because they don't know how to write and read. So they just send a message through me and then I go there … Once a month. two times a month, something like that. (A33, Ethiopia)

The absence of widespread availability of ICTs led to two things. The first is that participants had to design their own communication experiences without the use of ICTs. The second is the creation of privilege around communication technologies because of their scarcity.

But you see late 90s to 2000, it become more easier because we have access to use maybe home phone especially in the Khartoum area … But back at Southern Sudan—maybe because there was no home phones we just use when our parents or our family members are in the office, we use the office telephone actually. Like we use our own phone in Khartoum but there (Southern Sudan) we have to make sure that it is working hours so we can communicate with them during—what do you call it—in their working hours … From 2005 the mobiles were so spread out so everyone has mobile, it become more easier to communicate. It was anyone in all parts of Sudan. (A7, Sudan)

Landlines phones were only in offices. Some people had mobile phones. (A3, Sudan)

Yeah, we have the home phone. But mobile is, at that time, is very rare just for a work place … like airlines or telecommunication or government they use it. (A34, Ethiopia)

The lack of availability of ICTs was not just experienced by refugees from African countries of origin, but was also common to refugees from other parts of the world. However, it was evident that such lack of availability was more than a product of poor technical infrastructure and development, but had been deliberately designed by governments:

… it's hard to contact from Burma … you don't have [open] communication … when we write a letter the postmen [were not] working well … We have several [times we lost] our letter. (I2, Burma)

… we don't have [cell phone]. Also we don't have phone line. Just we communicate with, when we saw some people who came from our state and they will write a letter … Probably just one or two times every year … just we can tell we miss you and we want to see you, just like that. Because also we are afraid of the government. Yeah, we cannot tell anywhere about our situation or what's happened to us. Just only we miss you or we stay there, or something like that. (I6, Burma)

… as you know Burma is a very poor country. You can't use the telephone, internet if you are not the member of the government. If you are not rich you can't use at all because very expensive. Only people who, they work for the government, is a member of government and if they are related to the government. (I12, Burma)

I even didn't write a letter to them because I felt that it wasn't safe for them. (Mr E, Burma (pilot study))

I still feel very scared if I talk to my parents on the phone. (Ms. D, China (pilot study))

No mobile. It was not permitted to anybody to have a mobile phone when Saddam was the president. (M8, Iraq)

Only—I can remember—the people that use communication is walkie-talkie. Yeah, the military. Yes, I can remember that one. The police and the soldiers they use the walkie-talkie. They are the only means of communication at that time. (A18, Sierra Leone)

While, for many refugees, experience of ICTs was rare due to limited or lack of availability, technologies are also associated with power and privilege. Ruling bodies have successfully associated ICTs with fear, such that refugees are wary of them.

Exclusion by lack of accessibility

The minimal and negative experiences of ICTs that refugees have in their countries of origin are brought with them when they are forced to migrate. When refugees are displaced to intermediate countries, which have greater availability of ICTs at their disposal, there are still many obstacles to accessing and using them. Apart from the fear of using such technologies, those in refugee camps were often in geographically isolated locations, so the range of technologies that could be experienced was limited, and their reliability inconsistent.

> When I was in refugee camp, we are using radio—hand held radio. There is radio in the refugee camp in Somalia. (A25, Somalia)

> Sometimes you know you have to write a letter. Because sometimes in the country no [cell] network, because we are living in the city. (A41, Liberia)

> What I can tell you because the camp I was is in Kenya. You cannot contact people in the camp because there's nobody in the camp. There's no telephone in the camp so you just—it's like, isolated, so there's nothing in the camp … There seemed there's not [much] of technology … No mobile phones … You go to the city, so you just come to Nairobi contact your foreign wire, so you just stop there. You'd pay money. (A19, Kenya)

> … in our village, we didn't have anything—just only camera really … Not ours, just my friend … we didn't have any electricity as well. (I5, Thailand)

Refugees would often have to travel from their camps to urban areas to access a greater range of ICTs. However, this is only overcoming the physical barriers to access.

Exclusion by lack of affordability

Finances also pose a barrier to technology access, and, given that refugees, while displaced, have few opportunities for stable employment and income generation, the affordability of ICTs is a key issue.

> Yes, there were mobile access. It was a bit expensive, so mostly we meet. (A30, Sudan)

> Satellite telephone was also there but it was expensive and then unless you feel something burning, this is why you can go spend your money—it cost was expensive to use the satellite connection. (A7, Sudan)

… my grandparents stay in Burma … They have to come a long way to the city and they have to pay for—they have to pay [approximately AUD$5] per minute in Burma … just to receive the phone call. (I3, Burma)

Well, phone was really expensive. The only way you get a phone is they have someone overseas who send you money to get a phone. If we get a phone we have to buy a chip. The chip, too, costs money, we have to buy the phone you buy the chip. If you want to recharge you have to go to the booth and pay your money for like if you need a credit or $10 credit you pay and they will send the credit to you, they don't give you like a version number to put in. You only pay the money and they send the credit to your phone … We have a mobile but we didn't use it much … Then say we have money, we will buy credit. That's what we do when we use it. (A10, Ghana)

They contact us, yeah … Because in camp we didn't have enough money to contact them … Yeah, it was too expensive to contact in the other country. (I4, Thailand)

So because I'm refugee and we have hard life in refugee camp, so I have to look for my daughter for food and to education stuff because if you have money, yeah, you can have mobile. (A37, Kenya)

In addition to the geographical barriers to ICT access, refugees also experience financial barriers. Even if these are overcome, there are educational barriers to be addressed; that is, the lack of ICT familiarity and technical literacies inherited from countries of origin.

Exclusion by lack of literacy

Assuming that a refugee might be in a location where ICTs are available and accessible, and they have the money to pay for them, how do they go about using them if they have never had any experience of this? Respondents indicated that they would have to pay others to make a phone call for them, or write and send an email, as some were not literate and could not use computers.

At that time actually emails were available but I could not have access to the email because by that time it was not that easy to even own a computer. Although the internet café they start coming out in say mid 90s where you can go and pay your money. Then I can remember sending an email to the U.K., I wrote my email and then I take it to the post office and then they went and forwarded the email … So I remember like taking my message and then taking it to them so that they could type the email and then send it. (A7, Sudan)

When I was in Congo, some of my relatives went to Canada. When they reached there, they sent us an email address, and then they gave us their mobile number. Then from their mobile number we could contact them. We go to the internet cafe. It was costly. And it's only someone who's educated can … use the email. (A38, Congo)

In Thailand because we live in the refugee camp so we don't know how to use the phone. (I4, Thailand)

... when we use, the owner press for us, just [we show] the numbers and they press for us ... operate everything. (I6, Thailand)

I don't have [phone] because I use some money—I pay for other people ring. (A37, Kenya)

First you must ring the company then they say a PIN number in English. In English I couldn't understand. After this, when you press the hash key, you just start dialing your phone number. That time I knew how to use the phone card. Before, I didn't know the phone card. In Iran, I didn't know the phone card, but I used public phone, I used phone. I had to listen very carefully because I couldn't understand English at that time. (Ms. Y (on using an international calling card), Iran (pilot study))

Refugees reported having to use third parties to help them overcome (language and technical) literacy barriers to ICT access.

They used to sell mobile phones. So they have to teach you how to use it. That's how we learned this ... they will teach you free. A friend who has knowledge will also teach you how to do it. How to open it, how to put a SIM card inside, how to load all these kind of things ... I saw it from my friends. (A30, Kenya)

What this suggests is that the literacy threshold for ICT participation is too high for refugees to negotiate alone, and that they require the assistance of family and friends. It is also apparent that the design of these technological experiences has not been inclusive enough in considering the needs of refugees and similarly marginalized groups.

Conclusion

There is an important role for designers to play in minimizing experiential inequality. This can only happen with awareness and understanding of neglected groups such as refugees, who are so often overlooked in the design of ICT services despite the enormous benefits that access can potentially provide to them.

Although it is commonplace within Experience Design to discriminate between users, this practice should be applied to better understand experiential differences with a view to inclusion, rather than to ignore groups of users altogether. It is in the process of excluding that inequalities arise, while, conversely, the design of inclusive experiences explicitly attempts to address access barriers and lower thresholds to participation.

In order for refugees to become targeted users of ICTs, the design of accessible, robust, reliable, low-cost or free technology products and services are needed. Not only must physical and economic barriers be overcome, but educational ones as well. That is, technological experiences must be designed to be as inclusive and universal as possible to accommodate the lack of ICT familiarity and technical literacies refugees have inherited from their countries of origin.

PART TWO

Objects and Environments

Chapter 5

Narrativity of Object Interaction Experiences: A Framework for Designing Products as Narrative Experiences

Silvia Grimaldi

Most people use physical domestic objects, such as kettles, toasters, tables, and sofas, every day without any second thought. We are used to having these objects around. We may think of them when the time comes to replace them, but we don't usually look into the finer details of our interactions with these objects; they come to be part of the background. However, these are objects we interact with on a daily basis, and they allow us not only to fulfill practical tasks, such as toasting bread or boiling water, but also to say something about ourselves through our choices. These objects, partially because of their ubiquity, start to form part of our identity and of our personal narratives.

> We have, each of us, a life-story, an inner narrative—whose continuity, whose sense, is our lives. It might be said that each of us constructs and lives, a "narrative", and that this narrative is us, our identities. (Sacks 1998: 110)

I'm interested in analyzing our first interaction experiences with these mundane objects, the stage before the interaction becomes automatic; then to see how this can influence the way in which this personal narrative around the object is formed, and what role these objects might have in the construction of this narrative. The project analyzes two aspects in parallel: interactions with objects, and the narrative structures of fiction film examples. Following this analysis the aim is to create methods that can apply the findings from this comparison to generate designed objects that "direct" narrative product experiences.

The idea that experiences are described, remembered, and recounted as stories, so much so that it is almost impossible to talk about an experience or an interaction without "telling a story," has been explored in psychology as well as in design literature (Bruner 1991; Dewey 2005; Forlizzi 1997; Hassenzahl 2010; Löwgren 2009).

The field of narrative theory has also been expanding its remit from analyzing literary text to looking at a wider scope of interpretation of narrative. The term *narrative* has been used for a wider variety of mediums, from video games to immersive interactive environments. Real-life experiences, or the recounting or remembering of these experiences, have also been described as having narrative qualities (Abbott 2008; Bal 2002; Young and Saver 2001).

The concept of *narrativity* is important in this shift, as it moves the question from whether an experience *is* or *is not* a narrative to whether an experience *possesses narrativity*; this is intended as a quality, "being able to inspire a narrative response" (Ryan 2005). In addition, narrativity can be seen as a scalar quality, so an event or an experience can be seen as "more or less prototypically story-like," possessing more or less narrativity (Herman 2004).

Narrativity

The concept of *narrativity* lends itself to be adopted by designers because of its adaptability. If we look at an interaction with an object in narrative terms, we are looking at a sequence of events, which present more or less opportunities for being told as an interesting, engaging, and memorable story.

Figure 5.1 Micro-events in the interaction with a kettle.

When looking at a single interaction with an electric kettle, this could be analyzed in terms of *micro-events*: the user might look at the kettle first, then lift the kettle, open the top, fill it with water, close the top, replace the kettle on the base, switch the kettle on, wait for it to boil, hear the sound of the boiling water or the click of the switch or see the steam coming out the top, and then turn the kettle off, pour the water out, and replace the kettle on the base (Figure 5.1).

Each of these can be seen as a micro-event within the object interaction, and these micro-events could be manipulated, or *directed* in a story-like fashion by the designer. In a similar way to a film director, the designer could play with:

- The exact qualities of the micro-events, for example does a whistle alert us to the water boiling? What pitch?

- The way in which these are sequenced, for example a light might get progressively more red as the water gets hotter, or a red light might just turn on when the water boils.

- The meanings formed by interpreting these events, for example a whistle as a scream of distress as opposed to a whistle as an efficient call to attention.

In these ways the designer could influence the meaning that the user will attribute to the story of the interaction.

These micro-events could be looked at according to Desmet and Hekkert's "Framework of Product Experience" (2007), and the variations in the micro-events could be:

- On the level of an aesthetic experience, for example the impression we might get from the colors or textures of the object.

- On the level of experience of meaning, for example the interpretation we might give to culturally relevant details; or

- On the level of emotional experience, for example looking at how the micro-events make us feel.

- These three levels are obviously connected and influence each other throughout the product experience; aesthetic elements will contribute to our creation of meaning around the object, the meaning we form will inform our emotional experience, and so on.

This study proposes an additional level of experience, the narrative experience of an object. This narrative experience is influenced by all three levels described by Desmet and Hekkert (2007), and in turn helps to structure or organize our cognitive processes in relation to all three levels. The advantage of using narrative as a framework is that it would allow designers to apply different aspects of the product experience in a time-based way to design objects in order to direct a user's experience through the micro-events of the object interaction. This could create a highly *tellable* interaction (Baroni 2013), and thus lead to a coherent *story of use*, which has a high level of *narrativity*.

Agency

When we retell a story about an interaction with an object we often give the object human character-istics, such as a "stupid" automatic cash register in a supermarket, or the door lock that won't behave and let you into your office. It is hard to separate these human-like characteristics from the story; they are part of how we interpret events or happenings within our experience, and part of how we understand and remember the interaction.

In narrative terms, the object's perceived will amount to *agency*. Agency is what distinguishes a "happening," for example "it started to rain," from an "event," for example, "I decided to open my umbrella" (Abbott 2008). In the first example the event recalled is classed as a happening because there is no agency or will that decides to make this happen, while the second event clearly is the result of a wilful decision. Alfred Gell (1998) analyzed the idea of agency in relation to artefacts from an anthropological perspective, and concluded that artefacts possess agency when they allow events to happen "in their vicinity." In Gell's analysis, artefacts then acquire human-like characteristics when they are perceived as having influence on the course of events. We therefore tend to interpret, recall, and retell interactions with particular artefacts as an interaction between two beings, because in this narrative both beings (user and artefact) possess some form of agency.

Mieke Bal, in her book *Travelling Concepts in the Humanities* (2002), goes one step further, using her background in narratology to develop a narrative theory of interpretation. She starts from questioning the typical art–historical focus on the artist's intention when interpreting works of art; she then looks at the agency of the object and how the object itself communicates to the viewer, in ways in which the artist could not have predicted. This shifts the focus of our interpretation from the maker of the work of art to the actual work of art and its agency.

However, from here Bal takes the argument one step further: from the maker, to the object, to the viewer, through the concept of narrativity. Bal focuses on the relationship between the viewer and the object, and how the "story" of viewing and interpreting the object is created in the viewer's mind. This focuses the critique of works of art, and I am extending this to design, away from the artist's intention, through the agency of the object, and to the relationship between the viewer and the object. This relationship is not predetermined but can only be fostered by the maker's intention (Figure 5.2).

The focus on the cognitive activity of the viewer or user implies a narrative, because this activity necessarily happens through time, through an experience of viewing.

Narrativity is here acknowledged as indispensable, not because all pictures tell a story in the ordinary sense of the word, but because the experience of viewing pictures is itself imbued with process. (Bal 2002: 281)

This leads to a central hypothesis for this project: that objects perceived as possessing agency may have more potential for narrativity. In addition, this model points to the idea that a narrative is always created in a user's mind when interacting with an object, and this narrative is central to the way the user will interpret, remember, and approach the object.

Figure 5.2   Diagram of Bal's theory of interpretation.

Schemata

The idea that the process of story interpretation is an essential part of the activity of the viewer or user is central to constructivist conceptions of narrative. Bordwell (1985), in particular, when talking about the activity of the film viewer, states that the main activity of the (narrative fiction) film viewer is that of creating hypotheses about the way the story will develop, and then validating these hypotheses when the story develops as expected or disproving these when there are surprising turns of plot.

Bordwell explains that this process of story construction is possible because we already have some expectations about the way events develop in everyday life, but we also have expectations about the typical forms of stories, the typical forms of stories within particular genres of films, and the typical roles that agents such as characters, props, etc. might play. This is explained in terms of schemata theory.

Because, in film, schemata aid the viewer to reconstruct the story from the information presented on screen, and aid in the forming of hypotheses, the idea of schemata would be interesting to apply to the design of objects. Two of the schemata that Bordwell describes would be particularly valuable as a method of constructing narratives around object interactions.

Prototype schemata allow us to identify agents such as characters, props, and locales as contributing something to the story, for example a character with a gun might be perceived as criminal or as someone who could potentially perform a criminal act. These agents allow us to start making some hypotheses about the way in which they will behave, or, in the case of objects or locales, the way in which the characters might behave in their proximity, and then it is up to the filmmaker to either validate or invalidate these hypotheses.

Prototype schemata in film use the semiotic understanding of the audience to drop clues into the story, which may or may not lead in the right direction, but will nonetheless be understood by a "typical" (and culturally specific) member of the audience. In parallel, semiotic understanding is often used in design to give clues to users about usability and interpretation of objects; however, there is a potential for the designer to "play" with the idea of hypothesis validation or non-validation, which could lead to designs that reveal themselves with time to be surprising (Grimaldi 2008, 2006).

Template schemata represent abstracted narrative structures that allow the viewer to slot information into the right sequence when reconstructing a story. So a story that is told in an order that is different from chronological can be understood in the correct chronology because we have these template schemata to assist us in "filing" the information into the correct place. For example, a sequence of cause-and-effect, regardless of what order it is presented in the film, will have to be unraveled in the viewer's mind in a more or less chronological order for the viewer to understand which event might be the cause and which might be the effect. Incidentally, stories that are told in a way that is close to these template schemata are easier to remember, and, regardless of what order the story was told in the original film, viewers will make the story conform more to the template schemata when retelling or recalling.

Template schemata have to do with the understanding of the way time is organized within the film, and in a similar way could help in the understanding of time within the interaction experience, creating, for example, patterns of surprise and predictability within the experience, or creating different rhythms and "dramaturgical structures" to the experience (Löwgren 2009).

In addition, template schemata could help in the formation of cause-and-effect patterns, so that if an object behaves in a certain way we might ascribe a cause to that behavior through a template schemata. An everyday example of this is when the TV remote control is not working consistently, and we may try to turn it upside down; if it happens to work that time we tend to interpret that event as being the cause of the remote control starting to work again, and the next time we will try to turn the remote control upside down again to make it work.

Designers could use template schemata to organize micro-events within an interaction that happen over time in a way similar to a typical story structure; this might aid or foster the memorability of the object interaction, as well as the narrativity of the experience and the *tellability* of the object.

The result of applying these schemata to designing objects might be that the object actively encourages an increase in the gusto that someone might have in retelling the story of their interaction, thus fostering word of mouth and increased recall.

Analysis of film examples

The project is interested in outlining methods for designers to increase narrativity within the product experience. Therefore the idea is to analyze narrative elements of films in which the selected objects play a significant role, and then to apply these to the design of the objects themselves.

The first step in this process is to select a sample of objects and films and then analyze these in order to understand what elements could be incorporated into the object redesign. To select the objects a questionnaire was circulated online through message boards of people who were local, so that they could conveniently be involved with further stages of testing, and that were somehow interested in objects. More than 70 people replied to the questionnaire, which asked them to identify the first five domestic objects that come to mind and the three domestic objects they most enjoy using and why. Objects that could not be redesigned for technical reasons, for example TV sets, and objects that would prove testing problematic, for example beds, were discarded (Grimaldi 2012). The final selection was to be the kettle, toaster, sofa, and table.

As the overall project is still in progress, it is being piloted with the kettle. In order to identify films in which the kettle appears in a narrative role, a questionnaire was posted on the Internet Movie Database (IMDb) forums, asking forum participants, who tend to be film enthusiasts, to identify film scenes in which the object appears and plays a significant role. This method was preferred over trawling script databases for references to kettles, as the point was to identify those scenes in which the object had some sort of memorable impact, and resonated with the viewer, whether in the narrative construction of the scene or in the formation of meaning, as opposed to identifying scenes in which the object simply appears. For each object, four or five films were selected, taking care to have some variation in genres of films as well as in narrative roles the objects perform (Grimaldi 2013).

For the kettle pilot the films selected were

- *Vera Drake* (Leigh 2004): a historical drama in which the kettle helps establish the character of Vera as a caring individual, and helps to frame her activity of providing illegal abortions as a caring act.
- *Wristcutters: A Love Story* (Dukic 2006): a comedy in which the kettle's whistle is used as a device to cut from one scene to another.
- *A Tale of Two Sisters* (Kim 2003): a psychological horror in which a boiling kettle is used as a weapon.

- *Secretary* (Shainberg 2002): a comedy/drama/romance in which the kettle is used to establish a domestic calm scene but in that same scene is then used as a masochist's tool.

The film scenes were analyzed from different points of view. The first level of analysis followed McKee's guidelines (1999), looking at dividing the scenes into beats or actions and noting down the timing of those beats. Then each scene was analyzed in terms of conflicts and goals of the characters as well as any changes in values and turning points in the beats. In addition to the analysis based on McKee's framework, the films were also analyzed in terms of the role of the objects in the particular scenes, noting any points in which the objects change meaning or in which the meaning of the object influences our understanding of the scene, noting the perceived agency of the object.

Pictured in Figure 5.3 is the "kettle scene" from the film *Secretary* (Shainberg 2002). This scene unfolds as the opening credits finish rolling and it has been established that the protagonist has just left a mental institution and is trying to stop self-harming after coming back into the family home.

The "kettle scene" starts with a calm domestic evening setting, with the protagonist in a bathrobe making tea; the calm is interrupted by a violent fight between her mother and her drunk father. The protagonist grabs the now boiling kettle, calmly brings it up to her room, and proceeds to burn herself with it on her inner thigh. This seems to relieve her apprehension, ending the scene on a calm note. However, we as an audience know that her goal is to keep herself from self-harming, so this is a very ambiguous resolution to the scene as the apparent calm is actually a very negative development for the plot.

The kettle has a dual role in this scene: that of establishing a calm domestic scene, but also of being a catalyst for action—it is a loaded weapon and by being hot it is ready to use. The pacing of the scene is also interesting; starting out with longer beats, progressing through the middle of the scene in short

Figure 5.3   Scene from *Secretary*.

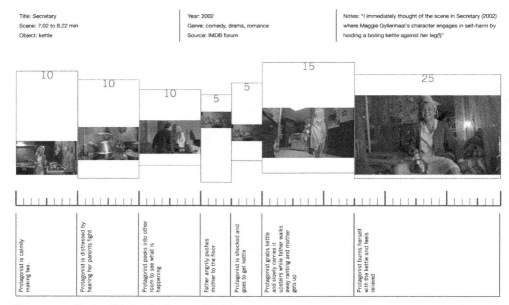

Figure 5.4   Beats within the "kettle scene" in *Secretary*.

beats with sharp editing and cuts, and then resolving in a long final beat in which the ambiguous nature of the restored balance is made evident.

The film examples are used as starting points for the redesign of the objects in different ways through the idea generation process for the new designs. Some of the narrative devices of the films are incorporated into the idea generation process. The roles or meanings of the objects are used as starting points for design, by looking, for example, at the role reversal between the kettle as a symbol of domestic calm and the kettle as an available weapon. And the timing and structure of the beats within the scenes is used as an organizing principle for the micro-events within the interaction experience (Figure 5.4). Each of these approaches could lead to different design outcomes based on the four films analyzed.

Analysis of product experiences

As a comparison to the film analysis, and also to act as a first stage of testing against which to test the final designs, participant research was used to analyze the interaction experience of using a kettle.

The participants were asked to film themselves using their own kettle at home. They then emailed the video to the researcher before their scheduled interview, so the researcher conducting the interview would be familiar with it. The interview was conducted in three phases. The first phase consisted of the researcher briefly interviewing the participant about their use of the kettle; the second phase was conducted while both participant and researcher watched the video of the kettle use, and the participants were asked to talk the researcher through the video.

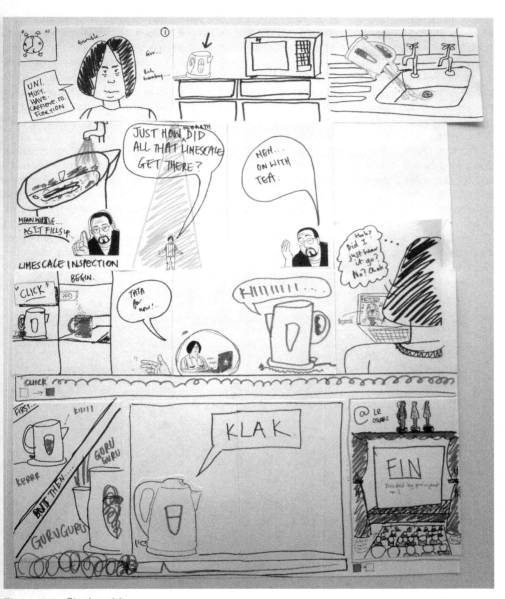

Figure 5.5 Storyboard 1.

It is interesting to note that the answers to the second phase were different from the first phase answers, proving the need for such triangulation and for the use of video. First of all the participants spoke more in depth about the details of the way in which they use the object, prompted by watching themselves on screen. But also the unexpected result was that the participants were more open, admitting to quirks of use, such as performing a "limescale inspection" before filling the kettle, or about always rushing to the kettle as soon as it boils, claiming "I don't like to let hot water wait, it defeats the point in my opinion." One participant even admitted to reorganizing all her kitchen things, putting the more expensive things to the front and hiding the cheap tea, although this obviously defeats the point of moving things around in the first place.

The third phase of the interview consisted in giving the participants drawing and collage materials, and asking them to create a storyboard of their use of the kettle (see Figures 5.5 and 5.6), followed by a few final questions about this storyboard exercise. One participant said that having to draw her kettle she realized that she doesn't really know where the on/off switch is located, nor what color this is: she remembers that the color of this light changes when the water boils, but is not sure from which color to what color.

This storyboarding exercise also forced the participants to divide their interaction experiences into micro-events and this information came in useful when mapping the micro-events within this interaction to see which ones could be acted upon or modified. Daniel Stern's (2004) work with visualizing interview data about "the present moment" was used to codify sequences of micro-events within the product

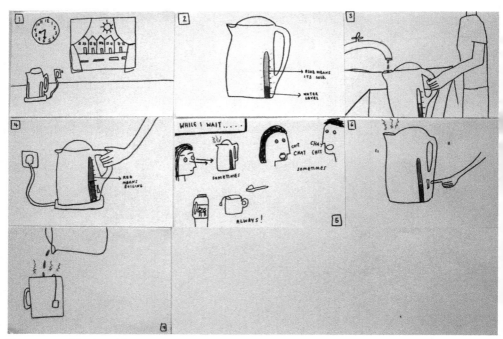

Figure 5.6   Storyboard 2.

interaction experiences, in a way that is similar to the film analysis shown above, so as to easily compare the data visually.

The information about micro-events in the kettle use and quirks of use that emerged from the participants is useful when redesigning the kettle to provide recognizable additional connotations.

Design applications

This section outlines the methods that are being used as starting points for design. The key point of the theoretical framework is that of measuring, at least in a subjective way, the tellability of the redesigned objects. The final designs will be tested against the initial objects to measure whether there has been an increase in narrativity of the object interaction.

The film analysis provides the raw narrative material to be adapted and adopted into the designs. This material comes from ideas around the form of the narrative (discourse) or the content of that narrative (story) (Abbott 2008). So, for example, the meaning of the kettle in a particular scene leads to a series of design ideas and concepts (content), which may be varied in terms of how the object is experienced in interaction (form) according to particular template schemata found in the films.

Some of the briefs that have emerged so far have to do with:

- *Role reversals*: the kettle is usually interpreted as a reassuring object, but also has the potential of being used a weapon; this reversal of roles is used in the designs through contrasting connotations and through timed sequences of changes. One sample design is a kettle the handle of which leaves a pattern imprinted on the user's hand, which could be seen as a scar but in a positive light.

- *Micro-event structures*: particular structures and timings of beats and scenes within a film are used within the kettle experience: the micro-events in the kettle experience are reorganized or timed so that particular events take more time and others are quicker, or so that there is a timing to a setting of the scene, climax of the scene and closure similar to that found in some of the film scenes. One sample design for this is a kettle that instead of signaling when the water boils it progressively starts glowing as the water gets hotter.

- *Narrative devices or tropes*: kettles are often used in films, and in particular, in the film analyzed, to cut from one scene to another, through the use of the whistle, the steam, and the sound of the water boiling. These time markers are used within the redesigned product experience as signifiers of changes in state or changes in meaning. One sample design is a kettle in which the whistle changes in sound, sometimes resembling a child's scream, giving a sense of urgency, and sometimes whistling in a pleasant pitch.

- *Symbolic meaning of the kettle*: the idea that a kettle can establish a character as caring or a scene as calm and domestic, is used within the redesign, both by being subverted, and by being reinforced or played with in an ambiguous way. One sample design for this is a kettle "clothed" in a knit sweater, with pockets to warm your hands.

The analysis of the participant interviews provides the raw material in terms of mapping the object interaction experience and in addition provides a ground to test the final designs against. The final designs will be tested again with the participants, following the same methods of the initial testing, and the interviews will then be analyzed and visualized in the same way as the original. This will provide a good ground for testing whether there has been an increase in narrativity of the interaction experience.

The final aim of the project is to provide designers with a series of methods they can experiment with in the creation of designs that foster more narrative experiences. This is not to be seen in contrast with other design methods or focuses, nor is it to be seen in opposition to other ways of using narrative within the design process, such as scenarios for empathizing with users (Blythe and Wright 2006; Wright and McCarthy 2008). It is instead intended to add a layer of understanding to the design of product experiences and to guide designers in the different ways in which they could use this additional layer.

Chapter 6

Centers of Experience: Bodies and Objects in Today's Museums

Xavier Acarin and Barbara Adams

Over the last two decades artistic practices have expanded to include projects that are explicitly participatory, community based, and socially engaged (see, for example, Bishop 2012; Helguera 2011; Thompson 2012). Both in and beyond the museum, artists have developed roles of directing, planning, and designing situations and experiences to be enacted, inhabited, and lived by various publics. Some projects target specific groups of people; others are planned to engage anyone who happens to venture within the institution. The narrative that underwrites these practices can be traced to post-minimalism and followed to relational aesthetics, through situationism, tropicalism, and institutional critique. Participation, interaction, engagement, and empowerment have come to codify these works, often propelled by a critique of the living conditions of our contemporaneity. We see this clearly in projects such as Thomas Hirschhorn's *Bataille Monument* at the 2002 Documenta, a participatory project that sought engagement with Kassel's Turkish community, or Paul Chan's *Waiting for Godot* in New Orleans during the aftermath of Hurricane Katrina. In these projects, there is a commitment to local communities that goes beyond the confines of established institutionalized structures.

Museums function as unique institutions in their contribution to the construction of collective identity, memory, and imagination. As such, museums face challenges in responding to our present conditions of emergency, inequality, and social conflict. In this chapter we observe practices realized inside the museum that elaborate the social realm of our existence. Starting with the origins of the museum, this chapter traces how the museum has evolved into a spectacular repository for today's social consciousness and the potential for creative practitioners to use and design the space of the museum to generate meaningful experience on the levels of the corporeal and social body. This effort is haunted by the ever-increasing commodification of experience that contributes to the museum's struggle for relevance and viability in terms of the pedagogical, the political and the ludic.

> Today ... it is historical becoming itself that the museums claim to protect, and they pose no longer as custodians of dead artefacts, but as mavens and cultural producers, self-appointed purveyors of the social-aesthetic imagination. (Kwinter 2008: 23)

Since the appearance of art museums resulting from the enlightened and revolutionary processes of the eighteenth century, and their (re)formation in the context of nineteenth-century colonialism and industrialism, the institution has been linked to an educational program (Bennett 1995). In addition to the basic aims of collecting, preserving, and exhibiting, there developed a general understanding of the institution as a place of knowledge. With the utopian impulse that emerged from the renaissance, the search for a better society was attached to an encyclopedic intention to comprehend the world. From Schiller to Dewey, the restorative power of art (and beauty) has been seen as a tool to bond social difference, promote cultural diversity, and expand human spirituality. Nevertheless, museums have also been used as propaganda machines, where economy and art meet to reinforce the national identity inside a modern official narrative (Duncan 1995). In this sense, the expansion of art institutions and venues, since the 1990s, has successfully achieved local and global gentrification from Bilbao to Abu Dhabi. In this context this chapter looks at the different formulations of the museum as a unique place to articulate an experiential encounter with art.

The modern use of museum space has its roots in the Germany of the Weimar Republic, where a group of artists, designers, architects, and museum professionals were innovative in the design of exhibitions considering and affecting the resulting experience of the exhibition visitor. Charlotte Klonk's study on this issue remarks on how the origin of museum display is directly connected to commercial exhibitions, from the nineteenth-century bazaar to the early twentieth-century fair (Klonk 2009). However, it is with the innovative design of the Bauhaus members where the modern use of space pushes the museum toward a new model: one that presents different narratives, along with the use of white walls, flexible space, ceiling lights, and the introduction of open windows to the exterior. This reworks the older model of display with the intention to include the viewer as a participant in the production of space.

During his time at the Landesmuseum in Hanover and at the Art Museum at the Rhode Island School of Design, Alexander Dorner developed a holistic approach to include context materials in the presentation of the collection. He called them "atmosphere rooms." Dorner believed that the division between art and science could be reconciled in the museum as the site of human creativity.

> The new type of art institute cannot merely be an art museum as it has been until now, but no museum at all. The new type will be more like a power station, a producer of new energy. (Dorner, cited in Cauman 1958: 9)

Dorner imagined the *Living Museum* as a new kind of institution that would hold past and present together, to show how the present is a result of the past, and to demonstrate "the psychic history of the human race" (Cauman 1958: 9). This innovative way to see the institution marked his time (1927–37) as director of the Landesmuseum[1] in Hanover, where he reorganized the collections to contextualize them as part of a sequence that would see the museum as "a history of expanding human thought and emotion" (Klonk 2009). Dorner proposed an adaptation of architecture and installation methods for each period showcased by the museum. These "atmosphere rooms" place the museum as a medium, an interpretative site where meaning is produced. His belief in a participatory model was based on the idea that, by including the public, the museum could provide a forum that would contribute to changing the social reality.

Dorner commissioned El Lissitzky (1927) and Lászlo Moholy-Nagy (1930) to design the contemporary rooms of the museum, although only Lissitzky could finish his commission, the *Abstract Cabinet*. This room was an example of a participatory layout,

There were sliding frames so that certain pictures could be moved. Sculpture was placed in front of a wrap-around mirror in the corner and there was a showcase underneath a blind window that needed to be turned if spectators wanted to see the entire display [...] No two people had the same view of the works on display and the perception of each individual was affected by the actions of others engaged with the display. (Klonk 2009: 117)

Klonk underscores the significance of this invitation to participate as a change in experience comparable to "what [it] would be like to act as a collective subject in a post-capitalist society in which interactive engagement counted more than individuality and interiority" (Klonk 2009: 118).

Overall, the idea of Dorner was to engage the visitor with the artworks through an activation of the exhibition space, which would recall the original context of the works.

Dorner's intention to cultivate a utopian space for human knowledge is opposed to the future understanding of the museum space as heterotopic, as defined by Michel Foucault. The activation through contextualization of the object was, for Dorner, a way to embrace the past and understand its evolution. For Foucault, the museum pretension "to enclose all times, all epochs, all forms, all tastes, the idea of constituting a place of all times that is itself outside of time and inaccessible to its ravages" (Foucault 1986: 26),[2] is part of the modern project that will reach its end in the post-World War II world.

It is through the work of Alfred H. Barr at MoMA, that the establishment and triumph of the "white cube" and the individual experience of art became the dominant model for modern art museums. Barr, who traveled and knew the German experiments in museum display through the 1920s, presented multiple exhibitions of the European avant-garde and created a narrative that now is taken for granted when thinking about the trajectory of American twentieth-century art. With the 1936 exhibition *Cubism and Abstract Art*, Barr fully realized his ideas. The show "was above all didactic rather than atmospheric" (Klonk 2009: 150),[3] and the intention of Barr's program was to disseminate a vision of art capable of establishing a correlation with the actual moment. Barr's program is opposed to that of Dorner as the experiences they promote are radically different. While Dorner involved the viewer in a participatory act, Barr's individual experience reinforced a way to understand art and its value inside the logic of the self. These models collided when MoMA audiences entered the *Bauhaus 1919–1928* show organized by Herbert Bayer in 1938 (for more on this, see Staniszewski 1998). The audience, accustomed to Barr's model, encountered an atmospheric exhibition that disrupted their viewing habits. Brian O'Doherty, reflecting some 40 years later, saw in the strategy behind the white cube a market model of display, "the wall becomes a membrane through which aesthetic and commercial values osmotically exchange" (O'Doherty 1999). The white cube constitutes a piece in itself as an isolated capsule creating an experience separated from the outside, clearly connecting to formulations of the museum as a sanctuary or mausoleum. The white cube is the art exhibition space par excellence that responds to a particular ideology of modern art expanded by the success of Barr and the MoMA.

While the white cube ideology was being developed at MoMA, another kind of experience was being produced elsewhere that understood the exhibition as an immersive environment in direct relation with the artist's intentions. The 1938 *Exposition Internationale du Surréalisme* at the Galerie Beaux-Arts in Paris and the 1942 *First Papers of Surrealism* at the Whitelaw Reid Mansion in New York, both organized by Marcel Duchamp, immersed visitors in a surrealistic environment.[4] In a similar manner, the *Fun Palace*, a project by Cedric Price and Joan Littlewood in the 1960s, situated the museum as a permeable institution where people and their actions effectively produce the space of the museum

(Lefebvre 1992). Price imagined an experimental laboratory in constant movement, where an open architecture allows the space to mutate and the visitors the chance to create:

> The activities designed for the site should be experimental, the place itself expendable and changeable. The organization of space and the objects occupying it should, on the one hand, challenge the participants' mental and physical dexterity and, on the other, allow for a flow of space and time, in which passive and active pleasure is provoked. (Price and Littlewood 1968: 127–34)

Hans Belting has defined the museum as an "island of time," as "the place for things left behind in the fight for the progress" (Belting 2001: 78). Following Belting, the museum is the encounter with things, places, and peoples. The increasingly virtual lives of our societies produce other forms of experience (for example, atemporal, mediated, disembodied), and the museum, as Belting argues, is one of the last holdouts that fosters and values direct, embodied encounters and interactions. Belting understands the experience of time in the museum not as a heterotopia as defined by Foucault as the space that creates a time apart. Rather, for Belting, the museum exists as an autotopia that "establish[es] and manifest[s] the identity and perception of places in today's world" (Belting 2001: 78). In this model, we remain tied to our realness even in the age of the virtual. Moreover, the museum is seen as a tool for action and being in the world—by experiencing objects, spaces, and people, our capacities as humans are revealed and the museum is expressed as a compensation "for the loss of real or time-resistant places that result from today's electronic networks" (Belting 2001: 78).

This model understands the museum as a meaningful hub in the democratic sphere characterized by active participation. This notion of the museum as forum, where global and local issues are discussed and debated, has been endowed with the possibility to rethink our present conditions. As Chantal Mouffe asserts,

> Museums and art institutions could make a decisive contribution to the proliferation of new public spaces open to agonistic forms of participation where radical democratic alternatives to neoliberalism could, once again, be imagined and cultivated. (Mouffe 2010: 326)

Sanford Kwinter echoes some of Mouffe's insights from a design perspective:

> When a major new museum, then, is not only built but, in fact, reconceived, and with a consciously philosophical view to addressing the future ways that humans will address themselves to the things they make, it must be realized that a critical political opportunity has presented itself … What is important are the relations a society permits its actors to maintain with art. (Kwinter 2008: 27)

The methods used to design and evaluate the experience of visitors have evolved and moved from pre-designed flow maps and surveys to forms of collecting data that incorporate feedback and adapt in accordance with the data itself. For example, eMotion, an initiative that uses a glove with sensors, can detect the time a person spends in front of a work of art, their heart rate, and skin variations.[5] This aims to demonstrate the ways in which visitors may be attracted to forms of art, despite their knowledge of it. Thus far, eMotion's research has included only sculpture and painting; extending it to installation and performance might tell us more about the ways audiences respond to works when they are invited to participate.

Understanding the museum experience has attracted attention not only from museums themselves, as they seek to increase attendance and widen their appeal, and not only from those interested in understanding our physiological responses, as with the example of eMotion above, but also from social researchers. These studies take into account "an interactive experience, resulting in a range of possible outcomes such as increased knowledge, as well as changed attitudes or enhanced social skills" (Dierking and Falk 1992: 173). The nexus of personal, physical, and social context converge in Falk's "interactive experience model," resulting in a typology of museum goers including: explorers who are curiosity driven and seek to add to their knowledge; facilitators who enable the experience and learning of others; hobbyists who are professionally tied to museum content; experience seekers who visit in order to immerse themselves in the atmosphere; and rechargers who are looking for contemplative or spiritual experience (Dierking and Falk 2011). Museums increasingly seek to capitalize on the wide range of visitors and in doing so, tap into the pervasiveness of the experience economy in which institutions, in order to remain culturally viable, orchestrate sensational and novel events for consumers (Pine and Gilmore 1999).

Visitors get naked and float in a saline pool at body temperature; the artist sits opposite a visitor and stares silently in the hopes of suspending time through a meditative encounter; visitors engage in conversation with "interpreters" regarding the theme of progress while moving through the museum's interior; the artist replicates a swingers' club in the museum where visitors can engage in sexual intercourse—these are just some recent examples of museums expanding the conditions of art reception through participation and interaction. The dematerialization of the work of art during the last decades has increased the experiential essence of artistic practices.[6] The object is no longer the center of art production and has become more like a tool or a furniture, a ritualistic object that facilitates the experience. As the importance of the object diminishes, galleries are transformed into spaces for bodies, which are seduced, activated, and realized. Challenging the art object, its visual condition, and its commodity status, the reception of experience-based works has shifted from the object to the subject.

One can trace a genealogy of practices and work methods in which artists have redefined the conditions of their work, their position as authors, and art's relationship with its audiences[7]. As artistic practice moves beyond the limits of the gallery and the museum, the museum seeks ways in which it might adapt to accommodate and facilitate these larger shifts. The museum galleries become spaces to be manipulated, transformed, and surpassed.

We situate the examples below in relation to this genealogy. The works of Marina Abramovic, Tino Sehgal, Carsten Höller, or Christoph Büchel resituate how we receive, relate, and perceive works of art. In these works, the visitor performs and there is no artwork without the visitor's engagement. This change in the ways of "doing" art, draws not only from a certain trajectory in contemporary art practice and discourse, but also involves the use and manipulation of the museum space, as the works can be read as commentary about the institution, its model, and its dreams. Museums have historically demonstrated influence in the formation of community identity by presenting objects as representative of a common heritage. The denaturalization of the objects inside the museum and the loss of their original context, precisely what Dorner was concerned with, follow a similar process in non-object art. The conservation and exhibition of these works will also be affected by the loss of their original context and each recreation will become a new piece, producing a whole new set of reactions, and extending the possibilities of different relationships. As Sol LeWitt remarked, "Successful art changes our understanding of the conventions by altering our perceptions" (1967).The dematerialization of the reception of these works places us in the space of the experience, the here and now where every single visitor relates differently with the work of art. If there were people crying in front of Marina Abramovic, this, she defends, is because she acted as a mirror, a shaman guiding participants in a ritualistic journey. There were many reactions to Abramovic's *The Artist is Present* (2010) from people getting naked to those throwing up, to still others mimicking Abramovic.

Sehgal's *This Progress* (2010) used the Frank Lloyd Wright ramp at the Guggenheim Museum of New York as an organic spiral activated by the conversations between a trained team of performers and those who visited the exhibition. Although Sehgal forbad participants to document the work in any form other than that of human memory, many participants disobeyed these instructions by making pirate recordings. Dorothea von Hantelmann argues "these forms of representation [imitation, impersonation, and enactment] interest Sehgal in contrast to the permanence of the material object and its documentation via images" (2010: 134). Because Sehgal does not allow press releases, catalogues, or any kind of contract or preservation guide, he marks a transition from the "archived event" to the "event of archiving" (Hantelmann 2010: 134). This can be seen as a democratization of the archive through participation.

The installation work of Carsten Höller and Christoph Büchel, can be differentiated from the previous cases of study in that they design the space or context for the experience, but they are not responsible for the performativity. In Höller's piece, *Giant Psycho Tank* (1999), visitors' bodies rotate together inside a saline pool. The experience was meant to be shared and negotiated by participants—an artistic intention that was altered when, after two weeks of his show at the New Museum in 2011, the NYC Department of Health restricted access to the pool to a single person at a time. The outcome was unplanned, yet expressive of the larger social fears and bureaucratic organization that characterize our times.

Christoph Büchel's work, *Element 6* (2010), invites visitors to engage in sexual acts inside the institution guided by the usual regulations of a swingers' club. The artist is, in this sense, a constructor not only of replicas (objects), but also of the dematerialized (non-object) experience. Again, the outcome is determined via the interactions of the bodies in attendance. The work creates a platform where various experiences are enacted from voyeurism to play to seductions to any number of other effects.

The experiences generated through these exhibitions articulate a role that differs from the traditional role occupied by the museum visitor. The work seeks to activate visitors and include them in the production of the work. In this context, the museum becomes a space for action, mediation, and social interaction. Gilles Deleuze in his essay "Mediators," remarks on the necessity of mediators in the process of creation,

> I need my mediators to express myself, and they'd never express themselves without me: one is always working in a group, even when it doesn't appear to be the case. (Deleuze 1997: 285)

The works presented here require the participation of the audience as mediators to complete the experience proposed by the artist. It is through the experience that the visitor fully participates and produces the work of art, reshaping the museum in the process. Moreover, the use of time to delimit the experience supposes a contrast with our high-speed rhythm of life. The museum succeeds when, as a laboratory, it cultivates experimental practices rather than promoting consumer behavior. From the ritual of the museum as a pre-industrial formative institution to the consumerism of the industrial institution, the museums of the immaterial economy are re-situated as live laboratories to generate experience.

This is an opportune time for museums to reconsider the experiential qualities of their institutions in collaboration with designers, art producers, and various publics. Museums today struggle to serve wide publics in meaningful ways that go beyond the experiences offered by commodity culture. In the field of design we see a similar concern emerging as designers "look at capabilities rather than commodities" (Busch 2014). The collaborative potential of sharing practices and expertise offers the possibility for the museums to become centers of experience.

Notes

1 For most of Dorner's time there the museum was still called "Provinzialmuseum," today it is the "Niedersächsische Landesmuseum."
2 This was not unprecedented, as the 1920 Berlin Dada Fair also took an experimental exhibition approach.
3 See eMotion's website at: http://www.mapping-museum-experience.com (accessed August 25, 2013).
4 This follows the arguments put forth by Lucy Lippard in the late 1960s and early 1970s. See especially Lippard (1973).
5 These genealogies have been explored along varying trajectories. See Bishop (2012) and Thompson (2012).

Chapter 7
Space, Experience, Identity, and Meaning
Peter Benz

In the "Prejudices" leading towards the main argument of the German architecture theorist's, Eduard Führ, essay, "Frankfurter Küche' und Spaghetti Carbonara" (2006) about the experiential quality (although the author doesn't use this terminology) of Margarete Schütte-Lihotzky's *Frankfurter Küche*, he describes a principal conflict between the architect's design intentions for a building and the experience of the space(s) by the public:

> In Architecture [discourse] it is common practice, to distinguish usage from production, living from building. One firstly builds [a building], then lives in [it]. The building is produced by an architect, who is identified as the artist: through an act of creativity he lifts something into existence, he shapes a piece of work, which did not—in identical form—exist before. The inhabitant lives in the building, after it has been completed. Inhabitants are contrary to the artist, they are not creative; they don't produce anything, they merely put up with it. They even are "anti-artists", they don't lift anything into existence, they consume the work by using it. [...] From the point of view of art theory, the usage of a built work of art, inhabiting it, is not only an inadequate method of reception and analysis of the work, it actually prohibits such. By living in it, the architecture is no longer perceived as a built artwork, but merely as a building, an instrument of everyday life organization and implementation. Everyday concerns over this and that don't allow the inhabitants either the leisure, or the proper—necessarily unemotional, distant—attitude to truly perceive artistically. The everyday cannot not be artistic, which is why art may only be perceived after the exit from the everyday, exterior from the living. (Führ 2006 [translation by author])

In the end of his extended investigation, Führ humorously concludes with an unexpected analogy:

> The usage of a building relates to Architecture like a football game relates to the pitch.
> It is always a singular game. Particular games cannot be repeated. One may play at the same venue, with the same players and referees, against the same opponents. Even if the same team kicks off, with the same player playing the ball in identical fashion to the same teammate, as a matter of fact each and every game immediately is a new game. Each game is concrete and singular. Every game

develops over time and within the space of the pitch. A game is about bodily participation, about the layout of a concrete narration. In a game of football, players interact, collaborate and compete in the usage of the pitch. (Führ 2006 [translation by author])

Führ thus essentially resolves the problem through acceptance of the bare facts of (everyday) life: an architect or other spatial designer may determine a spatial setup, and through the setup potentially also suggest particular rules and guidelines for use, yet ultimately it remains with the occupant(s) to give the space its functionality, and with that its (ever-changing) identity.

Common experience suggests Führ's line of thought to be not entirely off; however, that leaves designers of spatial situations and entities with a significant problem, as any attempts of determining particular spatial experiences for the occupants of a built environment would a priori be destined to fail. Even if the target audience could be limited to only one specific person, every time that person used the space it would instigate a "new game" with unpredictable outcome.

This isn't a new realization, a similar problem is, for example, outlined by Adolf Loos in his polemic essay "The Poor Little Rich Man" of 1900. It is the story of a rich man who has a house built artistically balanced to perfection by a top-notch architect of the day.

The rich man was overjoyed. Overjoyed, he walked through his new rooms. Wherever he cast his glance was Art, Art in each and every thing. He grasped Art when he took hold of a door handle; he sat in Art when he settled into an armchair; he buried his head in Art when, tired, he lay it down on a pillow; he sank his feet into Art when he trod on the carpet. [...]

The architect had forgotten nothing, absolutely nothing. Cigar ashtrays, cutlery, light switches — everything was made by him. [...]

However, it must not be kept a secret that he [the rich man] preferred to be home as little as possible. After all, one also wants to take a rest now and then from so much art. [...] (Loos 1982)

Finally the entire experience goes entirely downhill when the rich man celebrates his birthday, and gets a lot of presents from his family:

The architect's face grew noticeably longer. Then he exploded, "How do you come to allow yourself to be given gifts! Did I not design everything for you? Did I not consider everything? You don't need anything more. You are complete! [...]

Then a transformation took place in the rich man. The happy man suddenly felt deeply, deeply unhappy.

In this story the architect's (experiential) design intentions for the house come into conflict with the everyday life of its inhabitant: The architect provides a wealth of sensory experiences, yet denies the rich man even the merest personal token, thus ultimately rendering the entire spatial design meaningless. The inhabitant is not only unable to appreciate the (superior) artistic quality of the built experience, but in effect is even hampered in the pursuit of his everyday life.

Of course, both of the previous examples refer to one particular use of space only: "living in it," i.e. they are concerned specifically with residential spaces. It is intuitively agreeable that the residence of a particular person/family will always eventually take on features of the identity of its inhabitant(s), and thereby becomes recognizably "their home" — in difference to merely "a space in which somebody lives," and also in difference to whatever the architect's design intentions might have been. This is not merely an effect of placing personal presents—as the rich man wanted to in Loos' story—or putting up family pictures and displaying personal knickknacks, but can also be summarized in more abstract terms: a residence may be stylish, comfy, cluttered, messy, relaxing …

This spatial adaptation process usually results in the appropriated "home" developing meaning for its inhabitant(s): i.e. the inhabitants develop an emotional relationship with the space, and begin to identify with it—which essentially is a core purpose of many attempts at building brand identity: creating the setting for a meaningful relationship with a company's audience/clients/guests/visitors.

For example, the Intercontinental Hotels Group (IHG) is a British multinational hospitality corporation operating more than 4,500 hotels under several brands—the most important ones being InterContinental, Crowne Plaza, Holiday Inn, and Holiday Inn Express—in about 100 countries. The vast majority of IHG hotels are run under franchise agreements, implying that IHG effectively provides the name/brand for any of "its" hotels, together with the "identity," as well as guidelines and—to some extent—managerial support to articulate and realize that identity, but does not own the hotels as such (Interconti Hotel Group 2012).

As one of only few cities worldwide, Hong Kong is home to a total of nine IHG hotels, including all of its major brands: two InterContis, two Crowne Plazas, one Holiday Inn, and three Holiday Inn Expresses. With so many hotels of the same group in a geographically relatively small and very clearly distinct area, it is of necessity urgent—if not for IHG then certainly for the business interests of their franchise partners—to very distinctly articulate each of their brands' identities. Otherwise why would a guest stay at the InterContinental Hong Kong if the Holiday Inn Golden Mile (almost literally) just down the road provides a similar experience for a lesser price?

IHG recognized this issue early on, and—from 2007—over a period of two years went through a comprehensive worldwide relaunch of all its brands, which included articulating specific brand identities, and developing guidelines for their implementation/realization on site. These guidelines obviously define the various common issues of corporate identity—graphic appearances, etc.—but also go much further in detail on issues such as facilities, equipment, services, and particular spatial experience.

The core business of any hotel is the temporary lease of personal living space to the guest. The experience that this space—i.e. the guest room—provides to the guest therefore has to be of prime concern to any hotel management. In the case of IHG, with its multiple brands at varying pricing levels, spatial experience also has to be a paramount consideration in the articulation of (brand/hotel) identity, as, again, why should a guest stay in—and pay for—a room at the InterContinental Hong Kong if the rooms at the Holiday Inn Golden Mile are essentially the same, yet cheaper?

The general setup of the IHG hotels in Hong Kong—close geographic proximity, similar urban contexts, comparable ownership structures and clientele—is brought to an extreme in the suburb of Tsuen Kwan O where, within one month—on September 28, 2012 and October 26, 2012 respectively—a newly built Crowne Plaza and a new Holiday Inn Express opened in the closest possible vicinity of each other: they literally share the same driveway. Both hotels sit on the same building lot, are owned by the same holding company (Sun Hung Kai Property, Hong Kong), were designed by the same architectural firm (Richards Basmajian, Hong Kong), and—in a rare move by IHG—even have the same management team (Chan 2013). Thus—as all parameters are effectively identical—what makes the difference that would make the guest want to pay more at the Crowne Plaza?

IHG's management argues the difference is in the brand identities, which supposedly articulates through the guests' experience of their rooms: the Crowne Plaza is "an upscale brand […] offering business travellers high level of comfort, service and amenities" (Interconti Hotel Group 2012). Guests of this brand would be "travelling for success" (ibid.), which is supported through Crowne Plaza's signature "one-step-ahead service" (ibid.) and allows guests to feel "productive, accomplished and re-energized during their trip" (ibid.).

The Holiday Inn Express in return is "a fresh, clean, uncomplicated hotel choice offering comfort, convenience and good value" (ibid.) with guests that are "an unpretentious, ambitious, self-reliant, sociable group of people" (ibid.)—or, in short, as the brand claims: "Everyday Heroes" (ibid.).

The respective general brand guidelines also briefly touch on—among other things—the articulation of the spatial experiences of respective guest rooms. For example, at the Holiday Inn Express "guests enjoy the best possible sleep experience in a fresh uncluttered space of their own. [...] The real world bathroom is bright, fresh and up-to-date" (ibid.), as it provides "an invigorating bath experience with great shower pressure, plenty of room, and absorbent towels" (ibid.). The Crowne Plaza rooms instead feature the *Crowne Plaza Sleep Advantage*, which is established by a "designated quiet zone, luxurious and soft bedding, aromatherapy and a guaranteed wake-up-call" (ibid.).

Aside from these "hallmark experiences" (ibid.) promoted in its corporate publication materials in practical terms, IHG takes a very "mechanical" approach to the experiential design of its guest rooms: it developed a "brand book" that standardizes almost every imaginable guestroom feature in respect to the specific brand. For example, for each brand IHG defines the appropriate square meterage for guest rooms, standard items of furniture and equipment, as well as details such as bed sizes, TV-screen diameter, thread density of carpet flooring, items in the mini-bar, and specific "sensory experiences" like room scent and music blend.

Despite these brand-specific standardizations, in the first half year of operation of the two hotels in Tsuen Kwan O—from September 2012 to March 2013—the Holiday Inn Express had occupation rates of over 90 percent on average—in line with other IHG hotels in Hong Kong—while Crowne Plaza only achieved about 75 percent average occupancy. Apparently the experiences provided were neither distinct nor specific enough to prevent "target guests" of Crowne Plaza to book into Holiday Inn Express. While today's consumers may be prepared to put particular experiences over more traditional commodities during their purchase deliberations, if no distinct experience can be identified, quality or—as in this case—price still make the purchase decision.

All the various definitions in IHG's brand book establish quantifiable standards, which make all of their hotels "good hotels," but apparently they do not amount to a particular experiential design. Indeed, when asked specifically about any experiential features in their guest rooms, IHG management in Tsuen Kwan O could only name their "choice of pillow" program (Chan 2012) and their "signature shower" (ibid.)—both of which trigger sensory experiences, but do not necessarily pass the threshold of achieving "experiences"—i.e. a complex synthesis of sensory perception, cognition, and emotion (Desmet and Schifferstein 2011).

This appears in a context in which hotels strive to be "a home away from home"—while at the same time homes increasingly look like hotel rooms, as a visit to any of IKEA's show rooms around the world easily reveals—the spatial experience of hotel rooms poses a dilemma: an entangled set of somewhat fuzzy issues evolving around space, its experience, the identities they are intended to communicate in contrast to those they actually may create, and the meaning that develops from all of this for the guests.

Going back to our case: IHG are playing the part of the architect, having the interest and need to communicate a fairly specific brand identity through a spatial setup—which in Loos' story is represented by the "Art"—while the hotel guest is the rich man struggling to maintain his own identity within this "imposing" environment. Through living in the guest rooms, the guests come into conflict with the identities predetermined by IHG, and can ultimately not perceive the original intention any more, thus rendering IHG's efforts meaningless.

This dilemma is not least the result of a particular aesthetic notion that is present especially with architects—who consider themselves artists but also engineers—yet it is common throughout the community of visual arts practitioners: the notion that beauty is an ideal, universally recognizable state of harmonious order, established through the magic-like correlation of design principles such as balance, rhythm, contrast, and others. Such mostly static state of perfection inevitably is irreconcilable with the dynamic messiness that is our daily life, thus must lead to the effect as noted by Führ.

A resolution of the dilemma Führ therefore suggests a reconsideration of the aesthetic notion on which much of today's design practice is based on, namely a Pythagorean line of thought, favoring clear-cut geometric forms and numerical proportions and deducts a line of "practical aesthetics" starting of in the early eighteenth century in the writings of Anthony A. Cooper, 3rd Earl of Shaftesbury.[1] In *The Moralists* (1709) Shaftesbury outlines a concept of "practical aesthetics," which he developed specifically in contrast to a more prevalent "rationale aesthetics."

Nothing surely is more strongly imprinted on our Minds, or more closely interwoven with our Souls, than the Idea or Sense of Order and Proportion. Hence all the force in Numbers, and those powerful Arts founded on their Management and Use. What difference there is between Harmony and Discord! Cadency and Convulsion! What a difference between compos'd and orderly Motion, and that which is ungovern'd and accidental! between the regular and uniform Pile of some noble Architect, and a Heap of Sand or Stones! and between an organiz'd Body, and a Mist or Cloud driven by the Wind!

Now as this Difference is immediately perceiv'd by a plain Internal Sensation, so there is withal in Reason this account of it; That whatever Things have Order, the same have Unity of Design, and concur in one, are parts constituent of one Whole, or are, in themselves, intire Systems. Such is a Tree, with all its Branches; an Animal, with all its Members; and Edifice, with all its exteriour and interiour Ornaments. What else is even a Tune or Symphony, or any excellent Piece of Musick, than a certain System of proportion'd Sounds? (Cooper 1999: 51–2)

Shaftesbury admits to a concept of order as the basis for aesthetical considerations; however, he dismissed the notion that such order is established through "the force of Numbers, and those powerful Arts." Instead he contrasts a principle of "Unity of Design," which is not rationally deducted by connoisseurship, but may be "immediately perceived by a plain internal sensation," which also implies that such unity should be accessible to all, also without previous education.

Shaftesbury continues to elaborate on what constitute "intire systems," and how they establish their particular identities:

I know you look on the Trees of this vast Wood as to be different from one another:
    And this tall Oak, the noblest of the Company, as it is by it-self a different thing from all its Fellows of the Wood, so with its own Wood numerous spreading Branches [...] 'tis still, I suppose, one and the self-same Tree. Now shou'd you, [...], tell me that if a Figure of Wax, or any other Matter, were cast in the exact Shape and Colours of this Tree, and temper'd, if possible, to the same kind of Substance, that therefore it might possibly be a real Tree of the same Kind or Species; [...] I shou'd satisfy you what I thought it was which made this Oneness or Sameness in the Tree or any other

Plant; or by what it differ'd from the waxen Figure, or from any such Figure accidentally made, either in the Clouds, or in the Sand by the Seashore; I shou'd tell you, that neither the Wax, nor Sand, nor Cloud thus piec'd together by our Hand or Fancy, had any real relation within themselves, or had any Nature by which they corresponded any more in that near Situation of Parts, than if scatter'd ever so far asunder. But this I shou'd affirm, "That wherever there was such Sympathizing of Parts, as we saw here, in our real Tree; Wherever there was such plain Concurrence in one common End, and to the Support, Nourishment, and Propagation of so fair a Form; we cou'd not mistaken in saying there was a peculiar Nature belonging to this Form, and common to it with others of the same kind." By virtue of this, our Tree is a real Tree; lives, flourishes, and is still One and the same; even when by Vegetation and Change of Substance, not one Particle in it remains the same. (Ibid.: 80–1)

In other words, according to Shaftesbury the particular nature/identity of any object is not defined by its substance or its form—those could even change—yet through "such sympathizing of parts"; identity accordingly is uncoupled from any material articulation, yet instead is the result of a conceptual relation: not the parts as such make the object, but the "idea" that brought them together.

Here then, said he, is all I wou'd have explain"d to you before: "That the Beautiful, the Fair, the Comely, were never in the Matter, but in the Art and Design; never in Body it-self, but in the Form or Forming Power." Does not the beautiful Form confess this, and speak the Beauty of the Design, whene'er it strikes you? What is it but the Design which strikes? What is it you admire but Mind, or the Effect of Mind? 'Tis Mind alone which forms. All which is void of Mind is horrid: and Matter formless is Deformity it-self.[1]

To Shaftesbury this principal observation is also true for the human self:

You see therefore, there is a strange Simplicity in this You and Me, that in reality they shou'd be still one and the same, when neither one Atom of Body, one Passion, nor one Thought remains the same. (Ibid.: 106–7)

Like all other things, the nature of a person is not established through either his or her material physicality, or his or her emotional capacity, or his or her intellectual activity alone; only all of them in combination establish the identity of the self. Interestingly, body, passion, and thought, as listed by Shaftesbury, represent exactly the triumvirate of sensory perception, emotion, and cognition that are considered—in design practice today—the constitutional basics of what is "experience" (Desmet and Schifferstein 2011).
    Later in the eighteenth century, Shaftesbury's thoughts were followed up by David Hume in his *A Treatise of Human Nature* (Hume 1978: 284 [1739/40]), that introduces the notion of "impressions" (= perception) and "ideas" (= cognition) as two principal components to make up complex sensory experiences:

As the fancy delights in every thing that is great, strange, or beautiful, and is still more pleas'd the more it finds of these perfections in the same object, so it is capable of receiving a new satisfaction by the assistance of another sense. Thus any continu'd sound, as the music of birds, or a fall of waters, awakens every moment the mind of the beholder, and makes him more attentive to the several beauties of the place, that lie before him. Thus if there arises a fragrancy of smells or perfumes, they heighten the pleasure of the imagination, and make even the colours and verdure of the landschape appear more agreeable; for the ideas of both senses recommend each other, and are pleasanter together than when they enter the mind separately: As the different colours of a picture, when they are well disposed, set off one another, and receive an additional beauty from the advantage of the situation. In this phænomenon we may remark the association both of impressions and ideas, as well as the mutual assistance they lend each other (ibid.).

A little later, William Hogarth, in his *Analysis of Beauty* (1909 [1751]), also defines beauty—and with it identity—as an entangled relation of parts, which he summarizes in the observation:

[...] in shipbuilding the dimensions of every part are confined and regulated by fitness for sailing. When a vessel sails well, the sailors always call her a beauty: the two ideas have such a connection! (Hogarth 1909)

Contrary to his predecessors, Hogarth quite distinctly defines beauty in terms of a modern concept of "functionality" of the parts, and their contribution to the functionality of the overall entity.

Our necessities have taught us to mould matter into various shapes, and to give them fit proportions for particular uses, as bottles, glasses, knives, dishes, etc. Has not offence given rise to the form of the sword, and defence to that of the shield?
    And what else but proper fitness of parts has fixed the different dimensions of pistols, common guns, great guns, fowling-pieces, and blunderbusses; which differences, as to figure, may as properly be called the different characters of firearms, as the different shapes of men are called characters of men. (ibid.)

In the nineteenth-century ideas and concepts of the "practical aesthetics" were finally also transferred into architectural practice, namely by the German architect Gottfried Semper and his book of the early 1860s *Style in the Technical and Tectonic Arts; or Practical Aesthetics*. But already during his stay in London (1850–2), to where he had fled after his involvement in the German Revolution of 1848 had gone sour, he paraphrazed Hogarth in a letter to his friend Heinrich Hübsch:

After all what have I done in 48, that one persecutes me forever? One single barricade did I construct—it bore up, because it was practical, and as it was practical, it was beautiful. (Semper cited in Machens 2010 [translation by author])

From this brief historical excursion—along the lines provided by Führ—it appears viable to deduct for the purpose of our case that

- Identity is constructed through a specific and intentional relationship of parts.
- Experience is a construct of perceptional, cognitive, and emotional elements.
- Identity is experienced—in the context of (spatial) design—through the practical functionality of the design.
- Identity can be understood as a dynamic experiential "product" construed in real time while it is experienced.

The Finnish architect and theorist Juhani Pallasmaa in his essay "Geometry of Feeling" (2007 [1985]) comes to a similar realization when he develops the ideal of a phenomenological "Architecture of Imagery":

> The artistic dimension of a work of art does not lie in the actual physical thing; it exists only in the consciousness of the person experiencing that object. The analysis of a work of art is, at its most genuine level, an introspection by the consciousness subjected to it. The work of art's meaning lies not in its forms, but in the images transmitted by the forms and the emotional force that they carry. Form only affects our feelings through what it represents. [...]
>
> As architects, we do not design buildings primarily as physical objects: we design with regard to the images and emotions of the people who live in them ... [The] effect of architecture stems from more or less shared images and basic emotions connected with building. (Pallasmaa 2007: 242–5)

Pallasmaa thinks very much in line with his British predecessors but he introduces also a new "category," which he refers to as the "effect" of a building or its "meaning." While Shaftesbury originally developed his aesthetic theory in the context of his investigations into morality (McAteer 2011), thus is indeed concerned with the notion of "meaning," he does not explore how meaning is to be achieved or even purposefully designed.

At this point is seems useful to "leap" forward in this argument and to introduce some thoughts by Adrian Poole, a professor for English Literature at Cambridge University, who considered "meaning" in the context of identity in his Darwin Lecture *The Identity of Meaning* (2010):

> To summarize: within the whole range of the meanings of meaning both current and obsolete, the sense of intention or purpose or will to signify, communicate or make something happen is inalienable. So too is the sense of effect and impact and consequence, of meaning as something that passes between speaker and listener, between artist and audience, between lovers and between warriors. It is something that goes through a process in time, space and history. Against this there is the desire for meaning that lies outside vicissitude and even intentions, at least human intentions, a desire especially invested in great religious symbols that command widespread belief, such as the Cross and the Crescent. Yet even the most sacred objects of contemplation require stories to be told about them if their meanings are to be grasped. Meaning means interpretation in the sense that it requires and entails it. "Know what I mean?" Think of the way we appeal to such harmless, pathetic everyday fillers. Almost devoid of content, they mark the desire for connection, sometimes minimally, as who should say, "you know, like, uh, hey, man, I mean, cool, huh?"

Poole's deductions on the meanings of "meaning" provide ample touch points to integrate the notion of meaning with the theories of Shaftesbury and Pallasmaa, as well as with everyday design practice, namely the necessity of a story/interpretation, a narration for meaning to unfold, and the "sense of intention or purpose or will" to communicate. He even also highlights the importance of "everday fillers" that have the purpose of connecting the various parts of a story, thus establishing relationships and setting a particular tone.

For the case of the IHG hotels, it's quite safe to establish a failure in their attempts at producing meaningful guest relations, as neither the guest rooms of the Crowne Plaza nor the Holiday Inn Express instigate experiences that allow distinct identification. Guestrooms of both houses essentially allow for identical functionalities—to sleep, to shower, to watch TV, etc.—as do all guestrooms in all hotels of reasonable standard. The qualifications as provided in IHG's brand book consider the parts of the overall design, but they do not establish a coherent idea of the relation of these parts that in return could be a narrative and thus produce meaning, or—in Shaftesbury's analogy—they are all perfect wax replicas of the same tree, yet lack the "sympathising of parts" that is the nature of the original.

IHG does identify specific target guests, but those identities again are not reflected and articulated in the room designs: Crowne Plaza rooms do look "higher class" than Holiday Inn Express rooms, they are more spacious and designed more elaborately, but how these additional efforts reflect the targeted "business travelers" as opposed to the "unpretentious, ambitious, self-reliant, sociable" guests of the Holiday Inn Express remains unclear. Or, to argue along the analogy of Führ's football game: IHG establishes a playing field, but doesn't define whether this is a football pitch, a basketball court, or even a golf course.

Note

1   The following deduction is a condensed summary of a line of thought on a history of practical aesthetics from the paper by Eduard Führ quoted before. As Führ's paper is available in German language only, and was never formally published, I reiterate his thoughts for convenience of the English readership, but also extend and newly relate them to issues of Experience Design.

Chapter 8

Four Themes to (Phenomenologically) Understand Contemporary Urban Spaces

Lakshmi P. Rajendran, Stephen Walker, and Rosie Parnell

Our existence is always in relation with things in the physical world, a spatial relation that is fundamental for all our experiences. "We have said that space is existential; we might just as well have said that existence is spatial" (Merleau-Ponty 2002: 295). Often this spatiality of our existence is so obvious that it becomes almost invisible in our everyday living. Being subtle they tend to be remote from the individual's awareness, as physical settings are perceived as "backdrops" against which events occur (Proshansky et al. 1983). Largely, "spatiality tends to be peripheralised into the background as reflection, container, stage, environment, or external constraint of human behaviour and social action" (Soja 1996: 71). It is important, however, to note that any narrative that ignores the spatial dimension is incomplete and results in the oversimplified understanding of our experiences (Jameson 1991: 40).

Our spatial interaction with the physical world accommodates our fundamental need for reflecting one's self onto the outside world. We need to project something of ourselves onto the other in order to recognize or misrecognize ourselves in the other (Vischer et al. 1994: 104). It is the spatial relation and the experiences associated with it, which allow us to make sense of our own self by extending our self onto the outside world.

The primacy of spatial experiences lies in its power to enable things or objects to be connected (Merleau-Ponty 2002: 243). But technology has slowly and steadily acquired the power to (re)define our experiential understanding of the physical world by not only changing the characteristic nature of spatial experiences but also by conditioning our ability to perceive things. Paul Virilio (2001: 75) notes that people tend to be largely at "locations" where they cease to be moving bodies and become instead motionless objects that are subjects to the immediacy of actions "on the spot." The "violence of speed" (Virilio 2001: 76) of such actions additionally seldom allows deeper experiences, which is further heightened by the "reversal of two dimensions—a temporalisation of space and spatialisation of time" (Pallasmaa 2005: 21).

Amidst these dynamic transformations of our existence, it is essential to study people's urban spatial experiences to comprehend these new complexities and how they affect notions of identity negotiation in spatial environments. For this purpose this chapter presents a case study—based on a phenomenological approach—that aims to study the significance of everyday spatial experiences in urban spaces for identity constructions. Addressed to experiential designers and to others with an interest in spatial experiences, this study discusses the various implicit factors that affect contemporary urban experiences, and the emergent themes pertaining to spatial experiences and identity constructions in urban living.

Everyday spatial experience and identity

Places today are largely designed for promoting themselves as attractions where everyday spatial experiences are transformed as journeys into "hyperreality" (Baudrillard 1994: 149). Amidst these is hidden an underlying constant process of negotiation with the everyday spatial experiences so as to enact spatial tactics to find meaning within the environment through "performative constructs" (Butler 2006: 3). These spatial experiences allow one to extend one's self to identify with a particular place, in turn reassuring, reinforcing or restructuring one's identity through the place itself. In this context it is potentially significant to study "ordinary" everyday places that possess "multiple and shifting meanings rather than clarity of function" (Crawford 2008: 28).

Today, designers "in searching for meaningful ideas to use as generators of form, often push the purposive activities even further up the scale of predictability than they deserve to be" (Lawson 2001: 204). Consequently, contemporary places seldom offer spontaneity and freedom of experiential understanding, hence failing to accommodate the spatial tactics which offer ways of making connections, and finding meaning in otherwise abstract and alienating places (Leach 2005). These factors have had a great impact on our overall spatial understanding, and, as a result, the fundamental need for reflection of self in the environment has largely been suffering.

Definition of key terms

In psychology, identity is at "its core psychosocial: self and other; inner and outer; being and doing; expression of self for, with, against, or despite; but certainly in response to others" (Josselson 1994). Viewed in the context of relatedness, identity emerges from the continually redefined capacity to make use of and respond to context (Josselson 1994). Drawing from this explanation—while considering the physical context including the socio-spatial realm—identity can be understood as a sense of relatedness with a place, which gradually enables people to feel a "sense of identity" with the environment.

The notions of *space* and *place* used in this research are drawn from Robert Sack as two terms with blurred boundaries that are intertwined into one another by activities ad objects:

> Place implies space, and each home is a place in space. Space is a property of the natural world, but it can be experienced. From the perspective of experience, place differs from space in terms of

familiarity and time. A place requires human agency, is something that may take time to know, and a home especially so. As we move along the earth we pass from one place to another. But if we move quickly the places blur; we lose track of their qualities, and they may coalesce into the sense that we are moving through space. (1997: 16)

Study rationale

Building on the issues discussed above, this study probes the impacts of urban spatial experiences on the need to reflect one's self through identification with the physical environment. In the context of addressing the issues of globalization, multiculturalism, and alienation in urban cities today, the study aims to explore this problem through a case study conducted in Sheffield, United Kingdom. The study adopts a phenomenological methodology to establish significant connections between the everyday spatial experiences of a selected group of people and their constructions of relations with those. The research participants were 15 international students (coded as P1 to P15) studying research degrees in Architecture at the University of Sheffield. As students from different cultural backgrounds have varying perceptions of their spatial contexts, their spatial practices also differ. It is valuable to understand how these diversities are accommodated and/or adapted through myriad possibilities in physical settings that are often embedded in everyday spatial experiences.

As examples for the study urban outdoor spaces were selected based on the following factors:

a. Relevance to everyday life of international students

The identification of spaces of relevance to the achievement of the students' life purposes enable an understanding of how these spaces accommodate or allow everyday life and interaction, and how people individually respond to these spatial experiences.

b. "Undesigned" character of the spaces

"Undesigned" urban spaces closely related to the concept of "loose spaces" (Franck and Stevens 2007) were selected as they accommodate and encourage casual and spontaneous uses.

c. Familiarity/frequency of use

Spaces were also chosen for their frequency of use and general familiarity among the international student community, as that facilitated a more detailed discussion of spatial experiences.

Data collection

Data collection was carried out through in-depth qualitative semi-structured interviews with the participants, lasting between 45 minutes to 1 hour, employing tasks which included ranking images of 30 selected settings according to their perceived relatedness to respective participants. The participants were also to match selected images to words from a provided list of adjectives such as "comfortable," "safe," "pleasant," "complex"—to name a few—and to sketch the spatial aspects of places from their personal rankings to explain how they felt those places accommodated their identification with them.

To overcome the insufficiency of quantitative scientific methods, the architect Norberg-Schulz (1980) suggests phenomenology as an appropriate approach to explore the complex relation between person and world. In accordance with this line of thought, the analysis of the data gathered followed the Interpretative Phenomenological Analysis (IPA), which is specifically committed to the examination of how people make sense of their experiences and reduces the common tendency to fix experiences in predefined or overly abstract categories (Smith 2009).

Findings

The analysis and interpretation of the data allowed to identify four common "themes" that resurfaced throughout all the interviews: *Boundaries*; *(Re)Connection*; *Restoration*; and *Everyday Life*.

Boundaries

The primacy of boundaries is generally well accepted in architecture, for, "architecturally, to define space literally meant to determine boundaries" (Tschumi 1998: 219). The analysis showcases some interesting trajectories taken by boundaries—either suggestive or explicit—in participants' spatial experiences: boundaries define territories for individuals and events, thus not only clarifying the inside/outside, private/public relationships, but also offering significant cues for appropriate behavior/activities and/or communicating (personal/social) spatial constraints.

One of the participants recounted how she felt a strong empathetic attachment to a particular urban space, which stemmed from her sense of being a "passively active" part of the activities that she perceived as harmoniously fitting to this context:

> My mum was here during summer on a weekend, it was a sunny day and they had a stage here and lot of young people performed. Playing music all day, it was fantastic … and I almost felt I belonged there … with the people … with the activities … (P10)

For example, referring to an image of the hub outside the Student Union Building (Figure 8.1) largely characterized by informal interaction, the participant acknowledged its importance in student life, yet also hints on some deficiencies related to its fluidity and openness that lacks a sense of privacy, and in this case apparently created unease to the participant:

> Yes, it is a space, which is essential for student life but there's some discomfort, as the space is largely for movement. If it has … Hmmmm … I think it should have more elements like activities or seating areas or some kind of enclosure properly … (P11)

A similar need for privacy in open/public space is expressed by participant P1 when explaining her discomfort at a bus stop, linking the unavailability of seats with privacy issues:

Figure 8.1 Student Union Building, Sheffield: image discussed by P11.

In this place ... there are benches ... But it"s always occupied full ... or hmmm ... there is no privacy here ... I prefer that more ... For example I do not use the bus stop because no seating there also, it feels like people are always watching ... [P1]

Yet another participant started the sketch of her personal choice of space with a strong demarcating feature:

Is this a sort of enclosure? [I]
Yes, a fence. [P3]

Pointing at the space outside the fence she drew, she said:

This is anything outside my world ... [P3]

Two main observations could initially be distilled from these narratives:

First, particular activities—e.g. sitting, shopping, playing music—are perceived to demarcate particular territories. Social activities and the experience of other people apparently offer a wealth of sensual variation that create a pattern of spatial interaction, which in return allow the individual to delve deeper into other aspects of a context: if "time unfolds as change, then space unfolds as interaction" (Massey 2005: 61). Merleau-Ponty (2002: 243) defined space as "the universal power that enables things or objects to be." Pallasmaa (2005: 37) explains "creating this sense of presence through spatial experiences allows us to identify ourselves with the space; this place, this moment and these dimensions, becoming ingredients of our very existence." When integrated well with the activities within them, spatial experiences enable a strong sense of presence, that otherwise—in contemporary life with its multiple heres and theres—tends to be fractured (Wise 2012).

Second, explicit boundaries help to distinguish spaces from each other, while simultaneously allowing clear respective identity alignments—e.g. "my world" versus the "outside world." Spatial boundaries especially support a sense of secured association with a place when they allow the experiencer to fit in snugly and observe the world "outside" from a "secure" vantage point without attracting much attention to herself.

When explaining his favorite space, P6 sketched a frame around his drawing referring to it as a semi-covered space as seen from a first-person perspective (note the words "my legs" at the bottom) from which he could inconspicuously watch a landscape with people and activities (Figure 8.2):

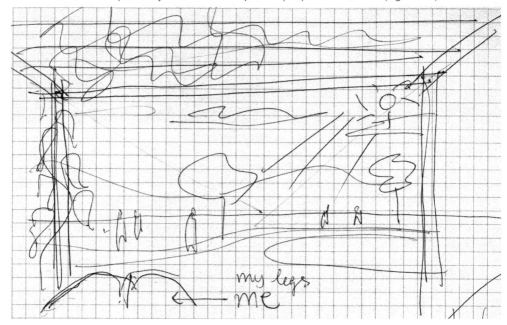

Figure 8.2 Sketch by P6 viewing the world from a secure point of view.

From here I can see what's happening around and there is nobody behind me … [P6]

Or, as another participant put it more definitely:

I don't mind being seen but I don't like to be in the center of attention … [P10]

Dovey states that "largely people feel out of place when not aware of "how to act" in that particular place" (2010: 32). In such situations boundaries allow people to "construct" for themselves a familiar position, a "secure base [that] is a safe haven to explore from and return to when the world feels dicey" (Gallagher 2007: 161). This observation also resonates with the prospect–refuge theory (Walmsley 1988: 74), which states that people feel most comfortable in landscapes where one can see and not be seen. These instinctive needs are to be addressed at all levels of territorial constructs—for example, through boundaries that potentially may carry rich symbolic meaning and, at the same time, implicit cues for people to "act."

(Re)Connection

Participants' narratives expressed an empathetic attachment with urban spaces that allowed them to recollect childhood memories, or otherwise resembled native places and/or previous experiences:

> This is my favorite personal space … I would like to have my place near the seaside … Maybe it's just the complexity of the work activities and the need for a complete oppositeness of calm and peace in sea, which I find very relaxing … [P2]

With further probing about the explanation:

> Maybe because I grew up on an island … a small one … all around it was sea … So maybe this is related to my childhood memory … [P2]

> I like the building … Old fashioned house similar to my grandma house … [P4]

> The atmosphere of the park is beautiful. Green space and water … Back home my house is close to the river and I have lived there for 23 years … My village also has similar bridge … So this reminds me my place, makes me more relaxed and peaceful … [P4; Figure 8.3]

> I feel like I'm at home here. There are pedestrian pathways where we walk down the market and we got shops on the right and left … and normally unlike shops here, the shop in my home country are only outside and people call … "Come to my shop …" "Come to my shop" … "I"ve got this …" "I"ve got that …" [P7; Figure 8.4]

Figure 8.3 Western Park, Sheffield: image discussed by P4.

Figure 8.4 Fargate, Sheffield: image as discussed by P7.

Another participant [P8]—in sketching his favorite place—chose a park and explained,

> I will say, I would have a park with more trees and seats under the tress and some place like a tent … similar to those in my village … it feels nice and relaxed … [P8]

In the first examples, places in Sheffield are likened to (even only vaguely) similar places that invoke pleasant memories, and thereby establish an almost instant relatedness. In the second case the thought of a tent—inspired by the place—evoked a sense of relaxation, despite it was not actually in the space he was describing; yet, the environment at hand struck him as suitable for such structure, and thereby evoked a sense of understanding of the place. Both these types of responses indicate the participants' tendency to search for spatial characteristics of familiar contexts to facilitate identification with their new Sheffield environment. It is interesting to note, in this context, the apparent possibility to link up places not just through their similarities but also through the differences in their spatial structures.

Apart from personal memories, also religious backgrounds appeared to play a significant role, when meeting people with similar religious beliefs, and the resulting social life emerged as an important aid for participants to identify with a specific urban environment. Describing the place of his personal choice one of the participant asserted the importance for the place to address his religious needs:

> … Any place is fine for me but then I'm a Muslim, my religion plays a very important part so where ever I'm staying now I have access to the Mosque so that would affect me, the way I relate to that place. The proximity to the mosque is important. [P7]
>
> Are you referring to the practical aspects of being close to a mosque? [I]
>
> Yes … but the point is: I need to pray and in a way helps me to mingle with my people … The social aspects I mean … When I go to pray, it makes me comfortable with my people. We meet say "Hi, Salaam" … [P7]

Restoration

Korpela et al. (1996), in their study on restorative qualities of places, explain that some properties of places prompt more positively toned emotional states, drive down activities, evoke sustained attention, and block negative emotions and thoughts. Such properties should be expected to encourage people to respond to places more readily, and accordingly—regardless of cultural background—a strong affinity towards restorative spatial experiences was observed in all participants' narratives.

Often the participants expressed the restorative quality of a place through its association to nature (see Kaplan 1995); otherwise specific spatial tactics were adopted to overcome stressful and complex conditions of places, which this study will focus on.

For example, participants described walking as one of the most prominent ways in which they would wish to maneuver through a space and experience its settings (Figure 8.5).

> The way I walk in the street is different … it's not stressful … it's not … I do not like when people are just walking in one direction … It's different when you have open spaces … when you walk more slowly … And you can really look what are around … [P5]

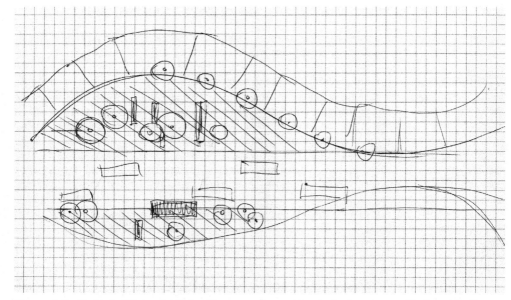

Figure 8.5   Sketch by P5 showing the walking space she would prefer for the purpose of feeling related to a space.

I would just want to walk over areas just to experience … [P10]

A relatively slower pace of movement is noted as an important criterion to engage meaningfully with the environment, reinforcing the urban dweller's implicit understanding of the significance of the fleeting present and its vanishing role for a meaningful existence (Boym 2001). A need for freedom in maneuvering through the space also emerged as a significant factor, which was largely described in terms of clarifying boundaries of movement, allowing choice of pace and pedestrian safety. Although walking often itself is a necessary act (Gehl 2011), it is the spatial dimension, which defines the appropriateness for rich experience and regulates "the human level of tolerance for interferences encountered" (Gehl 2011: 135).

One of the participants observed that a spatial experience that accommodated spontaneity to pause allowed her to be comfortable, as it relieved the need to be cautious while strolling in a public space:

For me this place is comfortable because this is where you can stop … It does not make you uncomfortable to stop there. [P3]

The same participant further compared this first place to another one and continued,

For instance in this place, if I would choose to sit here, it will look weird … If I stand here … it's okay in the pretext of watching the ducks. The space does not accommodate what I wish to do. [P3]

Figure 8.6   Public seating area, Sheffield: image as discussed by P5.

These experiences underlie the implicit yet strong desire for breaking free from the clutches of post-urban spatial behavior, which is arguably largely characterized by staged activity patterns. The participants' narratives of the experiences associated with the act of walking can also be interpreted in line with Michael de Certeau:

> The opacity of the body, in movement, gesticulating, walking, taking its pleasure, is what indefinitely organises a here in relation to an abroad, a "familiarity" in relation to a "foreignness". (1988: 125)

Participants ranked highly those places that allowed them moments of reflection and contemplation, for experiences associated with these places facilitated the interaction with one's self. For example, one of the participants also noted that, despite not having visited a particular place often, she identified with this place the most, since it provided her with a sense of personal restoration (Figure 8.6).

> I have been here only few times but in that time while I'm walking in the city and then I'm tired and just want to have a relaxing time … sitting in the bench … drinking coffee … Thinking about PhD, about me and many things and I think that's the way I'm relating myself with the place … [P5]

Amidst the busy and visually domineering places in the city center, it is the restorative quality of the space — in this case a common side walk seating area — that allows the emergence of sense of self in the individual.

McLeod established that the amount of information to be processed by the human mind in highly complex and dynamic contemporary urban environments is perceived as a combination of both intrusiveness and lack of boundaries (McLeod 1997). As a kind of counter-action and balance, participants showed an increased tendency towards seeking for simplicity in spatial structures. This became evident when participants were asked to sketch their personal choices of spaces, and many started their drawings with statements like,

I like the space to be simple ... [P9]

I want to see the physical world more clear and more tidy ... So much chaos in mind ... So want real life to be more tidy ... [P6]

I need to have clear space around me and I like to keep them clear. I tend to keep my space as free as possible ... [P10]

The place should be comfortable ... simple ... not complicated ... not too many things ... It blocks our imagination ... [P4]

Figure 8.7 Transition between the Sheffield University Library compound and Western Park: image as discussed by P3.

One of the participants also observed that the simplicity of spatial characteristics may play a significant role in experiencing places more deeply (Figure 8.7):

> Yes, it's just a set of steps there's nothing special about the space ... it's just that it is in-between two places having strong characters ... It's a simple transition between two completely different modes. [P3]

Everyday Life

Henri Lefebvre (1991: 169) stated that "man must be everyday, or he will not be at all," stressing on the significance and the essence of everyday life for human existence, and, not surprisingly, participants revealed a strong sense of connection with spatial experiences that were associated with everyday aspects of their life.

One of the participants, while attempting to locate his personal choice of place, began his sketch by questioning its physical context:

> Which is the place I have to consider? [P9]
> Any place, any context, the choice is yours. [I]
> So ... maybe this is my home ... and this is my office so this place should be between my home and office ... [P9]
> Oh, really? [I]
> Yes, that's what makes it more related to me. [P9]
> Is it more to do with familiarity? [I]
> Hmmm ... Yes ... But also we are leading a life between two points ... Destinations ... so the line is important and we have to enjoy it. [P9]

Although the usage of the term "every day" superficially reflects the timely frequency of activities or situations, the notion of Lefebvre's "everyday" is implicitly unconscious, and more complex than mere "familiarity." This may be noted in the way P9 defines the context in which he starts thinking about how he identifies with his space of choice. The participant unconsciously iterates that any space he would choose invariably would have to lie between his home and the office. This does not only reflect the need of frequency of visit to a space but also the need for the space to be a part of the journey (the line) between two important destinations in everyday life. This presupposes essence of everyday life to be inherently connected to spatial experiences that enables people identity constructions.

Everydayness was manifest in a variety of ideas throughout the interviews, yet it was particularly notable that in many instances it wasn't even necessary for participants to actively experience the space:

> I see this (park) every day from my window ... Sometimes ... when I'm so tired ... I just look into this space ... the bridge ... and it's pleasant too. [P2]
> Is this because you have visited and experienced this place? [I]

No, I think it's more because I see this place every day from place where I work, where I spend more time ... [P2]

Another participant stated

I will tell you what. Look at this window (in the picture) that's my place, that's my flat. This is a view which I see every day ... I get from inside my house, this part of the place ... [P11]

The respective spaces achieved significance in participants' everyday lives simply through viewing them from a distance, usually because they offer a kind of escape from the routines of everyday life. This is to some extent analogous with the observation before that also non-existent spatial structures may instigate relatable memories if certain characteristics of the environment point towards them. It also ties everyday qualities of spaces in with the restorative powers of space discussed before.

Discussion and conclusion

The various aspects discussed above following the narratives of the participants provide an idea of the multi-layered and overlapping nature of the four themes identified: implicitly and strongly inter-linked with one another they create meaningful spatial experiences which nurture a sense of self in individuals.

A participant recounted the spatial experience, which she felt she could identify herself with the most:

A coffee area with seats ... self-service or probably even like a proper coffee shop or a small van ... It should be pedestrian as its safe and make me relaxed ... [P11]
Does choosing coffee shop is synonymous for having a break? Or just a pause? [I]
Hmmm ... well ... Coffee for me is everything. It is symbol for many things ... It's like I have personal relationship with the coffee ... [P11]

Further probing into the participant's coffee habits revealed implicit connection with the socio-cultural aspects of her narrative:

A coffee area in a public space makes me feel good; it makes public space for me a better place ... or maybe some kind of a social thing ... Maybe I cannot see myself sitting in a public space doing nothing ... holding a cup is doing something ... Gives me a reason to sit in a public space. [P11]
Why do you think you cannot sit not doing anything? [I]
Probably whenever I sit without doing anything, it's just, I don't feel personal. If I'm busy doing something, I'm doing my own thing. [P11]

The above narratives of the participants epitomize the complexity of the multifarious factors, which influence the spatial experiences involved in relating one's self. The narratives overall also shed light on the qualities of a place, which are often implicit in enabling a deep relationship with the place, yet comprehendible only through the careful study of spatial practices. The study delineates how people tend to evolve their own meaning in their spatial experiences, but also hints that places are often designed for experiences, which have "pre-packaged meaning for consumption" (Dovey 2010: 26).

In a society of movement, it is important for spatial design thinking to consider the fact that "territories are subject to deterritorialisation and reterritorialisation, which are recombined into new assemblages" (Deleuze and Guattari 2004: 17). Often this requires places that provide people with spatial freedom to experiment with various spatial tactics to accommodate notions of self. Within the context of discussion on global sense of place (Massey 1991) and multi-territoriality (Petcou 2002) of societies today, the study sheds light on the potentialities of the repetitive element of everyday life, which can construct a sense of relatedness through familiarity and order. However, this sense of relatedness means nothing without the journey, the connection with the difference (Dovey 2010: 18).

"Architecture is our primary instrument for relating us with space and time, giving these dimensions a human measure." (Pallasmaa 2005: 17). Architecture also allows us to meaningfully connect space and time with a context. In opposition to the superficial relationship with the physical world inflicted upon people today and the kind of void we increasingly live in, it is proposed that design should aim toward creating places that offer a mixture of order and accident, called by Aldo van Eyck (1970) a "labyrinthine clarity."

> Design, in a way must put into doubt its search for all such, often well-intentioned, design solutions or self-deconstructions, to open the way to explore, discover, uncover, and expose the hidden dimensions of lived experience. (Wodiczko 1999: 16)

The design of places needs to allow room for "festival, the meeting, exchange, leisure, pleasure, mixture, contrast, mingling with 'others', comfort, solidarity, difference" (Castello 2010: 22). The results of this study highlight how spatial design "articulates the experience of being-in-the-world and strengthens our sense of reality and self; it does not make us inhabit worlds of mere fabrication and fantasy" (Pallasmaa 2005: 11). Places that nurture such spatial experiences become "profound centres of human existence" (Relph 1976: 43).

PART THREE

Interactions and Performances

Chapter 9

Co-Producing a Festival Experience: A Socio-Material Understanding of Experience Design

Sara M. Strandvad and Kristine M. Pedersen

In front of the tents groups of people have gathered—drinking, talking, gazing at the passers-by. The passers-by move past noisily, beers in their hands—laughing, singing, shouting. Music is playing loudly from the nearby venue where a local rock band has just entered the stage. The roar from the crowd rises and the sound of energetic drums transcends the bright evening. A couple starts dancing fiercely right next to a guy sleeping on the grass. The state of his appearance tells of several days of hard partying.

Capturing a festival experience is challenging, as the above short field note from the Roskilde Festival in Denmark reveals. Such a festival consists of strictly staged performances like rock concerts and of laid back social interactions of talking, dancing, and drinking alike. It involves times of intensity, and it includes periods of relaxation. It features carefully designed spaces of intense scenographies, and deliberately ridiculous theme parties on the adjoining camp sites featuring drunken teddy bears and storm troopers.

To somehow tie these impressions together, the Roskilde Festival experience has been labeled "The Orange Feeling" by the festival planners, in an attempt at combining the brand color of the festival with the socio-aesthetic experience of the festival performance. In the following we will engage in a discussion on the nature of festival experience, and to what degree it may be designed, suggesting that festival design represents an idea-typical case of a co-produced design of an experience. As such the case of Roskilde Festival also functions as an empirical frame for a wider theoretical discussion on how to understand co-produced experience designs in general, which we propose to approach as a socio-material process of enabling attachments. In particular we want to explore how social engagement and involvement can be designed by means of materials, and thus how festival experiences can be perceived as socio-material processes created by participants *and* festival planners respectively.

Experience Design

When Pine and Gilmore (1999) launched the concept of the Experience Economy, they put experiences on the agenda as crucial for economic growth in society. Since an interest in creating meaningful experiences for various purposes has continuously risen both among private companies and public institutions, and, accordingly, successful experiential designs have become sought-after samples for imitation and inspiration.

To explain when experiences occur, Pine and Gilmore declare:

> Companies stage an experience whenever they engage customers, connecting with them in a personal, memorable way. (1999: 3)

While companies may succeed in doing so by chance, experiences can also be created intentionally. To do so, Pine and Gilmore recommend that experience producers follow a principal to-do-list: create events which are unforgettable and have limited supply; sell the use of a product, not the product itself; put the customer at the center of attention; activate all five senses; and enable a sharing of the experience (ibid.: 11–20). They also outline a typology of four different types of experiences: entertainment, educational, aesthetic, and escapist. The so-called *experience realms*, which are differentiated by two criteria (participation and connection) to illustrate how customers may be engaged in various dimensions (ibid.: 30ff.).

While Pine and Gilmore believe that their recommendations will indeed produce valid experiences, they do not explain in detail how this is achieved; neither do they account for how experiences are actually created, nor for what happens during an experience. Instead, in their writings, experiences seem to occur as a more or less automatic response to a design, a position questioned by various scholars since (see, for example, Boswijk et al. 2007).

Second generation Experience Design

The critique of Pine and Gilmore's approach to experiences has been a major point in the development of a second generation within the literature on the experience economy (Boswijk et al. 2007; Prahalad and Ramaswamy 2004). Whereas the first generation—primarily Pine and Gilmore, but also others—focused on what companies should do, portraying customers as rather passive targets, the second generation focuses on customers' sensory perception, the creation of meaning, and the process of *co-creation*. That is, the second generation within the experience economy literature portrays experiences as something that rise from customers' active involvement.

Yet, also in the second generation of literature, customers' involvement is still mainly defined from the viewpoint of companies when co-creation is usually portrayed as a means for value creation (Humphreys and Grayson 2008). Hence, co-creation represents an asset for companies, not a fundamental feature of experiential designs as such.

As an alternative, in the following we will introduce a socio-material approach, turning attention to the performative scripts vaguely encoded in spaces and objects and those who encounter them, and suggesting that these attachments may provide the entrance point to understanding more principally how experiences are (co-)created.

A socio-material perspective

To consider the relation between material artefacts produced by festival designs and the practices of festival participants, this chapter draws inspiration from the work of the French cultural sociologist Antoine Hennion, who pioneered a socio-material, post-Bourdieuan stance in cultural sociology (Born 2010) in line with recent developments within science and technology studies. Working within the same paradigm as Latour and Callon, Hennion highlighted the active passion that cultural products give rise to (2001, 2007), proposing a sociology of *attachments* (Gomart and Hennion 1999). We employ this concept of attachment to address the production and encounter of experiential designs—exemplified by the case of Roskilde Festival—implying that experiences may be understood as a co-production of those who experience, and that which they experience.

Making attachments

In the socio-material approach, following the pragmatist tradition of the American philosopher John Dewey (1959), artworks may be studied by means of the experiences they give rise to. According to Dewey, the experience of art consists of a mix of *doing* and *undergoing*: an experience is not something which can be imposed on the subject or which the subject brings about. It is simultaneously something which overwhelms the subject and which the subject seeks to become overwhelmed by. In this sense, the experiencing subject is at once active and passive.

Dewey's description of experiences as a mix of doing and undergoing is paralleled in the work of Hennion (2001, 2007), who identifies a mixture of activity and passivity in the practices of music lovers. In his studies, Hennion finds that music lovers are highly knowledgeable about their musical interests, and carefully prepare when they set out to have musical experiences. According to Hennion, these individual practices of preparation are central to understanding the great experiences that music lovers have.

To explain the influential capacities of objects, Hennion uses the concept of *attachments* (Gomart and Hennion 1999). Attachments describe the performative relations that humans make to objects and situations. In other words, human agents actively use objects (also "intangible objects" such as tunes) to become passive and let the objects influence them. For illustration of his idea of attachments, Hennion uses the cases of music lovers and drug users, who both have refined practices of making objects carry them away (ibid.).

Co-production

The concept of attachments designates a dismissal of the subject/object distinction, as agency cannot be ascribed to only humans or only objects respectively because both become dependent and determining. Therefore, Hennion introduces the concept of *co-production* to demonstrate how objects are construed within the social practices which they are part of while at the same time forming those same practices (see DeNora 2000). Through the concept of co-production Hennion suggests that social relations and objects are constituted simultaneously. He further emphasizes not only the active role played by users in defining objects, but also the active role played by objects in forming social relationships.

In the case of Experience Design, rather than envisioning experiences as an automatic response to a design, or an occurrence caused by individual agency, the socio-material approach investigates the mutual constitution of a design and its experiencing subjects during the occurrence of the experience. As a result of this approach, an experience can be seen as the joint outcome of both, the users' individual qualifications and preparations, and the properties of the design.

In this line of thought objects can be said to have *affordances* (Norman 1988), or entail *scripts* and *programs of action* (Akrich 1992; Latour 1991), different conceptual constructs to explain object properties that are intended for specific uses. However, these concepts are not necessarily immediately effective for the experiential designer, as it still has to be understood how objects come to have these effects in practice. Thus, rather than assuming that an experience design can control users and cause one specific reaction only—the intended and desired experience—the socio-material approach would turn attention to the role played by users in constituting the experience. With the concept of attachment Hennion proposes that subjects seek to come under the influence of creative objects and thus gain an experience.

In the following we will introduce a number of examples from Roskilde Festival that can illustrate these theoretical points and show how experience in this case is a matter of co-production in which various socio-material designs enable a connection between participants' activities and the festival's program of action.

Roskilde Festival

Roskilde Festival is Denmark's biggest music festival, and has been a major venue of the Europe music festival circuit for more than three decades. Today, each year more than 100,000 people gather in the outskirts of the provincial town of Roskilde to listen to music, hang out with friends, and party for seven days in a row. Because of the festival's longevity, size, and annual line-up of acts, it has achieved iconic status in Danish and European youth culture, and participation takes on ritual characteristics.

The sheer size and impressive impact of the festival often leaves observers with a sense of intimidation, an image of consistency and massiveness, as if it was a natural force. However, if one leaves behind the thought of Roskilde Festival as a unified cultural institution, and instead focuses on its creation—the making and emerging of this huge event from an endless sea of the small decisions—the image of solidity gives way to an ever-evolving map of connections and porosity. This shift of analytical focus allows us to understand how the festival experience is "assembled" not only as a result of emotional impulses, but also as an outcome of strategy, planning, and active co-creation.

Designing the festival

Talking of design in regard to a festival experience is somewhat discomforting. The very idea of design implies a planned procedure and rationality that does not usually fit with our overall ideas of festival culture, which is liminal, impulsive, and social. The cultural paradigm by which we normally address festivals is based on an imbedded, structural, partly unconscious cultural phenomenon. The notion of "design" in return points toward the opposite, a strictness and strategic rationality, which can be difficult to recognize in the tumultous festival.

Most other cultural experiences have a distinct maker and a distinct experience subject or audience as basic entities to the design process, be it a movie, a book, a theater show, or a museum exhibition. Common to these cultural forms is that the designer or artist is the active creative part and the audience the consuming part.

This is not the case for the festival. The festival is a cultural form that requires participation and creative involvement for its realization. A festival without active participants from the audience is not a festival, a phenomenon that blurs the conventional lines of production and consumption. It is, however, interesting to try to understand how meaning is created when what we used to call "the audience" remain partly[1] consumers and spectators, and partly become active performers of the festival ritual.

The social experience

Overall the festival presents a range of different experiences to its 100,000 participants: music, art projects, DIY, restaurants, food parlors, street art, graffiti, performance art, to mention some of the central elements. However, the festival's main experience, the experience that defines its success, is the social experience, the experience of togetherness. In the words of anthropologist Victor Turner (1969) this experience could be described as the shared feeling of *communitas*. *Communitas* is the theoretical concept of the bonds that connect liminal entities involved in a given ritual. They share the same feelings of transformation and de-individualization, and thus experience a connection between themselves stronger than in other more ordinary situations.

Turner's description of the liminal ritual's social impact on those involved fits well with a modern festival like Roskilde. For example, Turner emphasizes that liminal rituals have the power to minimize traditional status and identity features, which is indeed one of the core criteria for any festival: the shared feeling of being equals in front of the stage—and in fact even on the stage. Similar correlations can be made between other liminal features of rituals and festivals. In both cases participants are separated from ordinary life; they dress specifically for the occasion; they share the same rather extreme living conditions; and they are more often than not under influence of alcohol and/or drugs.

Also a "rock 'n' roll lifestyle" and other more specific festival attitudes grown from oppositional youth culture are central elements in the overall festival performance, enacting a particularly extreme kind of communitas that involves—even inspires and readily sanctions—the performance and staging of transgressions like drug consumption, extreme drunken behavior, extreme extroversion, public nudity,[2] etc. However, while Turner's anthropological symbolism is relevant for understanding what cultural issues are being performed, it still doesn't enable us to fully grasp the mechanisms of engagement and involvement at stake at Roskilde Festival. Turner's communitas only enables us to understand the atmosphere of the collective, but not how the individual allows this to happen. Neither does Turner's point of view make it clear how the festival experience is actively materialized through the mundane change of outfit, purchase of tickets, the banal practice of drinking beer, and/or setting up a camp site.

Co-producing "The Orange Feeling"

"The Orange Feeling" is the slogan that intends to capture the socio-aesthetic experience particular to Roskilde Festival.[3] While this label was assumed for strategic branding purposes, and is framed and communicated through this particular wording, the actual experience of this feeling is developed and enacted in a far more multi-sited and complex environment than that of strategy and words.[4]

The Orange Feeling needs to be more than communicated—materialized and performed, often through hands-on-projects like "Build what here?," collective drumming sculptures, a shower show, or similar performance designs vaguely scripted and vaguely performed. Commitment and exchange are key when it comes to mobilizing the large crowds into being active participants, and thus the festival design seeks to enable this activation through co-production. According to strategic planner and architect of the festival, Jes Vagnby, his architectural designs for the venue are not important in themselves, but need to function as enzymes speeding up social interactions. A similar strategy is chosen for the many highly diverse activities and projects featured around the festival site: they all seek to engage visitors in creating experiences featuring themselves as the main act. In other words, the festival production is about staging and mobilizing the participants own self-expressions.

This mobilization is particularly visible in the micro-processes of the festival (co-)production. For example, a few years ago (2010) the central feature of the festival's website—before the start of the festival—was the prompt to "Make your own festival poster!" Visitors to the page were encouraged to upload a portrait, preferably showing off the "right" rock 'n' roll attitude, to create a personal list of favorite bands from the festival line-up, and then to convert this input—via a pre-designed template—into a customized festival poster, which of course was to be shared with one's digital network. Although a rather simple idea in itself, this little activity in the run-up to the festival allowed each individual member of the, in reality, largely anonymous audience to establish the visual impression of being the festival's star, enabled by the festival designers.

Another festival project is *Camp of the Year*, a camp creation competition, rewarding the camp with the coolest concept, most intense atmosphere, best design, weirdest costumes, and most outrages parties. Costumes and crazy camps have always been a natural part of the festival culture, but since the invention of the competition participants' co-production and participation are not only formally endorsed and staged, the festival planners can also influence the socio-aesthetics along the lines of the brand concept of The Orange Feeling by endorsing performativity, self-expression, community, and inclusion.

The photo gallery as an example of co-production

The various activities around the festival site all center around the notion of mobilizing co-production, but apart from that they are highly diverse. Engaging concerts are obviously the most central format at the festival, but other projects, for example, are about DIY music production; a small stage for visitors to act out their break dance moves; or even a hairdresser cutting her clients' hair while others watch. In many of these staged instances intermediaries employed by the festival instigate the activity and encourage others to participate, yet are not always clearly distinguished as employees. Who is paid for, and who is paying for the performance remains blurred, allowing both sides plausible deniability as to how an activity in the end develops.

All these mobilizations follow a sketched program of action in which participants—like actors—are choreographed to follow a vaguely defined common cultural script of transgressional youth culture. Yet, a festival like Roskilde consists of many venues, many concerts, many performances, and ultimately innumerable socio-aesthetic interactions, all happening simultaneously. Talking of the festival experience as a one-perspective interaction is thus misleading. Instead one has to think of the festival as a rhizomatic aesthetic script that guides the performances and attitudes of performers as well as participants.

As Hennion suggests with the concept of attachment, festival-goers need to perform and attach themselves to the sketched designs to gain experiences. Likewise, Callon (1986) states that it is not a matter of whether given roles are predestined, but a matter of how and if these roles are accepted.

The ambiguity and fuzziness of this enactment of roles becomes particularly evident in another festival activity, the Photo Gallery, an on-site space entirely covered by pictures taken of festival participants. The photos in the gallery are produced by a young photographer part-time employed by an earphone company that intends to engage with the festival audience.

His pictures of festival participants are captured during a night of wild partying, dancing, gaming, and drinking. However, the photos are not the result of passive observation or simple capturing of motives. On the contrary, it is evident that the audience actively stages themselves as performers: acting out, sneering, and posing provocatively (Figure 9.1).

In other words, the motives are neither authentic nor the opposite, since they truly capture the festival culture, but simultaneously create a stylized universe in which the right image is carefully choreographed in a collaboration between photographer and subject. The camera technology does not only capture the festival experience, it simultaneously produces the same festival experience. Following the thoughts of Hennion and Dewey this can be seen as a situation in which participants actively engage themselves in letting go. The technology of the camera acts as an attachment between the rhizomic festival script, and the here and now of the participants. They all need to work together for the purpose of co-creating a specific festival experience. Failing to participate—i.e. not co-creating the experience—would deny all

Figure 9.1   The photographer and his motive in the action: Both are working hard to create the right image of the *Orange Feeling*.

parties the experience of having been part of an experience that is special and therefore has meaning and ultimately value.

Conclusion

What is important for creating experience designs in the festival context is the ability to create atmosphere. But whereas atmosphere is often considered in terms of immateriality, it is here argued that atmosphere is created as material encounters between designed spaces, performative scripts, and humans reaching out to connect with each other. The performative articulations of the festival experience are thus not merely the expressions of some "inner condition" of an extrovert group of youngsters, yet neither are they the outcome of purely strategic guidelines—rather they are the result of a co-production between the festival organizers and their audience, and as such ownership of their collective design and their collective experience lies somewhere between the lines.

In more general terms, we would like to conclude that Experience Design does indeed not create experiences in themselves. The experiential design of for example an engaging concert, a relational artwork, or a drinking competition merely creates a platform for giving participation an aesthetic form. Experience Design thus functions as a platform for performative interaction. Important here is that these interactions are facilitated by both—vague cultural scripts, and specific scripts of material designs.

Engaging people in such co-produced designs demands that cultural context and material designs are being considered equally. Hennion's notion of active passivity appears very suitable to describe the mechanism of attaching to and participating in a designed experience for the purpose of letting it to let develop an effect on oneself. A successful experiential design is thus a platform from which the participants can seek to come under the influence and gain the experience of communitas and togetherness.

Notes

1 "Partly" in this context means "a certain ratio of the total audience," as not all visitors will be actively involved, but also "for a certain period of time" as people will actively participate for some time, but then again switch roles to become passive consumers, while possibly others in turn get active.

2 Since 1999 Roskilde Festival Radio annually organizes a "Naked Run" around the festival's campsite, in which participants compete in the nude for entry tickets for the following year.

3 The Orange Feeling is based on the signature orange color of Roskilde's main stage since 1978.

4 The "Roskilde Dictionary" on the festival's website explains: "Orange Feeling is Roskilde Festival—and it is what makes people return year after year. The orange feeling is hard to describe—it must be experienced. But watch out—it can be addictive" (Roskilde Festival, n.d.).

Chapter 10

CurioUs: The Logic of Performance

Amy Findeiss, Eulani Labay, and Kelly Tierney

One afternoon in December 2011, amidst the buzz of holiday shopping, commercial overload, and the Occupy Wall Street movement, three uniformed women appeared on one of New York City's busiest subway platforms and engaged commuters in the exchange of wishes and dreams. How did the CurioUs trio—three designers previously untrained in performance—come to capture the attention of passers-by in one of the world's most hectic cities?

Context

Every design needs a context, a place to live and influence, and for CurioUs it was the bustling New York City subway. The city's subway system is an integral mode of transit with room for improvement; while its level of service is usually sufficient to keep 5.3 million passengers moving through the city daily (Metropolitan Transportation Authority n.d.a), the experience is sullied by acts of littering, graffiti, and occasional violence. At the same time, informal entertainers on subway platforms introduce dynamic elements of performance that have the potential to shift the tone of the commuter experience from passive to participatory. Through the cultivation of a participatory atmosphere (Petersen et al., 2004), we believed that the underground experience could be redesigned to achieve a sense of community, stewardship, and safety.

This chapter will detail our assumptions about performance in public space, how we tested these through small-scale prototypes, what we learned, and how we applied our findings to the design of CurioUs. Through a structured design research process, we studied site-specific environmental triggers, performance practices, and cultural rules and norms for the purpose of designing a performative intervention that considered dynamic issues of staging, timing, and scripting as well as aesthetic choices such as costumes and props (Findeiss et al. 2013). The design development described in this chapter supports a context-led method aimed at understanding an unfamiliar context through distinct steps. CurioUs used a robust methodological system connecting modes of design research with those of several other fields—ethnography, performance, improvisation, and community organizing. This approach may also have value to other practitioners in developing new, transdisciplinary modes of working through design problems.

Research and assumptions

We designed CurioUs as a site-specific performance that would fill a gap in the offerings of the Metropolitan Transit Authority (MTA) (Metropolitan Transportation Authority n.d.b). Our objective was to test our own assumptions about the context (Anderson 2011), the performative nature of the subway platforms, and uncover relevant constraints to shape a new experience. It was necessary for us to understand the conditions and performance patterns of informal subway entertainers, through three areas of study: environmental conditions, skills needed, and cultural norms (see Table 10.1).

The site itself was designed for transit, not performance, and we wanted to discover the types of spaces that supported informal performers and the keys to their aesthetic decisions in this context. Although supported by an interview with seasoned subway performer Matthew Nichols (2011), our research in this area was largely based on both the first-hand observation of the Union Square station platforms, and that of other informal performers at work there.

A common pitfall of design research is to base research findings on faulty underlying assumptions. Like detectives on the lookout for clues, we declare our possible assumptions at the start of research in order to anticipate how they might bias our findings. In each area of study, we therefore identified basic assumptions, and organized these into a Research Assumptions Table (see Table 9.1), a guiding framework that captures and describes the core knowledge and activities we believed were needed to understand the context.

Table 10.1 Research assumptions

Environment study

A. We will be able to acquire a sufficient working knowledge of the formal system to better understand motivations and behaviors.	B. Observation will yield insights that will meaningfully define our tool.	C. We will gain sufficient access to subway musicians to understand their culture, motivations, and actions as it relates to the tool.	D. We will have sufficient understanding of the audience for our tool to ensure the design is relevant.

Skills study

E. Subway musicians are skilled musicians.	F. Subway musicians are skilled performers.	G. Subway musicians have high social skills.	H. Many subway musicians are active observers.

Rules study

I. Subway musicians recognize the culture they are a part of (and the rules that govern it).	J. Subway musicians are motivated by money or social currency.	K. Subway musicians want to increase audience participation in the hope to receive more money and or social capital.	L. Subway musicians understand the conditions to achieve their goals (of increasing money/social capital).

We began to understand these embedded assumptions as design constraints. Constraints limit the design field by providing the structure to a project, for example, by limiting participant action (in this case, of both performers and commuters) and creating actions that are fixed, binding, repeatable, and shared by all participants (such as the rhythm of traffic flows at two-minute intervals from when the train doors open to when the train doors close and the trains leave).

We then tested these constraints through the designerly process of prototyping, minding the three areas of study: testing environmental triggers; testing skilled practices; and cultural rules and norms.

Testing assumptions through prototypes

Prototype 1: Testing environmental triggers

How do informal performers facilitate interaction in underground public spaces?

Commuters on a subway platform are either taking a brief (less than two-minute) pause in their travels as they await their trains, or are entering a different atmosphere as they step off an arriving train before they leave the station. We observed that these environmental conditions would make commuters receptive to an upbeat performance, and to the possibility of participating in it. In our environmental observations it also became apparent to us that the performers on site had indeed developed differing approaches in dealing with their audience: some performers interacted freely through eye contact or speech, while others remained focused on the execution of their art.

First in the prototype *Thriller Footwork*, and later in *Breakdancing Silhouette*, we considered the spatial characteristics of the subway platforms used by performers in Union Square station. While MTA's Music Under New York (MUNY) program officially sanctions particular station areas for performers to use (Metropolitan Transportation Authority n.d.b), musician Matthew Nichols (2011) explained that informal performers adapt and use various additional spaces such as hallways and platforms beyond those sanctioned areas. Ad hoc spaces are often smaller, narrower, intimate, and transient; and they include tiled alcoves that act as acoustic shelters. We assumed that experienced informal performers such as Nichols chose these spaces intentionally; that these are inherently "good spots"; and that, based on level of experience and skill, performers can quickly assess a space for its effectiveness in order to choose one. Our review of these spaces also revealed the impact of intermittent flows of commuter traffic—hundreds of people getting on and off the trains at the height of rush hour—on performers' ease of movement or play and their visibility in the space.

The research phase was particularly important for us in determining an approach to facilitating interaction: what would it take to become the subway performer? We wanted to test the most basic assumption that performers must position themselves appropriately in the subway for the act of performing. We assumed that certain qualities of the CurioUs performance—in public space, with a level of interactivity, and without permission from the authorities—would require us to gain the same insights that had been acquired by experienced subway performers, including practical issues of space and timing.

Yet, what would happen if there was no subway performer at all? What if the commuters became the performers? In *Thriller Footwork* we tested the possibility to engage passers-by in an act of performance with minimal interpersonal facilitation. We approximated the characteristic transitory nature of subway platform space by using a semi-private, highly trafficked hallway space for testing: placing the prototype

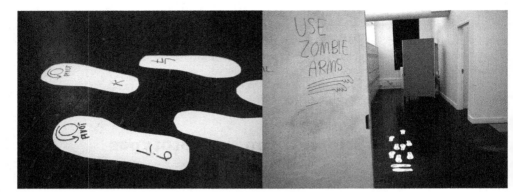

Figure 10.1   Numbered footwork details; footwork accompanied by written prompt at test site.

in the direct flow of foot traffic, we attracted a few dozen participants with footstep decals, visible in high color contrast to the floor. We played *Thriller*, a popular song by Michael Jackson, to recreate a musical atmosphere, as many subway performers (musicians and others) use music as a form of engagement. We used the iconic shapes of numbered dance steps to capture participants in an activity that they could explore on their own. In their line of sight, potential participants would see a large board with the written prompt, "Use zombie arms," accompanied by a sketch of outstretched arms (Figure 10.1). This acted as both a fun prompt for participation and as instruction.

All of these cues—the music, the written prompt, the visualization of arm movement, and the instructive footstep elements—drew people's attention to the activity in two ways. First, the song was instantly recognizable and upbeat; with the cues in place, some participants found it difficult to resist the temptation to dance, spending a few minutes trying the steps.

Second, the level of absurdity present in this prototype appeared to facilitate an openness to experiment. Both the immediate connection of *Thriller* and the low-fidelity quality of the cues lowered the barriers to participation. There was no pressure to interact because cues were unobtrusive, making participation opt-in. Those who chose to interact spent a few minutes with the challenge self-facilitating the dance instructions. The prototype appeared to exhibit a good level of complexity: simple enough to recognize and quickly learn (Figure 10.2).

From this prototype, we learned that, in relation to the environment, dynamic elements of the design could facilitate interaction. Placement of these elements was important, and our success was helped by situating our design directly in the path of passers-by, encouraging them to negotiate the space it occupied. While we had some success without a skilled performer, we also saw that the self-facilitation cues we provided were not enough to ensure the participation of many people. We realized that it wouldn't be enough to have the music, the performer, or passive activities. Ultimately, our final design would need simple and clear instructions, scripts, or written cues that could be quickly communicated and understood, and would most likely need to be communicated and reinforced by an "expert." This led us to the next area of study: skilled practice.

Figure 10.2   Participant engaging in prompts and footwork.

Prototype 2: Testing skilled practices

How do subway performers capture an audience from a sea of moving people?

It became apparent to us through observations and interviews that performers have a command of their craft through practice, experience, and public recognition. Performance skills, as well as an innate sense or ability to assess and choose staging areas appropriate for personal performance needs, construct an experience on the underground platforms. Performer and dancer, Rachel Lehrer (2011), explained that performers' abilities to engage audiences are reflected in their ability to socialize with audiences. We observed this first-hand in a pair of accordion performers whose ability to activate the subway platform space was initiated by becoming mobile themselves, wearing their instruments, walking the platform space, and making eye contact with the audience members.

Recognition of the need to activate an audience was a core concern for our second prototype, *Breakdancing Silhouette*. We aimed now beyond capturing the attention of small momentary audiences through quick, easy interactions, toward engaging them socially, personally, and individually through humanized cues like eye contact and gaze. *Breakdancing Silhouette* was inspired by breakdancing performance groups practicing on subway platforms and their ability to direct the movement of their arms and legs by sensing the space around them.

In *Breakdancing Silhouette*, much like in *Thriller Footwork*, we utilized a narrow hallway for its characteristic transitory nature, similar to that of a subway platform space. We gained access to the capacities of subway performers by modeling our observations of them on the platform and reproducing those dynamic elements in a controlled way. As a stand-in for the white-tiled back of a subway stairway, we used an 8-feet by 20-feet whiteboard-painted wall on which we drew in dry-erase marker the silhouettes of figures performing break-dancing moves. Again, we provided a short written cue: "Try and fill the shape."

Subsequently participants "filled in" or approximated the shape with their bodies by finding physical gestural markers (such as a head, arm, or legs) to mime the break-dancing form (Figure 10.3). The shape often required the cooperation of two or more people recreating a playful interaction, and encouraged participants to make awkward and silly positions, like they would, for example, in the party game *Twister*. We learned that a cue's tone, either written or drawn, must balance curiosity and novelty with provocation to be engaging.

The shapes we provided turned out to be ambiguous, and often did not have enough clues for a participant to recognize, yet participants often helped one another deciphering the puzzle. This was an unplanned response, but one we found greatly informative. In the final moments of testing, we observed one participant standing back to help guide two other participants, directing their movements like a human mirror and enabling successful completion of the activity. The interaction triggered by the first participant was a clue to a best practice of interaction: that "seeding" public interaction, using an actor who knows what to do, would be beneficial in training the audience to participate.

Much like the previously mentioned accordion players, we saw that participants searched for facial cues from one another in order to trigger responses. Reading subtle cues such as eye contact, direction of gaze, spoken words, and body position quickly enables participants to know what to do next.

Figure 10.3 Visual prompts suggesting postures and shapes.

This understanding directly affected how we approached scripting our movements and behaviors as performers on the platform in our own final design.

Successful prompts appear to elicit responses that are neutral and innocent. In addition to scaffolding an activity that augments skill through instructional guides and prompts, it is important that we "seed" public interaction in order to train audiences how to participate. As part of our kit of dynamic elements of performance, we would need to enlist a few "extra" performers to show the commuters how to act on the platform.

Prototype 3: Cultural rules and norms

What does it take to create spontaneous generosity in public spaces?

We began the third study with a set of assumptions around the motivations and actions of informal performers. We assumed that informal performers on subway platforms recognize the culture they are a part of and the rules that govern it; in other words, we assumed that these performers recognize each other as part of a community sharing similar types of goals. As such, we again assumed that performers are motivated to participate in the system by gaining either monetary or social reward. We also assume that the performers know how to manipulate conditions and audiences to achieve their goals. Both

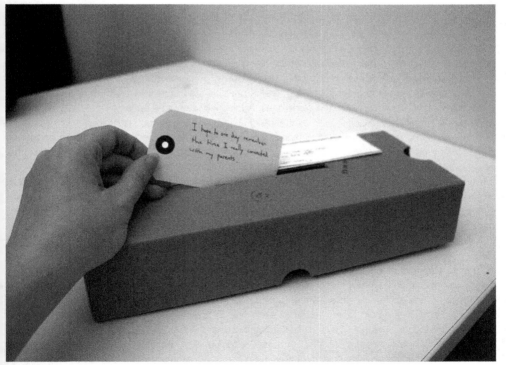

Figure 10.4   Participant submitting a memory.

performers and commuters are familiar with the environment (the platform), but in fact, may have little reason to engage one another based on their unfamiliarity and anonymity. In testing our assumptions about cultural rules and norms, we asked ourselves: How do we create successful interactions that promote generosity in this context?

In the third prototype, *The Memory Exchange*, we tested scripted elements in order to see how to elicit behavior and responses related to notions of community, interaction with strangers, gifting, altruism, the value of imagination, and the value in defining ideal future states. *The Memory Exchange* sought to better understand the challenges in engaging participants in aspirational exercises of memory recall and future visioning. Additionally, it tested participants' potential attachments to ideas, both concrete and ethereal. Finally, it simulated the act of "removing" such ideas, in order to gauge feelings of discomfort and attachment.

Participants were given handwritten instructions taped to a discarded box asking them to write down and submit "a memory they hope to one day have." Once the participant had submitted his or her memory (Figure 10.4) the final instruction was revealed—open the submission box and remove one memory at random, excluding his or her own. This was the end of the written instructions. Once the person had chosen and read the memory he or she had removed, he or she often asked the administrator of the test, "What now?" at which point the neutral, but frank, response was given, "Do with it as you will."

We observed a surprisingly high level of emotions and attachment to non-tangible concepts. Participants expressed enjoyment of contemplating their future and formed strong attachments to their contributions. Most participants were surprised when they realized their own memory would be removed by someone else, but liked the idea of contributing their memory to a collective. Others wanted to adjust their memory once it was placed in the box, to make it either better or less personal. Some participants became so attached to their memory that they expressed hesitancy and distress at the thought that their memory might be discarded by another participant.

The attentiveness of the participants illustrates a possible consistency in following cultural rules and a fear that others might not follow the same rules. Additionally, the value became not just a value of the memories themselves, but possibly an exchange of social currency through participation.

Although some participants were disappointed that their idea would not go towards something bigger, many participants were excited to be a part of an exchange and were eager to read other people's memories. Some participants were not satisfied with the initial memory they "removed" from the box and requested to select another memory. They expressed an expectation that they should receive a memory of equal or greater value, and were subsequently disappointed if the memory they received did not appear to be created with the same care that they themselves had used. Most of the participants gave significant value to the memory they removed from the box, asking for confirmation that they had permission to keep the memory they selected, despite being told they could do as they pleased with it.

This test is a blueprint for addressing abstract concepts, eliciting participation, and creating a meaningful exchange between an otherwise anonymous community. We posited that, by revealing the full process of the exchange earlier (letting participants know that their gift would go to someone and that they themselves would receive a gift in exchange for their participation), we could initiate more focused participation. This gave us additional assurance that the interaction and participation we hoped to achieve would be seen as valuable by our audience for CurioUs, the subway commuters. It also gave us an entry point into our primary goal of creating a sense of community and stewardship among the commuters. Up until this point, we were focused on understanding and testing the dynamic elements of performance—from environmental conditions to facilitation cues to facial and gestural triggers—and we now were able to bring this knowledge together with a tangible activity to bridge the divide between strangers.

Developing dynamic elements of performance from research insights

Our research with informal subway musicians began as an entry point into the commuter experience, while simultaneously considering the audience as recipients of the experience. While our hunch launched a suspicion that the informal entertainers on subway platforms were untapped and under-studied resources, our over-arching goal remained to influence the commuters by articulating and using the entertainers' dynamic elements of performance.

To elicit a desired reaction, design discovers, understands, and leverages social systems. It is these cultural rules and norms, skilled practices and environmental triggers that guide behavior and provide inspiration and opportunity for intervening within the systems that are all around us. Through action-led research and methodological unravelling of assumptions, we as designers were able to document insights revealing that informal subway performers are adept at prompting the participants in their spaces. Through clearly written, spoken, or performed instructions, a performer has the ability to shape experience.

Interaction, prompted through a novel and curious tone, draws out participation from a variety of audience members. Designed interactions that are short can limit poor performance and allow for a greater sense of accomplishment and fun. The more engaged a participant feels, the greater the chance they will linger. This aggregation of people seems to create momentum for a performance. Our next step was to bring the elements of performance and interaction together with a meaningful and relevant context.

Applied constraints: CurioUs final participatory experience

What happens when New York City subway commuters are asked to participate in an exchange of goodwill?

From the moment the CurioUs trio entered the subway station, commuters identified us as performers (Figure 10.5). Uncovered through our prototyping process, the dynamic elements of perfor-mance—designed movements, gestures, facial expressions, and cues for participation—were applied to the final experience with aesthetic considerations relevant to the context of time and place.

We had already studied an optimal subway platform, the L train platform at 14th Street, which was flanked on both sides by trains arriving and departing approximately every two minutes. We organized ourselves in a prime "spot," underneath a stairwell that functioned as our acoustic bandshell. The first set of cues, our visual appearance, was informed by atmosphere of holiday gift exchange during the political and economic climate of the time: concurrent with the Occupy Wall Street movement. Matching

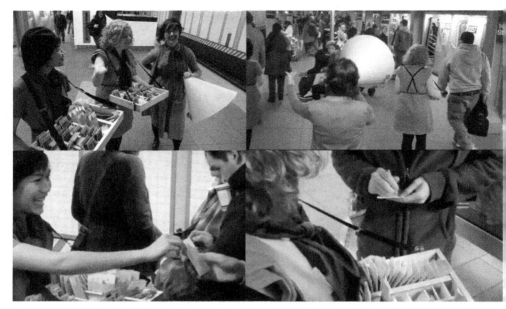

Figure 10.5   CurioUs performers in action.

costume elements, such as bright red lipstick and yellow-and-beige uniforms (inspired by the era of the New Deal), signaled the commuters to pay close attention.

In coordination with the automated announcement of a train arrival, one performer introduced the other two, whose roles as "Stewards" were to invite and facilitate the exchange of wishes and dreams. Next, the two stewards—each wearing a portable vending tray similar to those of old-time cigarette girls—extended the stage area by walking down the length of the platform, calling "Wishes!", "Dreams!" As we made eye contact with curious commuters, we offered the simple prompt, "Curious?" at which point participants either opted in or opted out. The stewards then explained the exchange and answered questions, while remaining in character with short quips ("Easy, handsome") and playful words of encouragement ("Ain't gonna hurt ya").

Those who appeared to want to participate were asked, "Might you trade a wish for a wish, a dream for a dream?" They were then offered from the tray an open envelope with a small card and golf pencil tucked inside. The card included a simple, playful prompt that read, "I would like you to have my ____ ." And while intended to be easy to fill out within two-minute waiting intervals, many participants took additional time, contemplating the gift they would give. Completed envelopes were sealed and then exchanged for another sealed envelope in the tray that had been prepared by someone else on the platform. Often participants were so excited about their exchange that they reported back to us, "I got snow!" or "Someone gave me their beard—and I'm trying to grow a beard!" Participants clearly saw value in the interaction, thanking us (and, in one case, offering to pay money) for the experience.

The activity quickly generated critical mass for two reasons. First, we had recruited and trained "seed" participants as extras and had them meet us on the platform to model the desired participant behavior. Second, the sight of participants mulling over the gifts they were about to give, or sharing what they had received, encouraged others—even those who had previously refused—to participate. Critical mass enabled an alternate social reality to emerge: a sense of togetherness between commuters.

Using staging, props, and scripted interactions, we were able to engage with participants visually, verbally, and through gesture. Our newfound ability to understand and predict environmental cues enabled us to appropriate the skills and best practices of performance, so that we were able to interact in an intimate, one-on-one manner, ultimately engaging 46 participants in sharing their dreams and wishes with fellow commuters within 20 minutes.

Reflection: CurioUs takeaways

By following a structured methodology and design process, we were able to create within a space unfamiliar to us an unexpected experience that was both poignant and socially relevant. We were able to change perceptions through action by intervening in a community's routine behavior. We learned how an activator can engage other community members by understanding the cultural conventions of the context in which they work. In addition, we observed that commuters understand their roles within the culture and understand the motivations of subway musicians: to gain money or social currency. We also utilized gifting culture to help elicit participation, to motivate participants to give careful consideration to the gift they were giving, and to instil value in the process.

The CurioUs trio did not simply ask for participation; we provided a service, designing a valuable experience based on research. By using design-led methods to discover and leverage the social systems of subway performers and commuters, we were able to apply a rigorous, mechanical-like process to create an ephemeral experience—pulling people from the habitual into a transitional space where the exchange of wishes and dreams could reveal a community.

Chapter 11

Designing for a Better Patient Experience

Gretchen C. Rinnert

Anna has Crohn's disease, an inflammatory disorder that tends to affect the colon and small intestines. Ulcers develop and cause pain and difficulty in digestion. Anna became ill in college and has battled this excruciating disease for more than 15 years. It has taken a toll on her body. In 2008, while living in Los Angeles, three fistulas became compacted in her abdominal cavity. She spent four long weeks in a California hospital where doctors bounced ideas back and forth. One day she was told medication was the best way to treat her condition; the next day a surgeon approached her and suggested surgery. They never quite decided on a plan and, in the end, they recommended she change hospitals. During this time she was not able to eat or even drink water. Her parents took her home to Ohio where she began seeing experts at one of the best hospitals in the country. Her new team of doctors presented her with only one option: surgery to remove her colon.

After a long surgery and many days in the hospital, she was sent home and instructed to take care of her incision and to come back for a follow-up appointment. Anna was told to eat and drink what she wanted. Several months passed and she lived a pretty normal life. Four months after her surgery she ate a hamburger and it became lodged in her intestines, blocked by scar tissue. Having no knowledge of warning signs or complications Anna waited to go to the hospital until she became very sick, vomiting and unable to eat. When she arrived, the doctors found her intestines twisted. They waited for her intestines to shut down and untwist, but they fully anticipated another surgery. Anna began doing online research and found that her prestigious doctors had failed to prepare her for possible complications from her surgery. From personal experiences detailed in online journals she learned that she should have been eating small meals and drinking additional fluids, and in the short weeks after her surgery she should have been massaging her incision to break up scar tissue to avoid the kind of intestinal blockage that she now had.

Much of the anxiety Anna felt was unnecessary. Anna is now healthy, but her patient experience was extremely stressful. She lost time waiting for answers, and her health was compromised by lack of communication. Many patients are faced with this same sort of experience on a daily basis. It is with absolute certainty that each person will face illness in his or her lifetime, and, if not personally, we will experience it as a caregiver to a loved one. Patients face many obstacles, but their experience could be improved by designing communication tools for patients and physicians.

Health 2.0 and online resources

During the past century we have seen tremendous medical advancements, and human life expectancy has nearly doubled. With these grand steps forward, health communication has remained esoteric. Doctors' appointments are rushed, confusing, and often overwhelming. When you add in the frustration of dealing with multiple doctors, pharmacies, hospitals, nurses, and treatment options, one can easily become baffled. Within such a context, how can patients digest, understand, and use complex and often intricate information?

Patients are seeking out information

Many patients search for clarification online, but acting as your own advocate can be extremely difficult. Google, WebMD, and online networks act as personal consultants, which has changed the face of medical communication. According to Jane Sarasohn-Kahn, a health economist:

> This movement, known as Health 2.0, can be defined as: the use of social software and its ability to promote collaboration between patients, their caregivers, medical professionals, and other stakeholders in health. (2008: 2)

This online communication is a lifeline for many patients. Wright, Sparks, and O'Hair describe online patient experiences and relationships as vital.

> For individuals facing illness whose support needs are not met by their traditional support network, the Internet allows them to find other people with similar health concerns and provides an opportunity to obtain support from a much larger network than would be possible in the face to face world. (2008: 160)

Patients are finding comfort in the experiences and wisdom of others who have been through the experience. Simply being told by a doctor is not enough; they want the details from someone who has first-hand experience. As we saw earlier, Anna used online research to understand and treat herself during her time in the hospital. This behavior is far from rare according to the polling of internet users by specialist company Pew Internet and others (Fox 2006: 8). Susannah Fox of Pew Internet further explains that patients are influenced by information they read online:

> 58% [of health seekers] say the information they found in their last search affected a decision about how to treat an illness or condition. 55% say the information changed their overall approach to maintaining their health or the health of someone they help take care of. 54% say the information lead them to ask a doctor new questions or to get a second opinion from another doctor. (Fox 2006: 15)

Some may worry that these online health searches could cause harm or have a negative impact. Their concern is warranted, as the larger the access to online information, the greater the possibility of being exposed to unreliable and less credible resources. According to a recent segment on NBC's *Nightly News* with Brian Williams (Snyderman 2011), this has been a particular problem in terms of vaccines and the recent rise in parents refusing to vaccinate their children. Many parents have no memory of the implications of infectious diseases that plagued the twentieth century before many vaccines quite common today were available to the public. These parents are gathering information from Google and risking their children's lives as well as the lives of people around them.

Fox found that only 15 percent of patients check the source and date of online health information, which means that 85 million Americans gathering health advice online do not consistently examine the information they gather (2006: 4). It is important to note the type of information they are gathering. The majority of patients are accessing user-generated health information online (Fox and Jones 2009). The bulk of this information is accumulated from various perspectives of medical thought—created by novices and health care professionals—whose date and origin have yet to be vetted.

This does not mean that all user-generated health content is dangerous or unreliable, but it does lack juried review and educated oversight. It is important to note that personal experience is extremely valuable and important. It has a strong place in health information. Knowing and hearing what another patient has encountered is reassuring and informative. It tells patients they are not alone or hopeless, providing confidence and inspiration. It also provides another level of information, detailed specifics and expectations for what lies ahead. Patient communities, such as DailyStrength.org, provide a place for patients to meet, share, receive support and help others.

Yet, one concern is that many patients do not have the skills needed to engage in online content, such as media and health literacies.

> Media literacy refers to the ability to understand and interpret media messages found on mediums which include television, newspapers, books, articles, blogs, web sites, portable devices, games, computers, cell phones, digital videos, photographs, illustrations, text messages, e-mail and the printed word. (Lane and Rinnert 2009: 1)

According to Richard Thomas, author, health researcher, and professor at the University of Tennessee Health Science Center:

> Health literacy is the ability to read, understand and act on health information. People of any age, income, race or background can find it challenging to understand health-information. (2006: 99)

When dealing with one's health and wellbeing it is imperative that the right information is received in a timely manner.

> Research shows that most consumers need help understanding health care information. Regardless of reading level, patients prefer medical information that is easy to read and understand. (Thomas 2006: 99)

This can be seen as an information design problem because it involves more than just managing complex information: "to present the right information to the right people at the right time in the most effective and efficient form" (Horn 2000: 16).

Despite the complex web of information that a patient will encounter in one simple Google search, there are plenty of data proving that patients are finding online health information to be valuable; however, currently much of the burden of finding good quality information is placed on patients. They must deal with their own medical crises as well as negotiate and judge what information they should use and how to manage it. We find ourselves in the midst of an elaborate design problem framed by complicated information structures, participatory culture, and health literacy.

Research statement and objectives

Our research question: How can designers respond to current medical communication problems and provide a better patient experience, reduce information anxiety, and improve comprehensive health outcomes?

Before beginning data collection, several hypothesis were developed in order to ground the research and provide focus:

- Patients do not know the process of their medical treatment and must continually call for updated treatment information, explanations, and assistance.
- Patients lack credible medical information that has been approved and certified by their physician.
- Patients seek support. They often deal with medical problems on their own or try to find help online.

In examining patient needs and experiences I have focused on how a tablet application could aid in patient communication. This application includes the following core functionality:

- Tools that show personalized medical information.
- Tools that provide patients with credible and transparent medical information.
- An internal support system that brings together online social networking capabilities.
- A personalized experience that helps patients document their medical journey.

Research strategies and visualization

Several strategies were used in order to define and frame this investigation:

- Research: An online questionnaire was presented to recent and current patients to test our hypotheses and collect data.
- Development: A concept map, user personas, and a visual prototype provided clarity allowing us to find connections, relationships and to see patterns from the data we had collected, and the secondary research we had gathered.

User research

The primary research used qualitative measures to reveal personal experiences through a web-based survey that was intended to collect information on patient experiences while under the care of a physician. Our goals were to

- Define health communication problems between patient and physician.
- Identify areas where design could aid in communication and comprehension.
- Define patient experiences, goals, and desires.

A call for participants was posted on several social networking sites as well as an online support group, DailyStrength.com. Participants were contacted through the online system, and their personal contact information was never collected. They were able to log in with complete anonymity.

In the end 87 adults participated on the online questionnaire, aged between 25 and 64. They answered 39 questions regarding patient experience, expectations, and technology exposure. Participants had to be adults who spoke English, over 18 years old, and a patient within the last seven years. Gender and ethnicity were not determining factors for inclusion in the study.

The questionnaire the participants answered consisted of both fill-in-the-blank and multiple choice questions. It was formative as it gained insight into the lives of patients, their experiences, and expectations.

Results

The beginning of our survey asked the patient about general demographic information, technology access, and media. Starting from Question 16 they were asked about their specific patient experience. The most revealing answers were found in the replies to Question 17: "What has been negative about your experience?" Thirty-nine percent of participants cited communication issues with medical

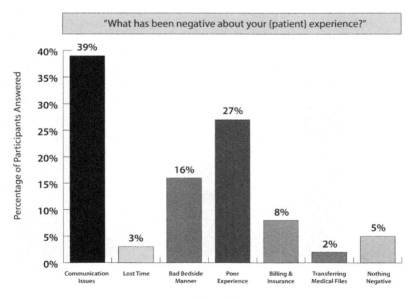

Figure 11.1   Detailed results to Question 17.

professionals, which included difficulty understanding, the use of medical jargon, and uncertainty in prognosis. Other answers included poor experience, bad bedside manner, loss of time, issues with billing or insurance, and problems transferring medical files. Only 5 percent of respondents said there was nothing negative about their experience (Figure 11.1).

Returning to the original first hypothesis, I found that patients tend to understand their medical protocol, but they often have questions nonetheless. The questionnaire confirmed that patients and caregivers use the phone as their main mode of communicating with their doctor. Question 36 asked patients: "When I have a question I usually: a. Call my doctor's office and speak with a nurse; b. Schedule an appointment with my doctor; c. Search online for answers; d. Ignore my problem and move on; or e. Email my question to my doctor or nurse." Fifty-one percent answered that they called their doctor's office and spoke with a nurse, 27 percent searched for answers online, and only 5 percent emailed their doctor directly (Figure 11.2). One frustrated patient:

> Neither my RE [reproductive endocrinologist] nor my OB [obstetrician] or their staff, do any communicating online or via email, and that's my preferred method of communication in almost every circumstance. It seems like calling in and having to talk to someone, leave a message, wait for a return call, etc. is very cumbersome and old fashioned.

In relation to the second hypothesis, when patients were asked, "Did you ever search online for supplemental information?", 91 percent replied "yes," and only 9 percent said "no." Those that responded "yes"

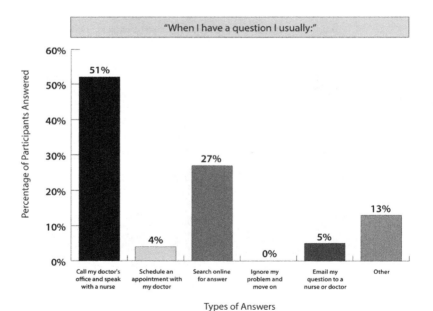

Figure 11.2   Detailed results to Question 36.

often elaborated lengthily, but generally their primary reason was that they needed more information or clarification after meeting with their doctor. Some patients consulted WebMD and others looked at online support groups. Those patients that did not look for supplemental information responded that they were overwhelmed with their situation, or that they did not feel a website would provide assistance. When asked if they relied on the information obtained online, the group was split: 53 percent responded "yes," and 47 percent said "no." When asked "How often do you use online resources regarding your medical prognosis and/or treatment?" only 9 percent replied "never." In contrast, 47 percent replied "less than once a month," and 44 percent replied that they searched online "between once a month and daily."

Questions related to hypothesis 3 brought about the following responses: When asked "Are you part of a support group?" only 27 percent responded "yes," while 73 percent said "no." The majority of respondents that participated in a support group experienced that as positive. One patient stated, "It has been extremely helpful to me just knowing that there really are people going through the same thing that I'm going through. People who can actually give me some advise and who really understand everything. It has brought peace of mind to me and it has also made it possible for me to share my experience and offer help to others! Another patient said: "Absolutely. The support and understanding (and advice) that I receive from other women in the same/similar situation has been invaluable."

Development

Following our questionnaire I employed three visual explorations: concept mapping, persona building and prototyping. Each of these approaches helped to understand the patient experience as well as model the end product.

Concept mapping

By developing a concept map, I was able to visually map the patient experience with the data we had collected (see Figure 11.3). The concept map placed all of the research in one view, giving a micro and holistic perspective on the project.

Personas

In order to define the project scope we developed two personas: fictional models of potential end–users that represent the target audience. Two types of patients were identified: those facing long-term, chronic care, and those facing short-term or elective care. Both personas have a consumerist view of healthcare, and were crafted to reflect the results of the previous survey. Our application will not hinder a patient with a paternalistic view, but it does not necessarily meet their needs and desires.

The first persona is Beth, who has Crohn's disease and will need long-term care and chronic pain management for the rest of her life. She is young and active, 36 years old. She has one child and is a strong member in her online support group. Beth is about to have surgery, and is preparing for the recovery and experience of losing her colon. She monitors her health carefully and wants feedback and communication from her physician. She is apprehensive about the surgery and needs confirmation that she is making the

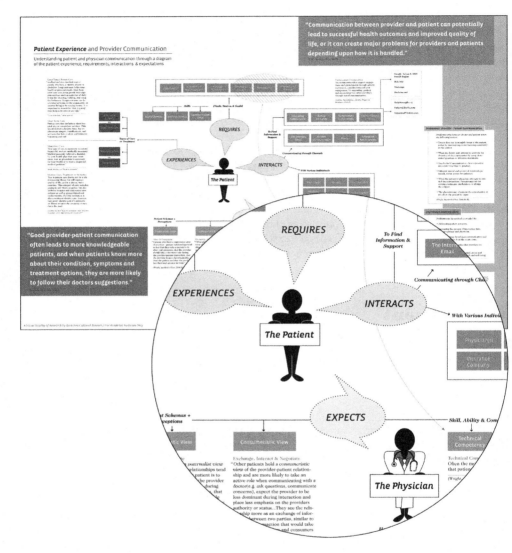

Figure 11.3   Concept map of the application.

right decision. She frequently visits websites like jpouch.net to read blogs from patients just like her. She desires to understand what will happen in the weeks ahead as she faces surgery and recovers.

Our second persona, Emma, is a fertility patient and will need short-term, elective care. She suffers from a genetic disorder that keeps her from getting pregnant. Her care is not covered by insurance and is considered elective because her infertility is not a life-threatening risk. Emma and her husband have been trying to conceive for many years and now they are moving to the most extreme fertility treatment, in vitro fertilization (IVF). A significant portion of their savings is at risk, and, with only a 40 percent chance for success with each cycle, communication and understanding are key. Emma must administer her own injectable medication. Comprehending instructions and following specific timing are critical, and if they are not carefully followed then US$12,000 could be wasted. Emma is nervous but enjoys hearing about successful IVF pregnancies. She does not discuss her fertility treatments with friends, due to the embarrassing nature of them. Emma frequently feels alone and secluded, and therefore welcomes the chance to communicate with others online.

Developing these two different patient personas allowed us to understand specific communication and education needs for patients with varying short-term and long-term medical experiences. We subsequently used these personas to revise and refine our concept map, and apply it more specifically to their narratives.

Prototyping and animated walk-through

Based on the outcomes of the initial two explorations, we developed a prototype for an iPad application called *The Patient Advocate*. The application is intended to connect patients with their doctors and

Figure 11.4 *Patient Profile and Health Log* page.

medical providers through visual and communicative tools that allow them to engage with their medical information, and it also provides a social networking space for patients.

The design phase of the project included the development of two artefacts: an interactive prototype for usability testing and an animated walk-through that describes the user pathway through the system. By this time in the project I had developed a relationship with Akron Children's Hospital, working specifically with the Lewis H. Walker, MD, Cystic Fibrosis Center. As I worked with the medical professionals together we found that Cystic Fibrosis (CF) patients had much to gain from a system like *The Patient Advocate*, and that through this new relation we would also have access to more realistic data and "soft information" to model our prototype after.

Accordingly, in the animated demonstration we follow a Cystic Fibrosis patient, Hannah, through the system to see how she may use the application. The following text aligns with the demo, explains the patient's experience within the application, and describes the core functionality within the context of use.

We see Hannah enter *The Patient Advocate* application using her iPad (to see the full demo visit http://www.flyingtype.com/patientadvocate). She enters a secure social network and database using her email and password. Once in the system Hannah visits the *Patient Profile and Health Log* (see Figure 11.4). On the left-hand corner we see a gray box containing her basic personal information shared to her network, and the rest of the screen is occupied by a daily health log. Each section can be expanded to customize and reveal more complex sets of data. This customized screen allows Hannah to quickly track data that will keep her aware of her body and changes as to how she's feeling. It can be tailored to each patient, their health and wellbeing, allowing the medical team to assign the key targets to be monitored. Warnings and alerts can be pushed to Hannah by her physician and caregivers if her health log shows problems—for instance if her weight has dropped, and if her use of her rescue inhaler has increased she may get a text message to schedule an appointment with her doctor.

Next we see Hannah visit the *Community Center* (see Figure 11.5). Here she can read recent discussions, articles, and content that her community members have posted. Hannah can participate as well. She may ask questions, share articles, advice, and videos. She can communicate through text-based chatting tools or join into a Google Hangout video-chat with her community. Hannah has contacts in three separate categories:

- Medical Team: physicians, nurses, social worker and a therapist;
- Support Group: a select group of patients, carefully matched with similar health diagnosis, within the same age group, and similar interests; and
- Family and Friends: family and friends the patient has selected to be part of her health network. This would usually be a smaller group of people close to her with access to information she chooses to share.

A research nurse, who organized the support group members, monitors the community on an as-needed basis. She can answer questions, provide feedback and upload content.

Next Hannah visits the *Patient Health Tracking and Chart*. This screen has three different sections: the first half is the patient self-monitoring, charted over time. Here Hannah's daily inputs are displayed, giving her feedback and a holistic view of her health. The next section shows Hannah's health goals, as established with her medical team, and efforts toward reaching these goals. She can also access

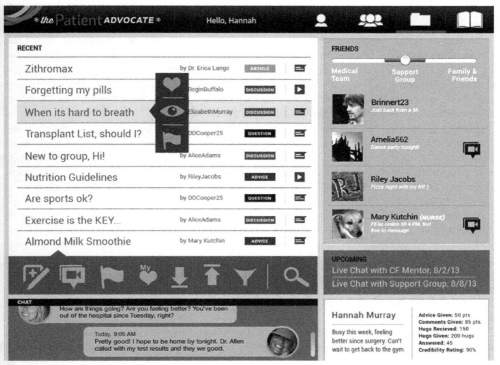

Figure 11.5   *Community Center* page.

instructions from her medical team from this interface. The last section is Hannah's medical chart. Here she can view her most recent test results, blood work, exams, and doctors' notes.

Finally we see Hannah visit the *Education Center*, an area of the application that provides an overview of her diagnosis, the top online resources, information on her medication and treatments, and any additional information her medical team would provide. This content is specifically curated by a research nurse in her doctor's office, customizing the information and thereby making it relevant to Hannah. When her medication and treatment list is updated, this screen will be refreshed with the latest information on dosage, warnings, and background information on the medication and/ or treatment.

Conclusion

The findings from the surveys, interviews, and visual explorations hint at what may be possible when the health industry employs the use of innovative technology such as the iPad along with a sophisticated application that could handle complex data sharing and communication, although at this point in the project a final conclusion would be premature. The *Patient Advocate* is a work in progress, and several more steps remain in defining the application.

Moving forward I will be working with Dr. Joel Hughes, a psychology professor at Kent State University with extensive research in health literacy, in patient self-management, and social support, and Dr. Anthony Sterns, CEO of iRx reminder. Together we will be developing the back-end database, and conducting usability pilot tests with real patients while seeking grant funding. So far I have completed two such sets of usability tests with CF patients at Akron Children's Hospital and have found an overwhelming interest and need for an application of this magnitude.

Many patients and their parents have expressed that they feel a lack of social connection with other patients, and experience much difficulty in communicating with their medical team. Doctors have expressed an interest in the medication and diet adherence functionality and how it could help their patients stick to their advised medical protocol. Children living with CF are poor self-managers. According to Dr. Nathan Kraynack, a physician at the Center for Pediatric Pulmonary Medicine at Cleveland Clinic, many adolescents and teen CF patients struggle with adherence to treatments and medications. This behavior places these patients at risk of a shortened life span or of needing a lung transplant prematurely.

Apple is currently looking for medical- and health-related iPad applications, because they carry great promise. Currently the iPad is being used by doctors as a digital notepad or for medical imaging, but primarily its use has been as a tool for doctors, not patients. It has also been used to help entertain patients. In 2010 Stanford Hospital and Clinics used iPads in place of televisions and laptops as a way to enhance patient experience during their hospital stay, to pass time as they waited in a recovery area (Stanford Hospital and Clinics, 2010).

In these contexts the *Patient Advocate* is an innovative concept because it seeks to improve all aspects of patient experience, from communication and sharing to understanding their own health and wellbeing. There are a number of healthcare organization, healthcare professional, and healthcare consumer needs that create significant market demand for the *Patient Advocate* application. There is a growing demand for mobile-health (mHealth) applications and technologies that support patients and healthcare providers on the go, especially for patients with chronic, life-threatening illness. Patients are obtaining health information online, and often sharing it with one another. Patients encounter communication problems on a daily basis that include: understanding their health information, accessing their personal records, and managing and sharing their health updates with doctors, nurses, and caregivers on a regular basis. Patients often learn after-the-fact and respond to health needs in a defensive manner. After much research and testing my collaborators and I continue to believe that by putting more control and credible information in the hands of patients, better health outcomes may be obtained while creating a less stressful patient experience.

Chapter 12

Designing Mobile User Experiences: A Framework for a Design Methodology

Claus Østergaard

Human–computer Interaction (HCI) has had an increasingly growing interest in developing and improving methodologies for designing mobile interactive systems, as mobile media have become an integrated part of everyday life, and as it has become a collective habit to never leave home without our mobile phone (Richardson and Wilken 2012; Wilken and Goggin 2012). A design methodology can be defined as the development of a method with focus on the process rather than the final product (Edelson 2009: 115; degreedirectory 2013). Since the beginning of the twenty-first century the field of mobile user experience has aimed at further developing the methodologies for designing mobile interactive systems by focusing on the different contexts of the interaction situation. That is, how the constantly changing contexts affect the mobile user experience as the users physically move around (Tamminen et al. 2004).

This discourse has also resulted in a rather rich discussion on the definition of *user experience*. Even though there does not seem to be a joint understanding and definition of user experience, the following aspects seems to be part of the vast majority of the definitions: The *user*, the *contexts of interaction*, and the *system* (Wigelius and Heli Väätäjä 2009; Roto 2006; Jumisko-Pyykkö et al. 2008). The general definition of the term "user" of a mobile system covers the user's needs, previous experiences, state of mind, as well as expectations to the mobile system (Roto 2006: 24).

The "contexts of the interaction" are commonly accepted as the *environmental context*, the *social context*, the *temporal context*, and the *task context* (Wigelius and Heli Väätäjä 2009). The environmental context refers to the physical objects, their apparent features, and the environmental surroundings they are found in (Jumisko-Pyykkö et al. 2008). The social context takes note of other people in the user's physical surroundings, and the interactions between them and the user (Jumisko-Pyykkö et al. 2008; Østergaard 2013). The task context focuses on the given task as well as the possible interruptions that could occur during the execution of the given task (Jumisko-Pyykkö et al. 2008), while finally the temporal context describes the time available to complete the task (Roto 2006: 55).

The mobile "system" is commonly accepted to be the device that runs the (software) product that is under examination (Jumisko-Pyykkö et al. 2008), which in the case of this chapter will be a mobile concept.

The fluent interrelations of the three aspects mentioned above make mobile user experiences complex to investigate, as the experience is: (a) dependent on the given user's internal state of mind and previous experiences; and (b) based on the changing contexts as the user moves. As both of these aspects are very unstable in nature, Wright et al. argue, that "it is not possible to design the experience, it is only possible to design for the experience" (2004: 52). Therefore, it is important that the methodologies for designing mobile user experiences are user-oriented and consider the ever changing contexts.

This understanding of mobile user experience has resulted in various design methodologies including focus on designing low-fidelity and high-fidelity prototypes (De Sá and Carriço 2008), participatory design focusing on involving specific user segments such as elderly people (Stößel 2009), as well as focus on usability design (Duh et al. 2006). In difference to all these methodologies, this chapter proposes a design methodology that is not aimed at specific user segments like elderly or young people. Nor is it aiming at designing specific prototypes with specific tasks. Instead, the chapter proposes a design methodology that is applicable across user segments, user tasks, and prototypes based on specific concepts of mobility. This is achieved by designing for ever changing contexts with special considerations for the environmental and social contexts of the usage situation.

Background and motivation

The chapter draws on empirical data collected through a series of five workshops held from 2012–13. The workshops were aimed at designing user-oriented and context-aware mobile concepts for theme parks, thus the workshops were restricted to focus on the interaction between the user and the user interface in a given environmental and social context.

Context-aware mobile-user experience in theme parks is an evolving niche within the domain of mobile-user experience, as theme parks around the world have a growing interest in designing and developing such mobile concepts for their guests (Irvine 2010). According to Pine and Gilmore, services—whether being person-to-person services, self-service, or location-based and context-aware services—facilitate the overall experience for the guest (Pine and Gilmore 2011: 17, 5). Context-aware mobile concepts therefore have the potential to enrich the visiting experience especially within the closed circuit context of theme parks, as they provide service information to the guests based on automatically obtained location, time, and other contextual information of the user (Glushko 2010: 234).

However, the challenge for context-aware mobile concepts is to integrate with other service contexts of the park (Glushko 2010: 219). Glushko argues, that, more often than not, context-aware mobile concepts are not integrated but simply added as a digital service layer to the already complex service context, which results in a non-consistent experience for the guests (Glushko 2010: 246). Thus, from a design perspective, the particular problem of context-aware mobile concepts is their relation with the environmental context (Glushko 2010: 233) for the purpose of securing a coherent user experience.

Additionally, considering the previous definition of mobile-user experience, further issues for consideration are: (a) the users' needs and expectations to the mobile concept; as well as (b) the social context of the interaction (Jumisko-Pyykkö et al. 2008).

Principally, of course, the task context needs to be considered; however, in the workshops that are the basis for this chapter the specific task was not the primary goal, as the focus was to design experience-oriented mobile concepts rather than task-oriented mobile concepts. Similarly, the temporal context was also considered of lesser priority in this particular circumstance.

Based on the above-mentioned challenges and considerations the following hypotheses for the workshops were established:

Hypothesis 1: The mobile concept needs to integrate with the environmental context of the theme park.
Hypothesis 2: The mobile concept has to consider the needs of the users based on the environmental context.
Hypothesis 3: The mobile concept must integrate with the social context.

Considering the three hypotheses, the research question for the workshops was: How do we design user-oriented and context-aware mobile concepts for theme parks that integrate with the park and successfully enhance the visiting experience?

Workshop setup and methodology

The following workshop setup and methodology is the result of five iterations of the workshops held during 2012–13, which were organized and facilitated by the author of this chapter, and was developed based on the theory of mobile user experience as accounted for previously. The workshops were made up of participants with a wide variety of professional backgrounds including students from different universities, service design and tourism professionals, marketing professionals, representatives of app development companies, as well as professionals from other industries and businesses.

Table 12.1 The workshop activities

Activities	Content and purpose
1. Experiencing the environmental context	Experiencing and getting to know the park.
2. Identifying points of interaction	Identifying points of interaction for negative and positive experiences
3. Idea generation	Generating ideas for mobile concepts based on points of interaction. The result is a concept for a smartphone app
4. Environmental context	Considering how the concept integrates with the changing environmental context
5. Social context	Considering how the concept integrates with the changing social context
6. Mobile context	Considering the hardware and software limitations.
7. Sketching mobile concepts	Sketching the mobile concepts via mock-ups.
8. Presentation of concept	Each group presents their mobile concept as well as their reflections on the design process.
9. Evaluation	Debriefing and evaluating the workshop.

Each workshop lasted for a full day (7.5 hours), and was made up of nine activities (as shown in Table 12.1). The participants had limited time to work on each activity, which will be elaborated further below. The tight time limitations and various deadlines were intended to ensure that participants focused on the current activity instead of diverting their attentions between the current, past, and future activities (Sims 2006). Also the participants were divided into groups of five, to simulate the typical size of guests' groups in a theme park (Durrant et al. 2010; Østergaard 2013). The groups were not supposed to change throughout the entire workshop.

The progress of the workshops was documented by videos and photos, and after each workshop the participants were gathered for a discussion and evaluation of the methods and processes, producing in total 12.5 hours of video, 252 photographs, and records of five interviews/follow-up discussions. The empirical data were then analyzed using the *grounded theory method* for its inductive approach to generate themes and patterns (Strauss and Corbin 1990).

Workshop: Experiencing the environmental context

As the first workshop activity, the participants spent two hours in their groups experiencing the particular theme park under investigation by the workshop, getting to know the setting and facilities. More specifically the purpose of the visit was for them to first-hand experience the environmental context as well as the social context during the theme park visit, as these two contexts have the greatest impact on the visitor experience (Wigelius 2009).

Workshop: Identifying points of interaction

After the visit the participants gathered in a room not far from the park for the rest of the workshop. Based on the participants' visiting experience, they were requested to spend 45 minutes identifying points of interactions with other guests, amusements, rides, staff, etc. in the park. This was intended to generate the basis for the idea generation in the next activity.

To facilitate the identification of interactions the participants were asked to map their journeys in the park in a "customer journey map": participants were provided with a standard map of the theme park into which they marked the identified points of interactions based on their personal experience. Additionally, they were asked to note whether each of the interactions was a positive or a negative experience. This effectively led to the participants establishing their emotional state of mind at each point of interaction, a condition that is often affected by the users' previous experiences with theme parks as well as their expectations (Roto 2006: 24) (Figure 12.1).

As first-hand observation during the workshops and later the video evidence revealed, the second activity of the workshop functioned especially as a social activity that facilitates dialog among the various group members as they tended to have individual opinions on the different points of interaction, and the group needed to establish a common position first. This discussion also worked well to establish a notion of common experiences and expectations for each interaction, which in return proved to be useful starting points for the third activity, the idea generation.

Figure 12.1   Customer journey mapping on a map of the theme park.

Workshop: Idea generation

Based on theories on convergent and divergent creativity thinking, this activity focused on generating ideas in 45 minutes for mobile concepts that could enrich the visiting experience (Cropley 2006). Most

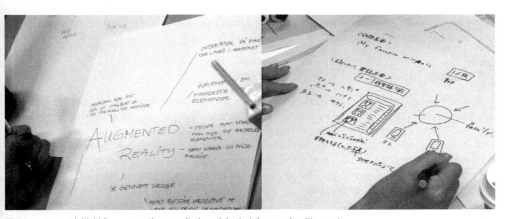

Figure 12.2   Initial idea generation results in quick sketches and written notes.

often the participants used the points of interactions previously identified negative experiences as the starting points for generating ideas that could turn the negative into a positive experience. Additionally, this process usually took into account the participants' shared previous experiences in theme parks, positive and negative experiences with mobile app usage situations, external mobile concepts they either like or dislike, etc.

The participants often found a pattern across the identified negative experiences—such as lack of information, or lack of entertainment—thus they often generated ideas for mobile concepts that could address several points of interaction within one intervention/application. The participants were asked to note down their ideas quickly, and to potentially clarify them with rough sketches (Figure 12.2).

Workshop: Environmental, social, and mobile context

In line with the original workshop hypotheses, after each group had established a series of rough concepts ideas, the following three activities focused on exploring the possible integration of those ideas into the environmental, social, and mobile contexts of the particular park for 45 minutes each.

To instigate the discussion about the environmental context, participants were asked to consider the following question: "How can the environmental context potentially support and integrate with the mobile concept, and vice versa?"

When discussing the social context, the goal was to consider how any of the proposed mobile concept ideas would affect the social interactions and behavior of the mobile-users in the park.

These first two considerations were supposed to be largely based on the first-hand experience of the personal visit in the first activity as well as the consolidation and interpretation of those visits in the preceding discussions. In this aspect those two considerations differed from the third discussion item on mobile contexts, as that needed to consider an external influence, the specific hardware and software limitations and possibilities of different mobile devices.

Essentially participants needed to contemplate if and how a mobile device could support the intended functionality of their concepts. Would the mobile device, for instance, be able to run computer-like graphics if that was part of the concept? Was the mobile device required to have a camera to support the concept? Was GPS technology required, or speakers, or headphones support etc.? In doing so, the participants determined minimum technical requirements for their concepts that could later be applied to different devices.

Workshop: Sketching a mobile concept

In the first clearly design-oriented activity the participants visualized their final mobile concepts via low-fidelity mock-ups, as these are easiest for most participants to engage in, are cheap and quick to do, in difference for instance to digital prototypes (Buxton 2007).

Accordingly, the participants were handed large printouts of a smartphone template with a blank screen on which they could draw their concept visualizations in 45 minutes (Figure 12.3). In doing so the participants were reminded to consider, for example, the size of the screen when designing the interface, as for instance a larger screen allows the users to see more information at one time. Or, if participants designed a concept for an activity that gathered more than one user around the mobile device, they were asked to think about the size and direction of texts or photos shown on the screen,

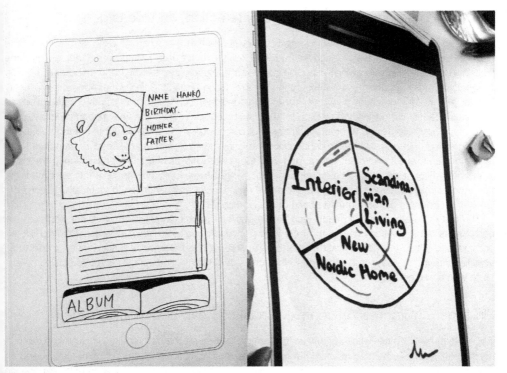

Figure 12.3   Examples of participants' mock-ups.

etc. All in all, the aim of this activity was to reflect on the effects specific technological setups would have on the development of their concepts.

Workshop: Presentation and evaluation

At the end of the workshop all participants would come together and take turns in presenting their mobile concept to each other very briefly (15 minutes in total only), including their process throughout the workshop, and how their reflections on contexts affected and changed the mobile concepts. The presentations and the workshop were finally wrapped up with a debriefing and evaluation section of 45 minutes.

Findings and discussion

After completion of each workshop, the data accumulated from then were screened and analyzed, leading to the following summary findings.

Findings: Theme park visit, points of interaction, and ideas generation

Analysis of the gathered data provided significant evidence that the initial unbiased visit at the theme park under investigation was indeed instrumental for the entire rest of the workshop, as only the first-hand experiences had at that occasion enabled the participants to fully understand and reflect a "normal" visitor's exposure to the interactions on site. Such understanding was important to identify "actual" points of interaction of visitors, rather than "designed" or "assumed" points of interaction, as one could identify them merely based on previous experiences or common imagination or knowledge. The shared visit also helped to create a platform for discussion when all participants contributed to the "customer journey" map. All participants found especially this mapping exercise to be very helpful to remember and reflect on when, where, and why they had good or bad experiences during their stay in the park. From their mapped experiences participants were usually able to "extract" a theme most commonly centered around especially the negative experiences which then could materialize in concrete ideas and concepts during the third phase of the workshop.

The first three activities seemed to work well together, to complement each other and to "lead" the participants smoothly from one to the next step. As all information needed was essentially collected or produced within the different activities—through first-hand experience or discussions—these three activities integrated easily, and allowed participants with different backgrounds and interests to collaborate with equal qualifications.

Findings: Environmental context, social context, and mobile context

The next three activities were somewhat different in nature as they all required including "external" considerations: while the discussion of environmental and social context could still be partially based on the previous visit—but needed to take into account nonetheless personal knowledge and experience beyond that, for example for technical issues—certainly the elaboration on mobile context was not initially informed by the theme park experience. Insofar participants had to draw from other sources and make connections to the task at hand. It also turned out the three contexts, which may be separate in theory, in reality overlap in many ways at many occasions:

> We decided not to use the camera and Augmented Reality because of the many guests [walking in between the smartphone-camera and the building that was intended to come alive via Augmented Reality].

Another quote exemplifies how the participants rethought their concepts, when thinking about ways how their idea could apply to the environmental context:

> We changed [our concept] to use stickers on the wall inside [the building] instead of GPS, as we expected poor GPS signal indoors.

These examples show how initial ideas needed to be changed or even abandoned, when they were confronted with the respective contexts: when considering the setting of a proposed idea (= the environmental context), the inside of a building, it becomes evident that a different technology has to be applied if the mobile concept is to remain context aware, and that in return affects the mobile context, which in theory should only be reflected later in the process. Similarly the environmental and mobile contexts might support another idea—like augmented reality on another building—yet the social context makes this impossible. A strict separation of the different context discussions thus doesn't seem feasible or practical.

Similarly, the sequence in which the three contexts were considered led to difficulties: Concepts that initially related well with their environmental and even social contexts, suddenly required changes because of requirements imposed by the mobile context, changes which then however affected the original position within the other contexts. Common reflections on this would go along the lines of:

We found that some of our original ideas did not work to integrate with the social and environmental aspects and context. So we had to rethink and reconsider our ideas.

And there we thought: If there is video and audio [as part of the concept], and there are 25–30 people around … this will annoy everyone.

The last quote exemplifies how participants at first wanted to use the built-in loudspeakers of a device for an activity. This would have been easily supported by the mobile context, as almost every smartphone has built-in speakers. But when the participants then thought of the environmental and social contexts they realized, that they had to change the concept to use headphones instead due to the noise from other guests (social context) as well as the rather small room (environmental context).

Situations such as these clearly show how the three contexts deeply affect each other, which the participants also reflect on:

It [the three contexts] sets limitations to what we can achieve with our concepts, because we had to relate it [the mobile concept] to three different contexts … and how they relate.

This observation aligns with previous research that suggests the tight interrelatedness between the environmental, social, and mobile context in understanding mobile user experience (Østergaard 2013).

Nonetheless it makes sense to keep the three activities with their respective focuses separate as this more gradual approach forces participants to revisit their initial concepts again and again from different angles, thereby verifying their validity, or otherwise prompting their "guided" revision. When the participants were to acknowledged new possibilities or limits of their developing concepts at a later stage, they had to move back to the previous Idea Generation activity, or even the customer journey maps, and adjust and verify their designs.

This iterative approach required the designs to continuously evolve throughout the entire workshop. By providing the participants with three distinct assignments one at a time, they were required to repeatedly evaluate their outcomes from changing points of view. This didn't necessarily stop them from considering individual aspects of another focus occasionally also within the "wrong" context, yet the important notion for the methodology of the workshop is that of "repeated re-consideration." It is within these workshop activities and due to these repeated reconsiderations that participants are required to reflect most intensively on their ideas, which is probably the reason why in these activities the most innovative concepts are being born.

Based on the findings the step-by-step introduction of the three contexts is of essential importance, also because keeping each activity separate establishes the particular perspective that is to be taken on at a time (Sims 2006). However, the specific sequence in which the distinct contexts are discussed could be varied—it is not important in which order the contexts are considered, it is merely important that they are considered one after the other, again and again—and participants are allowed to cross context-boundaries within each section as long as they eventually find back to the particular view currently under discussion.

Findings: Sketching

The Sketching activity appeared to be the favorite of many participants, where they could act out their creativity in drawing the mock-ups of their mobile concept (see Figure 12.3) and visualize all the past discussions and reflections. However, the findings also show that the participants continued to reflect and develop their concepts up until into this final design activity:

> We ended up thinking that it was unpractical for several people to gather around one mobile phone, because it is limited how much information the screen can display. So if there is some kind of quest to complete, the children will hold the mobile phone. Otherwise the parents will hold the phone and read out loud for the children.

This quote exemplarily shows how the participants adopted some last-minute changes to their design when during its visualization they realized that the proposed interface didn't fit the screen of the mobile device. This then lead to a reconsideration of the various contexts, and eventually to an intervention in the realms of the social context that newly introduced two distinct types of users—children and parents—with different roles and interactions. This example may be taken as evidence how the final visualization and other preparation for the presentation become effective as final thresholds for assessment and evaluation of a design.

Findings: The workshop as a methodology in general

The division of the workshop into activities created a systematic framework for the participants to continuously reflect on previous design decisions, and thereby to methodically revise their outcomes. Participants came to realize that new design decisions had consequences on previous as well as future design decisions, which—if applied consistently throughout a design process—will help reduce and focus any concept in development as well as add more complexity and validity to it in the process:

> We had to reconsider many things during the exercises, but the exercises did also give us new ideas as the exercises made us narrow down the ideas, because we had to consider the ideas in other contexts.
>
> I liked that first we just came up with all different kinds of ideas, and then we had to reduce the ideas throughout the workshop. Some things we had to rethink and thereby get to the same result but in a different way.

The discussions during each activity resulted in continuous new iterations of the mobile concept. Each of the new iterations was based on reflections, and discussions of reflections between the participants, which increased the "depth" of the consideration. Especially the exchanges during the middle part of the workshop—during the activities that required sequenced integration efforts of initially casual ideas into specific environmental, social, and mobile contexts—resulted in innovative ideas.

All reflections and discussions were based on the first-hand experience of the design objective at the beginning of the design process, as well as on the participating "designers'" previous experiences, mental states, and expectations (Roto 2006: 24). The findings from the workshop also show that experiences are not exclusively an individual knowledge, as the participants were able to construe new meanings from their experiences through exchanges with the other participants. In that way, the design activities also functioned as a social design experience as the meanings emerged from a social interaction (Battarbee and Koskinen 2005).

The timeframe for the workshop was given from the beginning as 7.5 hours, which put all participants under constant time pressure:

> It was a fast-paced process. But it was cool, because it made it possible for great ideas to emerge, because we are under pressure.

> The flow was very good, and the link between the individual exercises made sense.

It could be argued that such pressure might limit or reduce the creativity of the participants, yet as a matter of fact it seemed to positively "push" participants to their limits instead. Nonetheless, it could be considered to develop an extended version of this workshop format over the period of two days: the first day could focus on the first three activities—experiencing the park, identifying points of interaction, and generating initial ideas—thus giving the participants plenty of time to develop a deeper understanding especially of the environmental and social contexts of their design objective; the second day might afterwards be solely dedicated to further developing the initial ideas into more founded concepts through the process of repeated reconsiderations outlined above. However, any changes to the timeframe would have to be balanced carefully as simply giving the participants proportionally equally more time for each activity might in fact compromise the design progress, as rigid time frames are found to enhance creativity (Amabile 2002).

Conclusion

The findings and discussion show that it is possible to develop a workshop-based methodology for designing user-oriented experiences that leads the designers through a sequence of phases, thereby providing a structured procedural frame work suitable to facilitate the entire design process from the initial understanding of the design objective, through the early idea generation via an iterative sequence of considerations and reconsiderations towards a design result of complexity and validity. The findings also reveal that while the maintenance of the framework is principally important, such structure should not be too rigid as to still allow the participants the opportunity to consider issues from other activities of the process outside of their proposed sequence. Based on the experience of five workshops conducted the methodology can be condensed to the following three phases, each of which may comprise one or more activities (Figure 12.4):

1 understanding;

2 integrating;

3 designing.

Understanding includes the individual steps of first-hand experiencing the design objective at hand; the generalization and analytical interpretation of the experience, as well as the generation of initial design ideas that establish the outcome of this first phase, and are the "material" to further work with in the second.

Integrating is made of a complex and time-consuming iteration of considerations and reconsiderations that forces the participants to measure their initial ideas against a sequence of different contexts. Any changes to a design to accommodate one particular context will almost inevitably lead to the necessity to re-measure the new idea also against contexts the design had previously "passed" already—and the re-measurement may indeed lead to yet another change of the new design. To avoid participants getting lost in this process it is necessary to provide at least some minimum guidance by defining clear view points from which to evaluate the design-in-progress.

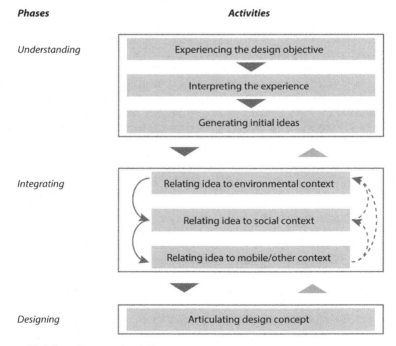

Figure 12.4   Workshop phases and activities.

The final phase, *designing*, leads the participants to articulate their previous process in a coherent design concept. While in principle at this point the idea should have matured enough to not entirely disintegrate anymore, there is the possibility that particular discoveries made only during the final articulation may require the design to be tested once again through the "fire of integration."

The ambition of the original workshop was to develop a methodology to facilitate the design of mobile-user experiences. Even though the workshops focused on theme parks as their case, and has thus far only been pilot-run for this purpose there seem no reasons to assume that variations of this methodology couldn't just as well be applied for other user-centered experiential design problems.

Chapter 13

Suspending Reality: A Disruptive Approach to Designing Transformative Experiences

Tara Mullaney

What are the key characteristics of an experience? According to Pine and Gilmore (1998), in their seminal article "Welcome to the Experience Economy," experiences engage individuals in a memorable event that is inherently personal, engaging them on an emotional, physical, intellectual, or even spiritual level. Indeed, they suggest that experiences can be treated as distinct economic offerings, unique from goods and services. For example, when an individual buys a good, he or she purchases a tangible artefact, and when a service is purchased, he or she purchases a series of intangible activities carried out on his or her behalf. However when the individual purchases an experience, he or she is paying for a memorable event in which he or she engages in an inherently personal way.

Despite the relatively clear distinctions that Pine and Gilmore make between goods, services, and experiences, designing memorable experiences is not a simple and easy feat to accomplish. In his book, *Experience Design* (2010), Hassenzahl looks closely at the inherent qualities of experiences, and investigates what it means to design for experience. He emphasizes that experiences are emergent, subjective, holistic, situated, and dynamic. According to him, experiences cannot be reduced down to their underlying components, nor fully explained by them; however, they can be shaped through the careful crafting of elements. Furthermore, specific experiences cannot be guaranteed to be achieved because they emerge from a variety of aspects, many of which are beyond the control of the designer. All of these characteristics, taken together, make designing experiences a difficult undertaking. Despite this, there are some clear guidelines for how to approach experience design.

One of the basic tenets of Experience Design is to consider the experience before the product. The premise behind this is that without a clear understanding of the experience, the products we design will never be able to properly shape experiences, let alone create new and novel ones. According to Hassenzahl, it helps to conceptualize an experience as an emergent story, i.e. "a narrative that summarizes feelings, thoughts and actions," and that one must "set the story straight before we can start thinking about how we can create this story through a technology" (2010: 63). This is sometimes difficult for designers, because we tend to focus upon the tangibles, since these are what we traditionally have been trained to create. Taking the metaphor of "experience as story" further, Hassenzahl classifies an experience designer as an "author of experience." The designing of a product can only occur after having outlined the desired emotional and cognitive content of the experience, the action involved, its context, and its temporal structure. Then, each and every detail of the product must be scrutinized according to its potential to create or destroy the desired experience (Hassenzahl 2010: 68–9). This notion of scripting an experience is essential, as is being able to detail the story with a rich understanding of the people it is being authored for, and the context it will be implemented in.

While Hassenzahl clarifies how we might attend to designing for experiences, it is less clear how one decides what type of experience to design. There is clearly a difference between designing supportive experiences for existing products and services, and coming up with transformative experiences which might challenge our daily routines, or provide a new way of approaching an issue or condition we generally take for granted. Supportive experiences are driven by existing product and technology structures. In contrast, transformative experiences are first conceptualized through the designer's imagining of possible alternatives to current conditions (whatever they may be), and the qualities of experience that the designer wishes to create for the user, without the constraints of technology and society grounding these ideas.

Nelson and Stolterman (2003) describe design as being interested in what is "ideal" and what is "real," where the "real" is grounded in the details and relationships of everyday life, and the "ideal" is focused around imagining how the world ought to be. User-centered design (UCD), a commonly employed approach in designing new products and experiences, places a strong emphasis upon the role of the "real" within the design process by focusing on understanding people and creating "designs that work" (Koskinen et al. 2011). While this approach to design has provided us with powerful tools for understanding people and creating designs that solve problems, Koskinen et al. (2011) suggest that UCD's focus on problem-solving has left many important sources for imaginative designs unused.

Designing experiences around existing products and infrastructures limits a designer's ability to "set the problem." Schön defines problem-setting as the process by which designers define the decisions to be made, the ends to be achieved, and the means to get there (Schön 1983). I believe that the difference between a supportive experience and a transformative one comes from whether the designer is too grounded in the "real" and focused on problem-solving versus taking a problem-setting approach and critically questioning, what the "ideal" may be. One of the main challenges for designers wishing to create transformative experiences is moving beyond the assumptions and perceptions that they have about existing products or services within the area that they are attempting to evolve, through the creation of something novel.

In order to create transformative experiences, as designers we need to move towards problem-setting, where we question what the problem really is, and how we might rewrite the script, aka the experience, so that the current experience is transformed. This type of work requires being able to re-imagine better futures instead of trying to disrupt existing ones, to look at problematic conditions from different perspectives, and to view existing structures, systems, and products with a critical lens. So how might we take a problem-setting approach to designing experiences? In this chapter, I explore the idea of "suspending reality" within the design process as one approach that a designer can take to develop ideas about what is "ideal." In this moment of suspension, designers can merge ideas and concepts together in a way that doesn't exist in our current reality, allowing them to imagine what could be in a more open and imaginative way.

To illustrate my points, this chapter presents project work done by a group of international students studying Interaction Design at the Umeå Institute of Design (UID) in Sweden to make the case that suspending reality within the design process is one way to facilitate the design of transformative experiences. Presenting the project as a case study, I will highlight the methods I used, as the main studio instructor, to "suspend reality" within the students' normal user-centered design process, the outcomes of these methods, and the overall outcomes of the project. In addition, I will analyze the impact of this approach, by presenting examples of where students noticeably shifted their framing as a result of the methods, and through the evaluation of the experiential qualities proposed in final designs of a selection of the students' work.

Case: Transformative transactions

UID is known within industry for the quality of work that its master's students produce, which results in a wide variety of companies asking for project collaborations with the school. Depending upon the needs and interest of the school and the company, collaborations take place in the form of sponsored term projects with one of the design programs. In the Master of Interaction Design (IxD) program at UID, each term has a main project, which explores a different facet of Interaction Design.

In this particular case the Brazilian bank, Itaú, contacted UID with the desire to have the students look at how a bank's role in society can be made more relevant, and how it could build lifelong relationships with its users and inspire new behaviors. Based on a shared interest in thinking conceptually about what banking experience could be, UID formed a collaboration with Itaú for the ten-week Interaction Concept term project in which second-year IxD students explore user experience at a conceptual level.

As a researcher at UID, my current work focuses on designing patient experiences within health care (Mullaney et al. 2011), while my past research has looked into developing richer interactions between people and everyday objects (Mullaney 2010). My background in designing experiences and interactions, as well as my interest in critical design, led me to become the main instructor for the Interaction Concept term project at UID starting in 2011. My experiences teaching this course in 2011 and 2012 made me aware that it can be difficult for the students to think conceptually when the majority of their other projects are highly user focused and driven by insights gathered from user research. Since banking in today's society is dominated by big brands and rigid structures, I wanted to ensure that the students could step beyond these perceived constraints in their designs. In order to do this, I decided to keep the project brief as open as possible. Instead of giving the students a specific user group or a specific area of banking to focus upon, in collaboration with Itaú and the IxD program director, we decided to ask the students to work within four thematic areas in relation to banking: Transformation, Transparency, Thoughtfulness, and Tangibility.

The students were tasked with exploring whether it is possible to establish a relationship between a bank and its clients, not by money but through understanding the life of each of its clients, and how a bank might be able to help its clients accomplish their personal goals, may they be financial or not. Additionally, the students were asked to promote transparency in the way bank clients perceive their finances and financial relations with other people, and to consider how tangible interactions could influence the perception of banking systems, with reference to the increasing digitization of money. The final deliverable for the project was to create a new banking experience, which had a tangible component to it, and was grounded in the technological constraints of today. In addition, we asked them to provide a physical "experiential" prototype of their design.

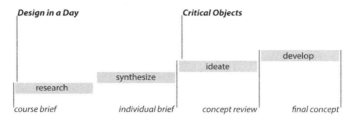

Figure 13.1   The students' project timeline including the two designed disruptions.

The project was structured with a traditional design process timeline, starting with a research phase where the students explore the project topic and gather information, followed by a synthesis phase where the students pull their research together into focus areas for their design work, leading to an ideation phase where the students develop a wide variety of design ideas based on their particular area of interest, and finishing with the final development phase during which the students commit to one design idea and develop it into their final design (Design Council 2005). However, since the students are very familiar with UCD methods and regularly work within a problem-solving framework in their design projects, I decided to disrupt their normal routines by facilitating two "extra" workshops during the project timeline.

Drawing inspiration from critical design, and the equal importance of designing for the ideal as well as the real within design practice, these workshops were designed to disrupt the students normal problem-solving process (Figure 13.1), with the aim of getting them to rethink the rigid constraints of banking today and ideate around new possibilities for interaction with these institutions. The premise was that by allowing the students protected time within the design process to set aside the real constraints of the project and to just play with the "ideal", it would trigger the students to think critically about the assumptions, preconceptions, and givens about the role of a bank in everyday life.

Design-in-a-Day

The first disruption was a workshop entitled *Design-in-a-Day*. It was held on the first day of the project, and its aim was to challenge the students to dive into the project by asking them to take action and create designs of new banking experiences before they had done any in-depth research on the topic, with the goal of kick-starting the students' research and ideation around the topic of new banking experiences. For the workshop, they worked in pairs on a high-speed design project, where the normal ten-week process was shortened to six hours only. Their designs needed to roughly follow the guidelines of the course project brief, but didn't have to strictly follow its constraints. The workshop was seen as a brainstorming exercise to allow the students to imagine what could be possible as topics to work on in this project, without having to commit to them.

The results of this workshop were very varied, but brought up topics that the students found personally interesting in relation to banking. Three representative outcomes of the workshop are exemplified in Figure 13.2:

Figure 13.2   Images of results from the Design-in-a-Day workshop: a) a responsive digital money token being loaded; b) the secure credit card; c) the experience of exchanging electricity credits for sunglasses.

a. A system that incorporates some of the advantages of cash money in a digital money world through the creation of responsive physical tokens. These tokens are designed to visually represent the amount of money they hold based upon their thickness. The more money on the token, the thicker it grows, and vice versa.

b. New forms of credit card security through pin code security measures enabled on the card itself, not on the terminal.

c. An electricity-credit system for homeowners in which you may generate your own electricity at home, and convert your surplus into money to buy items at stores.

Overall, the results of the workshop demonstrated that the students had looked into a broad variety of topical areas related to banking without being restrained by current banking systems. Some concepts were definitely conceptual and explorative, while others were technologically driven by current real-world problems. As the instructor, the workshop was a useful tool for me to see which students might have trouble stepping outside of a problem-solving framework, such as the individuals that created the secure credit card design. Overall, I found that the workshop served its purpose of having the students think openly about the types of experiences they could strive to create within the project.

Indeed, some of the ideas that arose in this workshop were visibly present in the students' final designs. For example, one student was triggered by the idea of banking electricity in the workshop, and decided to explore how a bank could take a more active role in informing its clients of their environmental impact. His final result was *Carbon Currency*, a system where the bank analyses your purchases relative to their environmental impact, and provides you with a carbon currency badge that will help you meet your short- and long-term carbon consumption goals, and allows you to compete with others participating in the same program. Building upon the current data mining capabilities of banks, this student saw an opportunity to re-frame the role of the bank into an ecological powerhouse by providing its clients with access to information about their environmental impact, something usually reserved for governments and industry.

Critical Objects workshop

The second disruption was a three-hour workshop entitled *Critical Objects* that was held at the start of the ideation phase, four weeks into the project. Taking inspiration from critical design, which uses speculative design proposals to challenge our preconceptions and givens about the role products play in everyday life, and questions the limited range of emotional and psychological experiences offered through designed products (Dunne and Raby 2011), this workshop was designed to help the students enrich their banking experience ideas by drawing on rich details of existing everyday behaviors and interactions, and mapping them onto a hypothetical product.

In preparation for the workshop, the students were asked to define a life topic and a banking topic relevant to their project focus area for the class to ideate around. Some examples of the students' life/bank topic combinations were: making a wish/saving goals, shared living/expense account, and your future self/retirement savings. The workshop was set up as to allow the whole class to brainstorm around every student's topical area. Each student was given ten minutes for their project, with the first five minutes dedicated to brainstorming around the qualities and behaviors related to the student's life topic (and the objects that live there), and the remaining five minutes were spent combining aspects of the life topic with their banking topic and coming up with possible designs. The students were again encouraged to be open to all possibilities, no matter how absurd or unrealistic they might seem, and not to worry about the constraints of the project in their brainstorming.

While the format of the workshop was not the most successful because there were too many students and not enough time to dedicate to each one's ideas, the results that came out of the workshop were still rich and insightful. Most of the ideas generated were impractical or impossible in the real world, yet the linking of real-world life experiences to banking concepts helped the students begin to think about the qualities of interactions they wanted to facilitate within their designs.

In looking at the students' final results, it is possible to trace the impact this workshop had on some of their designs. For example, the student who was interested in future forecasting and retirement planning used the workshop to brainstorm around the life topic of "your future self" and the banking topic of "retirement savings," which generated ideas that ranged from a magic mirror that shows you where you will end up based on your financial actions of today, to a belt that tightens on your waist in response to your spending activities. Her final result was *Mino*, a small ambient device that displays predictions of its users' future based on their current behavior (Figure 13.3). *Mino* allows its users to monitor their financial data in relation to other aspects of their life: health, social life, as well as global scenarios such as inflation. In the end, *Mino* is not so different from the idea of a magic mirror that shows you what your

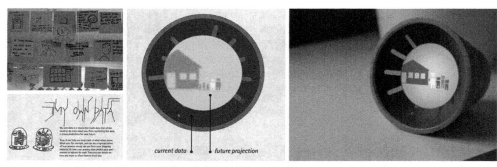

current data   future projection

Figure 13.3   The development of *Mino:* a) *Critical Objects* workshop results, b) final design concept, c) end result.

life will be like in the future, however the final concept is fully grounded in the reality that banks and social network sites collect and store large amounts of personal and statistical data about their users, and that complex algorithms can make quite accurate predictions about the behavior of specific user groups.

Impact analysis

So what was the impact of the workshops on the project outcomes? Did these disruptions help facilitate the students to create transformative banking experiences?

The students' final design concepts reflected a wide array of ideas around how our current banking experiences could be reframed and transformed. Some students focused upon how we can simplify our relationship with complex banking information by taking this information out of the computer and presenting it in new sensorial ways, while others looked at issues related to the increasing digitization of money, or how we might re-imagine the role of the bank in our lives. Both of the design concepts I mentioned already, *Mino* and *Carbon Currency*, take the existing capabilities of banks, and provide new ways of interacting with them. These concepts carefully balance the real and the ideal within their designs, and provide experiences that are conceptual, yet grounded in their understanding of human behavior.

Throughout the course of the project, the students began to look at the design process in new ways. Instead of relying solely on user research to drive their designs, they used it in more of a supportive way. Where they would normally do in-depth fieldwork at a bank to study client behaviors and experiences, the students instead now focused more on developing their ideas through brainstorming with other students, and distributing questionnaires that asked about peoples' perceptions of the bank and how they might want to change their current relationship with money. These forms of research provided the students with details that ensured the experiences they were creating were contextually relevant and understandable while allowing them to take a problem-finding approach rather than a problem-solving approach within their designs. Not only were the students encouraged to think critically about banking experiences, we also asked them to do the same with their design process by requiring them to design their own project briefs.

One example that exemplifies this criticality of both banking experiences and design process was a project entitled *Lost in Transaction*. This student decided to take a critical approach to the project, and place emphasis upon the imagining of new social values, and how these might create new products and interactions. She decided to focus on the theme of "consumerism as religion," and to create a series of objects that would invite new forms of bank-driven experiences. She also decided to employ a variation of the Design-in-a-Day workshop in her own design process, which she called "Idea-in-a-Day," for which every day she sketched a new idea of a design within her focus area. From this approach, she was able to generate 15 rich design directions that she then mapped for the behaviors they facilitated. The end results of this project were five objects, each one aligned to a new, religious-esque bank behavior: invitation to reflect, give guidance, highlight life transitions, bestow peace and wellbeing, and offer comfort.

As we have seen with *Carbon Currency*, *Mino*, and *Lost in Transaction*, the temporary suspensions of reality that the two workshops provided served as touch-points to influence the directions that the students took in their larger projects. The results presented here demonstrate that the students were able to conceptualize new banking behaviors and experiences, providing ideas that are idealistic and yet richly grounded in reality. Their concepts are not attempting to solve a particular problem within today's banking systems for a user, particular user group, or banking service. Nor have they designed "value-added" experiences onto these systems. Instead, these students have imagined a wide variety of possible, new, transformative banking experiences, drawing from insights into human behavior, banking systems, and technological trends.

Discussion

As it is possible to trace ideas that arose in the workshops all the way to the final design outcomes, I suggest that the workshops achieved their desired role, to trigger the students to think beyond what the banking system currently is to what it could become. Furthermore, by allowing the students to have the space and freedom to conceptualize the ideal without being constrained by reality, I argue that these workshops helped to get the students to shift their framing of the bank experience, stepping away from their traditional problem-solving approach to a problem-setting one. Based upon the design results presented, momentary suspensions of reality within the design process appear to be a valid approach to helping designers come up with truly transformative experiences.

Chapter 14

Understanding and Designing the Meal Experience and its Psychological Consequences

Werner Sommer, Felix Bröcker, Manuel Martín-Loeches, Annekathrin Schacht, and Birgit Stürmer

Recently the authors have started an ambitious line of research about the effects of the meal context on cognitive and emotional processes; the results obtained so far are summarized in the present chapter. Currently the team is cooperating with top gastronomy in order to investigate the meal experience and its persistence over time. For this chapter the authors have teamed up for the sake of discussing the translation of basic research about psychological aspects of meals into application.

The effects of a delicious dinner are wonderfully described in the story *Babette's Feast* by Karen Blixen. Babette, a humble maid in a Norwegian village and—unbeknown to the villagers—an excellent cook, invites her pious and austere masters and their relatives and neighbors to a lavish dinner. As the dinner unfolds, the villagers—against their intention not to be seduced by worldly pleasures—begin to thaw and warm up to each other, forget old wrongs, and rekindle ancient loves while life acquires an almost mystical quality.

Arguably, very few human activities are as important and multifaceted as those related to food. For good reasons—from satisfying the elementary needs for nutrition to providing spaces and places where gastronomy unfolds as a form of art designed to elicit unique experiences of the customer—the food industry is the biggest of all industries. The provision and consumption of food can be viewed from several sides. At its most simple level, it is about nutrition. Through this lens, the exchange of food is a business that trades material goods. In addition, food and its constituents are a major factor for physical health, mental wellbeing, and cognitive development (Meiselman 2013; NEMO Study Group 2007; Portwood 2006). However, and of special concern in this chapter, meals are very important elements of social and family life (Flammang 2009; Jones 2007), and the experience of meals is a prime source of human pleasure (Rozin 2005). Whereas a lot is known about normal and abnormal aspects of energy regulation and food consumption, much remains to be understood about the psychological and social aspects of having a meal.

In the following we will distinguish between: (a) the meal situation, that is, the material aspects of the meal; the food of which it consists, its material ingredients and social context, (b) the meal experience, that is, how the meal situation is subjectively experienced by the consumer; and (c) the psychological consequences of the meal situation or the meal experience on cognitive and emotional processes and states that are not about the meal and its context, such as changes in mood, creativity, or empathy.

Efforts to shape the meal experience by creating specific meal situations are probably as old as humankind; sharing food in an organized and ritualistic manner is a uniquely human behavior not observed among animals (Fischler 2011; Jones 2007). Research on the meal experience is complicated by the multitude of possible meal situations, ranging from a hasty breakfast at home, a simple snack in the office, an informal lunch with colleagues in a canteen, dinner with family or friends at home or in a restaurant (basic to gourmet), all the way to a formal banquet at a wedding ceremony or a diplomatic summit. These different kinds of meals and different contexts—meal situations—likely yield a wide range of meal experiences. In addition, the particular experience is influenced by the personality of the individual, his or her previous mental state (e.g. mood or mind set for weight control), and may further be affected by events that are difficult to predict or control, like the course of social interactions with dining partners and restaurant staff, slow service, or a hair in the soup. A similar argument could be made about the psychological consequences of the meal experience. Considering such complexities, isn't it hopeless to get a grip on understanding the psychology of meals? Understanding the meal experience, like all science, requires the isolation of essential factors from myriad random variations. The application of scientific methods and principles can provide a deeper understanding of this critical aspect of human life and may allow the purposeful design of meal situations in order to create pre-planned meal experiences and psychological consequences.

Meals are experienced on different dimensions and in varying degrees, including tastiness, novelty, or the degree of which the food taste conforms to the eater's expectancy. The eater's sensation, the way he or she perceives and evaluates the food as well as the degree to which food impresses the eater is related to both the food itself and the context in which the meal is consumed. Context might be a particular physical environment—for example, a restaurant on a tower. Context might as well be social, for example an event like a wedding providing the occasion for the meal. In some cases the memory of the meal experience, for example of a gourmet dinner, may persist for a long time.

For a long time, designers of restaurants and other eating places—architects, interior designers, and their clients—have strived to create certain physical environments, which may affect the meal experience and its psychological consequences. These places range from street vendors, fast-food places, cafeterias and canteens to gourmet restaurants, serving different needs and allowing for rather different experiences (e.g. Hurst and Lawrence 2005). However, the scientific study of meal-related experiences has to a large extent been limited to sensory judgments of food—often in isolated laboratory situations (Meiselman 2008). Unfortunately, there is very little scientific work about the psychological consequences of meals. We argue that knowledge about the meal experience and the psychological consequences of meal situations is important to optimize the purposeful design of food, meal serving places, and their procedures.

The meal experience

In gastronomic practice, as well as in home cooking, a main aim is the "tastiness" of the dish. However, the sensation of "taste" or—better—its flavor, is determined by many other sensory modalities in addition to gustation: its smell, temperature, texture (known as somato-sensation), sound (during biting and chewing), and color. The great chef Auguste Escoffier (1846–1935) was well aware that the context in which a meal is taken has strong effects on the tastiness of the meal beyond its sensory qualities. For this reason, Escoffier enhanced the meal situations by serving the food in luxurious environments, on fine tableware, and having waiters wear tuxedos. Modern-day chefs such as Ferran Adrià (Adrià, Soler, and Adrià 2008), Andoni Luis Aduriz (2012), or Heston Blumenthal (2008) continue in the tradition of paying attention to context. These chefs not only emphasize the multisensory qualities of the food they prepare by, for example, playing the sound of ocean waves when serving oysters (Blumenthal 2008); they also take great care in designing the restaurant environment, such as the space available, or the inclusion of the sights and sounds of the nature outside. Food may (re)evoke feelings when it is associated with childhood memories or it may elicit surprise when, for example, color and taste combine in unexpected ways, or when hot and cold receptors in the mouth are stimulated simultaneously. By the sophisticated elaboration of the meals and the meal serving contexts, top restaurants may create deeply moving and unique experiences similar to those induced by other fine arts. These examples demonstrate the scope of what is possible in creating meal experiences. Everyday meal experiences are by comparison much humbler but, by virtue of their ubiquity, highly important.

A sizeable body of scientific research has addressed contextual effects and their influence on the meal experience (see, for a recent review, Meiselman 2008). A home meal leads to higher ratings of a food product, for example an ice cream, than a standard laboratory environment (e.g. Boutrolle et al. 2007). The environment in which food is consumed is associated with expectations of food quality. Expectations are highest for meals consumed at home or in a restaurant, more modest for school and military canteens, and relatively low for airlines and hospitals (Cardello et al. 1996). Food in institutional settings is rated lower in quality than in restaurant settings (Edwards et al. 2003; Meiselman et al. 2000). The same food, if part of a wider range of choice, is rated higher than when choice is restricted (King et al. 2004; King et al. 2007; Kramer et al. 2001).

Although meals are generally considered to be a social human activity (Rozin 1996), sociability (aka commensality) during meals differs widely, with a much higher frequency of solitary meals in work situations than outside of work (Sobal and Nelson 2003). Research on the effects of commensality has shown that in company people tend to eat more (de Castro and de Castro 1989) and meals last longer (Sommer and Steele 1997). A social situation may also decrease the acceptability of some dishes (King et al. 2004).

Overall, studies have shown that contextual effects are very powerful determinants of the meal experience. However, this area of research has usually focused on the food itself and its acceptability rather than on the experience of the meal context, such as the restaurant interior, the service, atmospherics, or the social situation.

Finally, a promising line of research applies the principles of subjective utility to the meal experience. The value given to any type of experience is determined not merely by the sum of the individual elements constituting the experience (such as the sum of the experiences of all dishes in a meal), but—importantly—by their combination and sequence along the whole experience. Thus the experience of the very last dish in relation to the preceding ones during a multi-course meal seems to be of special relevance for the pleasure or displeasure assigned to the entire meal experience (Rode et al. 2007).

The psychological consequences of the meal

Meals may have consequences that transcend the impression made by the taste, smell, texture, etc. of the food and the experience of the meal situation. Thus, it is sometimes thought that business contracts or conflicting positions may be negotiated more easily during a meal, that "creative" people may readily seek and discuss new ideas while eating, and that a candle-light dinner may foster pair bonding. However, there is very little academic research on meal effects on social outcomes and psychological processes. As an exception, Danziger, Levav, and Avnaim-Pesso (2010) reported that judges' sentences became more severe as time since the previous meal lengthened. Unfortunately, it is not clear whether this is related to the physiological benefits of food consumption (e.g. glucose availability) or to fatigue due to the time on task. The special social significance of a meal has been indicated by Kniffin and Wansink (2012) who reported that more jealousy was aroused in spouses of persons who had a meal as compared to a coffee with an opposite gender acquaintance.

A starting point for scientific research about psychological effects of meals and their crucial determinants may be based on the assumption that meals affect cognitive performance and social interactions via emotions and mood states. Previous research has indicated that positive mood enhances creativity (Baas et al. 2008), cognitive fluency (Mitchel and Phillips 2007), and memory (Bless and Fiedler 1995; Lyubomirsky et al. 2005) but impairs cognitive control (van Steenbergen et al. 2009; for an alternative view see Stürmer et al. 2011).

Recently, we conducted an initial study on the psychological effects of a meal situation (Sommer et al. 2013). In the first step, we measured the consequences of a typical lunch situation in a restaurant, in company and with ample time as compared to a quick business-style lunch alone in an office. We felt this to be a good starting point for better understanding the influence of the meal context on several psychological variables because it compared two meal situations that are often found in daily life. In order to see whether these typical situations impact psychological states and processes in any way, in this first attempt we did not try to isolate specific factors of the meal situation. Importantly, because food and its contents may have a direct effect on psychological states and processes, we wanted to preclude any differences between the meal situations in the kind and amount of food (or drinks) consumed. Therefore, we assembled an experimental group (EG) and a control group (CG). Both groups consisted only of women in order to avoid the complication of sex differences, and they ate exactly the same type and amount of food. Hence, the only difference between the groups was the meal context.

First, a baseline session with several experimental tasks was conducted at noon. On a second day, around the same time, there were two kinds of meal situations: The women of the EG went to a standard Italian restaurant with a (female) friend or acquaintance of their choice who was conveniently available. They could choose pasta or pizza from a menu of about 15 items and had one hour to finish their meal. The women of the CG were selected to be similar to the EG in terms of eating preferences and weight. They also went to the restaurant, but picked up a meal from the take-away counter, which was the meal chosen by the partner from the EG. Hence only women of the EG, but not of the CG, could choose their meal. Another difference between the situations was that the 15-minute walk between the restaurant and the lab occurred after the meal for the EG and before the meal for the CG. The CG participants took their meal to a standard office at our department—sized for one person—where they were to eat the food within at most 20 minutes, without the company of others. Immediately after the group-specific meal situations, there was a second experimental session with the same tasks as in the first session.

A mood questionnaire (Steyer et al. 1997) was completed by participants at the beginning of each experimental session. As self-reported on the questionnaire, the EG was significantly calmer and less wakeful than the CG in the session following the meal. That is, the restaurant meal situation seems to have been subjectively relaxing.

As mentioned, there were several tasks in each of the two sessions. The Simon task aimed to elicit cognitive conflicts and provoke erroneous responses. This task involves pressing a button with either the left or right index finger, depending on the shape of the particular stimulus presented randomly in varying spatial locations on a computer screen. As expected, performance was better when the screen location matched the required response button than in case of a mismatch. This so-called Simon effect is interpreted as a consequence of a conflict between different responses activated by stimulus location and stimulus shape, which has to be detected and resolved by a mental control process to select the correct response (Kornblum et al. 1990). As compared to the baseline sessions, the CG demonstrated a diminished Simon effect after the meal whereas it was not attenuated in the EG. We suggest that in the CG there was improved cognitive control over response conflicts in the second session, possibly due to practice; in contrast, in the EG there was no such improvement over cognitive control after the restaurant visit.

In both test sessions preceding and following the meals we also recorded the electroencephalogram (EEG). We were interested in the processing of incorrect responses (errors) committed in the Simon task. Shortly after an incorrect response, a negative-going deflection occurred in the EEG, the so-called error negativity (Ne; Falkenstein et al. 2000). The Ne has been related to performance monitoring such as response conflicts or response (in)correctness. Performance monitoring processes are seen as essential elements of cognitive control. As it turned out, the Ne after the meal was smaller in the EG than the CG (Figure 14.1). Following the Ne to incorrect responses there was also a positive-going ERP-component, the error positivity (Pe). The Pe has been related to the conscious perception of committing an error (e.g. Leuthold and Sommer 1999). Just as the Ne, also the Pe was diminished in the EG relative to the CG (Figure 14.2). That is, the EG demonstrated lower cognitive control and less awareness of errors than the CG.

In a second task, we measured brain responses to facial expressions of emotions. Faces of men and women were presented that showed happy, angry, or neutral expressions. Interestingly, the brain responses to angry faces relative to neutral faces were larger in the EG than in the CG starting at less than 200 milliseconds after the onset of the face on the screen. In previous research, similar very early emotion-driven increases of brain responses have been found when the capacity to control such situations was diminished by an additional task (Rellecke 2012).

Together, these results indicate the existence of two potentially related effects of the restaurant meal situation relative to eating alone in a small office space during a relatively short period of time. First, the restaurant meal was subjectively more relaxing than the office meal. Second, after the restaurant meal, cognitive control and error monitoring was diminished for those who ate with company and in a restaurant setting relative to the meal in the office.

To the best of our knowledge, our study is the first ever to assess the psychological consequences of a meal experience. Importantly, the effects found are unrelated to the kind and amount of food consumed because this was the same in both groups; similarly we had made efforts to control for

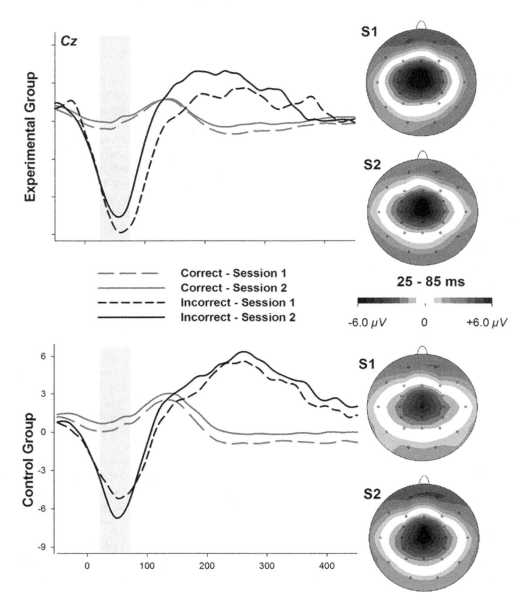

Figure 14.1 Response-synchronized ERPs from the Simon task. ERPs at electrode Cz, superimposed for correct and incorrect responses and Sessions 1 and 2 and for the EG and CG. Topographies of the Ne as the difference between incorrect and correct responses are depicted to the right of the waveforms (25–85 ms).

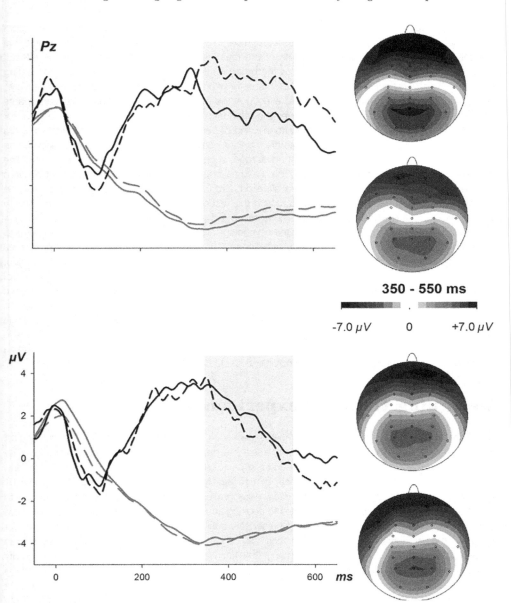

Figure 14.2   Same as Figure 14.1 but for electrode Pz (please note changes in voltage and time scales). Topographies of error positivities (350–550 ms) are shown to the right of the waveforms.

weight, food preferences, age, and had excluded participants with depression, ruling out these factors as causing the effects found. Because we had compared two typical meal situations as a whole, we cannot tell at the moment, which elements of the meal situations were responsible for the effects. Among the potentially important factors are the broader office versus restaurant environment, eating alone or in company, and the 15-minute walk before or after the meal in the CG and EG, respectively.

One may have expected more "positive" effects on the psychological processes of the participants who ate in the restaurant situation. However, the attenuation of cognitive control may be negative for certain purposes, such as when close self-monitoring of performance and detailed attention to errors are required, such as in laboratory and factory work or numerical processing. In other situations, an attenuation of cognitive control may be of advantage, such as when social harmony is desired. The example of our study shows that: (a) meals may have psychological consequences that do not concern the meal itself and last longer than the meal situation; and (b) these consequences may be specific. In our opinion, it would be highly desirable to extend this research area into various directions in order to learn more about the effects of meals on emotional, cognitive, and behavioral functions.

A possible research agenda concerning the psychological consequences of meal situations and meal experiences might investigate the following questions: What are the affected psychological processes and functions? In addition to the processes assessed in our first study, one might consider, for example, pro-social behavior, language processing, creativity, memory, or mental speed. What are the temporal dynamics of these factors? Although methodologically challenging, it would be interesting to see at what point during the meal particular psychological effects emerge and how they develop over time. What are the crucial elements for the effects? As pointed out above, we have compared two situations as a whole and cannot differentiate between the specific elements and variables contributing to the effects. If these elements can be identified through systematic experimental variations, they can be utilized for designing meal experiences in order to achieve psychological effects desired by the consumer.

Designing the meal experience

Many trades are involved in designing meal experiences and—*nolens volens*—their psychological consequences. The food industry aims to optimize the marketing effectiveness of their products by designing suitable sensory qualities (and attractive packaging) of the food they aim to sell. Similarly, restaurants and other eating establishments aim to satisfy the expectations of their customers by providing meals directed toward specific tastes, visual presentation, nutritional value, and freshness, to name a few. Here the design question relates to cooking and meal preparation. However, it should have become clear from the review above, that even sensory qualities are strongly influenced by context. For example, the "delicious" smell of an old cheese may be experienced as body odor when presented in isolation (Blumenthal 2008). Hence, Meiselman (2008) has warned against assessing the sensory quality of food in isolation and disregarding the context in which it is actually eaten. Thus, in optimizing airplane meals, for example, one should measure the food experience in an airplane situation and in the context of the whole meal rather than in a clinical lab environment where just a sample of the food in question is presented.

Restaurant design has to consider functional constraints, for a start. A fast-food restaurant or a canteen has to be able to serve hundreds of people and provide the option of finding seating and rest rooms quickly. It has to be easy to clean and should not be too comfortable if the company wants to have a high fluctuation in order to generate more money in a short time. Fine dining places have a more inviting interior in order to make people feel intimate and relaxed. Nevertheless functional demands must always be fulfilled, in order to run the restaurant smoothly.

Hurst and Lawrence (2005) suggested an interesting classification of meal serving places, from "raw" (street vendors and fast-food places) to "medium" (family restaurants and cafes) to "well done" (high-class gastronomy). Meal serving places of different categories serve different purposes. Thus, during a busy day, lunch may be eaten just to provide calories and nutrients and little emphasis is placed on social communication—a case for "raw" eating places. On other occasions people want to discuss issues of interest over lunch; here a relaxed atmosphere may be desired which presumably fosters new ideas— here the "medium" type may be more suitable. Yet, at other times, dinners serve mainly social purposes, such as when guests are treated, birthdays are celebrated, or when social/romantic relationships are to be initiated, deepened, or repaired; here the choice would be on "well done places." Although such a rough classification of restaurant designs is plausible and intuitive, its optimization and fine-tuning may benefit from systematic study and quantitative analyses, as exemplified by our experiments.

Restaurant design often prepares the customer for the sensual pleasure of food consumption by creating a fitting atmosphere. Thus, restaurants serving organic produce might use natural looking materials for their interior design in order to indicate its approach to food, whereas an Italian restaurant might provide an Italian interior. If this is done successfully, the context may also affect the meal experience. Just as the sound of waves reinforces the taste of an oyster, interior design is able to reinforce matching food qualities: Bell, Meiselman, Pierson, and Reeve (1994) reported that Italian food served in an Italian environment is perceived as more authentic. However, the design has to be well balanced, as the quest to create authenticity might easily lead to an over-styled, unnatural setting.

Our meal experience is influenced not only by the interior design but also by the very tableware. Glasses, plates, and cutlery have significant impact on our perception and valuation of the food we eat (Spence et al. 2013) and should be taken into consideration in designing the physical environment.

As mentioned, chefs are also starting to think more about the meal experience as a whole. But usually they are concerned about what is happening on the plate or how the food interacts with the customer. Providentially, there are also designers and artists (e.g. Sanderson and Raymond, 2008; Vogelzang 2009) who concentrate on the eating experience as such instead of the food as main protagonist.

An interesting issue in this context is the design of private homes and their eating places. Since private homes are the place where most meals are eaten (Holm et al. 2012), the opportunity they provide for eating in company and for having a pleasant meal experience is very important. With increasing cost pressure on housing, the available space for cooking and eating has come under pressure as well. In more spacious residences, there may be a separate dining room. However, in the typical present day home, eating now usually takes place in the living room or kitchen. In many cases, however, apartments are so small that it compromises opportunities for family meals or inviting guests for dinner.

Just as knowledge of the context effects on the meal experience allows to optimize the designs of meals and eating places, knowledge about psychological consequences of meals will allow to custom-tailor meal situations. At the moment, research about the psychological consequences of meals is in its infancy. The optimal design (and choice from the perspective of the customer) of an eating place and of the procedures at this place might be very different if the aim is to foster concentrated learning and understanding of difficult material, creative processes, social interactions, general wellbeing (e.g. in rehabilitation or recreational contexts), or—indeed—the supply of nutrition with minimal cognitive and emotional impact. From our own study we may derive a preliminary suggestion: If concentrated work and diligence are desired, it may be preferable to keep lunchtime short rather than to indulge in an extended restaurant meal. In contrast and in line with everyday experience, a meal in a restaurant in agreeable company seems to be indeed appropriate for relaxation from tension.

Eating design should combine different elements to create an overall experience. It should use interior design, cooking, food design, product design, and insights from sociology, psychology, biology, and history of food and its consumers. Together all these elements may contribute to creating or selecting meal situations that are well designed to fit one's personal needs and interests.

Acknowledgement

We deeply appreciate the helpful comments of Amanda B. Clinton on a previous version of this chapter.

Further Readings

As outlined in the Foreword, one purpose of the collaborative efforts in this publication was to attempt to establish some common theoretical ground. As it turned out—and as is evident in the reference lists of the various chapters included in this book—this proved to be difficult, if not impossible. Experience Design as a discipline in its own right is still too young, too much in flux, and has a yet too disparate background as to have developed a coherent theoretical framework, and with it a commonly accepted canon of texts.

As in the Experience Design arena itself, the contributors to this publication come from backgrounds across the academic scope: Architecture, Archaeology, Computer Sciences, Interaction Design, Product Design, Psychology, Visual Communication, and more. It seems evident that with such varied backgrounds, and, deriving from those very different approaches, much varying intentions and expectations in the notion of Experience Design, it seems futile and potentially even presumptuous to come up with any attempt to propose further readings for this area, as quite obviously it would always depend on the angle the new reader would wish to approach from.

Yet, while it may not be possible to establish a common reference list between those various disciplinary backgrounds through discussion, a comparative examination of the reference lists provided with the chapters of this book proves quite interesting.

In total ten texts were referenced by more than one contribution. Maybe not surprisingly, the text with most citations is:
Pine, B. Joseph II, and James H. Gilmore. *The Experience Economy*. Updated edition. Boston, MA: Harvard Business Review Press, 2011.[1]

Second most citations were achieved by what probably is to be deemed an "experience-classic":
Dewey, John. *Art as Experience*. New York, NY: Perigee Books, 2005.

The only author represented by two texts in this "most cited list" is the cognitive scientist and advocate of user-centered design Donald A. Norman with:
Norman, Donald A. *Emotional Design: Why we Love (or Hate) Everyday Things*. New York, NY: Basic Books, 2005; and
Norman, Donald A. *The Design of Everyday Things*. New York, NY: Basic Books, 2013.

Further texts cited by more than only one contribution are:
Desmet, Pieter, and Paul Hekkert. "Framework of Product Experience." *International Journal of Design* 1, no. 1 (2007): 57–66.

Forlizzi, Jodi, and Katja Battarbee. "Understanding Experience in Interactive Systems." *DIS '04: Proceedings of the 5th Conference on Designing Interactive Systems: Processes, Practices, Methods and Techniques*. New York, NY: ACM, 2004: 261–8.

Gell, Alfred. *Art and Agency: An Anthropological Theory*. Oxford: Oxford University Press, 1998.

Hassenzahl, Marc. *Experience Design: Technology for All the Right Reasons*. San Rafael, CA: Morgan & Claypool, 2010.

Redström, Johan. "Towards User Design? On the Shift from Object to User as the Subject of Design." *Design Studies* 27, no. 2 (2006): 123–39.

Shedroff, Nathan. *Experience Design 1*. Indianapolis, IN: New Riders, 2001.

This list can obviously not claim any representative validity in statistical terms, yet the simple fact that different academics/professionals from around the world found these same texts valuable should justify their recommendation for further reading.

While only ten authors' specific texts were cited more than once throughout the chapters of this book, a small number of further authors were referenced for different texts. Among them are

- Katja Battarbee and Ilpo Koskinen, who often join up with each other and/or with Jodi Forlizzi to write about issues in Interaction Design/User Experience Design;

- Hendrik N. J. Schifferstein, who works with Paul Hekkert and Pieter Desmet from a background in Product Design;

- Tim Brown, CEO of IDEO and advocate of Designing Thinking theory;

- American psychologist Mihaly Csikszentmihalyi;

- French philosophers Gilles Deleuze and Henri Lefebvre;

- French sociologists Bruno Latour and Antoine Hennion; as well as

- Finnish architect Juhani Pallasmaa.

This list of researchers can by no means be seen as comprehensive or generally accepted, yet the authors' repeated citations throughout this book and beyond indicate that they are probably worth a further look into if interested in the notion of Experience Design.

Note

1   Contributors may have cited from different editions of the same text. For the purpose of easier accessibility the latest edition of the referenced texts is listed here.

References

Part One: Positions

1 Fundamental Aspects of Human Experience: A Phenomeno(logical) Explanation

Anolli, Luigi. "The Detection of the Hidden Design of Meaning." In Luigi Anolli, Starkey Duncan Jr., Magnus S. Magnusson, and Guiseppe Riva, eds. *The Hidden Structure of Interaction: From Neurons to Culture Patterns*. Amsterdam: IOS Press, 2005: 23–50.

Baldwin, Thomas, ed. *Maurice Merleau-Ponty Basic Writings*. London: Routledge, 2004.

Bate, Paul, and Robert Glen. *Bringing User Experience to Healthcare Improvement: The Concepts, Methods and Practices of Experience-based Designing*. London: Radcliff Publishing, 2007.

Battarbee, Katja. "Defining Co-experience." *DPPI '03: Proceedings of the 2003 International Conference on Designing Pleasurable Products and Interfaces*. New York, NY: ACM, 2003: 109–13.

Battarbee, Katja and Ilpo Koskinen. "Co-experience: Product Experience as Social Interaction." In Hendrik N. J. Schifferstein and Paul Hekkert, eds. *Product Experience*. London: Elsevier, 2008: 461–76.

Carman, Taylor. *Heidegger's Analytic: Interpretation, Discourse and Authenticity in Being and Time*. Cambridge: Cambridge University Press, 2003.

Coxon, Ian. "Is Change as Good as a Holiday? Using Metaphysical Bonds to Design Enduring Change." In Carla Cipolla and Pier Paolo Peruccio, eds. *Changing the Change: Proceedings*. Torino: Allemandi Conference Press, 2008: 497–508.

Dewey, John. *Art as Experience*. New York, NY: Berkley Publishing Group, 1934.

Feenberg, Andrew. "Experience and culture: Nishida's path to the things themselves." *Philosophy East and West* 49, no. 1 (1999): 28–44.

Forlizzi, Jodi, and Katja Battarbee. "Understanding Experience in Interactive Systems." *DIS '04: Proceedings of the 5th Conference on Designing Interactive Systems: Processes, Practices, Methods and Techniques*. New York, NY: ACM, 2004: 261–8.

Fuad-Luke, Alastair. "'Slow Design'—A Paradigm Shift in Design Philosophy?" Presentation at the *Development by Design Conference*. Bangalore, India, December 1–2, 2002.

Gadamer, Hans-Georg. *Truth and Method* (Wahrheit und Methode). 2nd edition. London: Sheed & Ward and Continuum Publishing Group, 1975.

Gallagher, Shaun. *How the Body Shapes the Mind*. Oxford: Oxford Scholarship Online, 2005.

Haraway, Donna. *Simians, Cyborgs and Nature*. London: Free Association Books, 1991.

Heidegger, Martin. *Being and Time* (Sein und Zeit). New York, NY: Harper and Row, 1962.

Latour, Bruno. "Pragmatogonies: A mythical account of how humans and non-humans swap properties." *American Behavioural Sciences* 37, no. 6 (1994): 791–808.

Latour, Bruno. "Why has critique run out of steam? From matters of fact to matters of concern." *Critical Inquiry* 30, no. 2 (2004): 225–48.

Moran, Dermot. *Introduction to Phenomenology*. New York, NY: Routledge, 1999.

Nielsen, Lasse N., Sven D. Poulsen, and Ian Coxon. "When a Patient Goes Home: Meaningful Lessons in Designing for the Patient Experience of Cervical Radiculopathy and Stroke Paralysis." Presentation at the *Design4Health Conference*, Sheffield, UK, July 3–5, 2013.

Redström, Johan. "Towards user design? On the shift from object to user as the subject of design." *Design Studies* 27, no. 2 (2006): 123–39.

Ricoeur, Paul. *The Rule of Metaphor: Multi-disciplinary Studies of the Creation of Meaning in Language*. London: Routledge & Kegan Paul, 1978.

Van Manen, Max. *Researching Lived Experience: Human Science for an Action Sensitive Pedagogy*. 2nd edition. London; Ontario: Althouse Press, 1997.

Varela, Francisco J. "Neurophenomenology: A methodological remedy for the hard problem." *Journal of Consciousness Studies* 3, no. 4 (1996): 330–49.

Willis, Peter. "The things themselves in phenomenology." *Indo-Pacific Journal of Phenomenology* 1 (2001): 1–21.

2 Experience as Excursion: A Note Towards a Metaphysics of Design Thinking

Bogost, Ian. *Alien Phenomenology, or, What it's Like to Be a Thing*. Minneapolis, MN: University of Minnesota Press, 2012.

Bjögvinsson, Erling, Pelle Ehn, and Per-Anders Hillgren. "Design things and design thinking: Contemporary participatory design challenges." *Design Issues* 28, no. 3 (2012): 101–16.

Brown, Tim. *Change by Design: How Design Thinking Transforms Organizations and Inspires Innovation*. New York, NY: Harper Business, 2009.

Connor, Steven. "Introduction." In Michel Serres, ed. *The Five Senses: A Philosophy of Mingled Bodies*. New York, NY: Continuum, 2008: 1–16.

Crang, Mike, and Nigel Thrift, eds. *Thinking Space*. London: Routledge, 2000.

Cresswell, Tim. *On the Move: Mobility in the Modern Western World*. London: Routledge, 2006.

Csikszentmihalyi, Mihaly. *Flow: The Psychology of Optimal Experience*. New York, NY: Harper Perennial, 1991.

Desmet, Pieter, Paul Hekkert, and Hendrik Schifferstein. "Introduction." In Pieter Desmet and Hendrik Schifferstein, eds. *From Floating Wheelchairs to Mobile Car Parks, Selected Work from TU Delft: A Collection of 35 Experience-driven Design Projects*. The Hague: Eleven International Publishing, 2011.

Harman, Graham. *Guerrilla Metaphysics: Phenomenology and the Carpentry of Things*. Chicago, IL: Open Court, 2005.

Highmore, Ben, ed. *The Design Culture Reader*. London: Routledge, 2009.

IDEO. *Human-Centered Design Toolkit: An Open-source Toolkit to Inspire New Solutions in the Developing World*. Palo Alto, CA: IDEO, 2011.

Jantzen, Christian. "Experiencing and Experiences: A Psychological Framework." In Jon Sundbo and Flemming Sørensen, eds. *Handbook on the Experience Economy*. Cheltenham: Edward Elgar, 2013: 146–70.

Jelsma, Jaap. "Technology and behavior: A view from STS." *User Behavior and Technology Development* 20 (2006): 61–70.

Kelley, Tom, and David Kelley. *Creative Confidence: Unleashing the Creative Potential Within Us All*. New York, NY: Crown Business, 2013.

Klingmann, Anna. *Brandscapes: Architecture in the Experience Economy*. Cambridge, MA: MIT Press, 2007.

McDonagh, Deana, Paul Hekkert, Jeroen van Erp, and Diane Gyi. *Design and Emotion*. Boca Raton, FL: CRC Press, 2002.

Moggridge, Bill. *Designing Interactions*. Cambridge, MA: MIT Press, 2007.

—*Designing Media*. Cambridge, MA: MIT Press, 2010.

Norman, Donald A. *The Psychology of Everyday Things*. New York, NY: Basic Books, 1988.

—*Emotional Design: Why We Love (or Hate) Everyday Things*. New York, NY: Basic Books, 2005.

—*The Design of Everyday Things*. New York, NY: Basic Books, 2013.

Pine, B. Joseph II, and James H. Gilmore. *The Experience Economy: Work is Theatre and Every Business a Stage*. Boston, MA: Harvard Business School Press, 1999.

Schmitt, Bernd. *Experiential Marketing: How to Get Customers to Sense, Feel, Think, Act, and Relate to Your Company and Brands*. New York, NY: Free Press, 1999.

Serres, Michel. *Genesis*. Ann Arbor, MI: University of Michigan Press, 1995.

—*The Five Senses: A Philosophy of Mingled Bodies*. New York, NY: Continuum, 2008. [Originally published in French, *Les Cinq Sens*. Paris: Éditions Grasset et Fasquelle, 1985.)

Shanks, Michael. *Experiencing the Past: On the Character of Archaeology*. London: Routledge, 1992.

Shedroff, Nathan. *Experience Design 1*. Indianapolis, IN: New Riders, 2001.

Simonsen, Jesper, Connie Svabo, Sara Malou Strandvad, Kristine Samson, Morten Hertzum, and Ole Erik Hansen. "Situated Methods in Design." In Jesper Simonsen, Connie Svabo, Sara Malou Strandvad, Kristine Samson, Morten Hertzum, and Ole Erik Hansen, eds. *Situated Design Methods*. Cambridge, MA: MIT Press, 2014 (forthcoming).

Sundbo, Jon and Per Darmer. *Creating Experiences in the Experience Economy: Services, Economy and Innovation*. Cheltenham: Edward Elgar, 2008.

Sundbo, Jon and Flemming Sørensen. *Handbook on the Experience Economy*. Cheltenham: Edward Elgar, 2013.

Svabo, Connie. *Portable Objects at the Museum*. PhD thesis. Roskilde University, 2010. [Accessed on 27 March 2014 at http://rudar.ruc.dk/bitstream/1800/5583/4/Svabo_Portable%20Objects%20at%20the%20Museum%20(small%20file).pdf].

Thrift, Nigel. "Inhuman Geographies: Landscapes of Speed, Light and Power." In Paul Cloke, ed. *Writing the Rural: Five Cultural Geographies*. London: Paul Chapman, 1994: 191–250.

Tschumi, Bernard. *Architecture and Disjunction*. Cambridge, MA: MIT Press, 1994.

3 How Much Time Does it Take for Experience Design to Unfold?

Acuna, Alejandro, and Ricardo Sosa. "The Complementary Role of Representations in Design Creativity: Sketches and Models." In Toshiharu Taura, and Yukari Nagai, eds. *Design Creativity 2010*. London: Springer, 2011: 265–70.

Brown, Tim. "Design Thinking." *Harvard Business Review* 86, no. 6 (2008): 84–95.

Cain, Rebecca. *Involving Users in the Design Process: The Role of Product Representations in Co-designing*. Doctoral dissertation, Faculty of Social Sciences and Humanities, University of Loughborough, 2005.

Crilly, Nathan, Anja Maier, and P. John Clarkson. "Representing artefacts as media." *International Journal of Design* 2, no. 3 (2008): 15–27.

Darses, Françoise, and Marion Wolff. "How do designers represent to themselves the users' needs?" *Applied Ergonomics* 37, no. 6 (2006): 757–64.

Desmet, Pieter, and Paul Hekkert. "Framework of product experience." *International Journal of Design* 1, no. 1 (2007): 57–66.

Ehrlenspiel, Klaus. *Integrierte Produktentwicklung. Methoden für Prozeßorganisation, Produkterstellung und Konstruktion* [Integrated Product Development. Methods for Organizing Processes, Product Design and Construction]. Munich: Hanser, 1995.

Elsen, Catherine, Anders Häggman, Tomonori Honda, and Maria C. Yang. "Representation in Early Stage Design: An Analysis of the Influence of Sketching and Prototyping in Design Projects." *ASME 2012 International Design Engineering Technical Conferences and Computers and Information in Engineering Conference*. Chicago, IL: ASME, 2012: 737–47.

Ingold, Tim. "Anthropology is Not Ethnography." In Ron Johnston, ed. *Proceedings of the British Academy: Volume 154, 2007 Lectures*. London: British Academy, 2008: 69–92.

Jones, John C. *Design Methods: Seeds of Human Futures*. Chichester: John Wiley, 1970.

Lai, Justin, Tomonori Honda, and Maria C. Yang. "A study of the role of user-centered design methods in design team projects." *Artificial Intelligence for Engineering Design, Analysis and Manufacturing* 24 (2010): 303–16.

Law, Effie L.-C., Virpi Roto, Marc Hassenzahl, Arnold Vermeeren, and Joke Kort. "Understanding, Scoping and

Defining User Experience: A Survey Approach." *CHI '09 Proceedings of the SIGCHI Conference on Human Factors in Computing Systems*. New York, NY: ACM, 2009: 719–28.

Luck, Rachael, and Janet McDonnell. "Architect and user interaction: the spoken representation of form and functional meaning in early design Conversations." *Design Studies* 27, no. 2 (2006): 141–66.

Morris, Betsy. "Steve Jobs Speaks Out: *Fortune* Senior Editor Betsy Morris Interviewing Steve Jobs." In *CNN Money* (2008). [Accessed May 30, 2013 at http://money.cnn.com/galleries/2008/fortune/0803/gallery.jobsqna.fortune/index.html]

Oehlberg, Lora, Celeste Roschuni, and Alice Agogino. "A Descriptive Study of Designers' Tools for Capturing, Reflecting On, and Sharing User Needs and Conceptual Designs." ASME IDETC/CIE 2011. August 28–31. DETC 2011-48661 (2011).

Olsen, Tonje O., and Torgeir Welo. "Maximizing product innovation through adaptive application of user-centered methods for defining customer value." *Journal of Technology Management & Innovation* 6, no. 4 (2011): 172–92.

Osborn, Alex F. *Applied Imagination*. New York, NY: Charles Scribner and Sons, 1963.

Postma, Carolien E., Elly Zwartkruis-Pelgrim, Elke Daemen, and Jia Du. "Challenges of doing empathic design: experiences from industry." *International Journal of Design* 6, no. 1 (2012): 59–70.

Redström, Johan. "Towards user design? On the shift from object to user as the subject of design." *Design Studies* 27, no. 2 (2006): 123–39.

Van Someren, Marten, Yvonne Barnard, and Jacobijn Sandberg. *The Think Aloud Method: A Practical Guide to Modelling Cognitive Processes*. London: Academic Press, 1994.

Von Hippel, Eric, Stefan Thomke, and Mary Sonnack, M. "Creating breakthroughs at 3M." *Harvard Business Review* 77, no. 5 (1999): 47–57.

Wilkie, Alex. *User Assemblages in Design: An Ethnographic Study*. PhD dissertation, Goldsmiths, University of London, 2010.

Yang, Maria C. "A study of prototypes, design activity, and design outcome." *Design Studies* 26, no. 6 (2005): 649–69.

4 Experiential Equality and Digital Discrimination

Abdul-Rahman, Alfarez, and Stephen Hailes. "Supporting Trust in Virtual Communities." In *HICSS '00: Proceedings of the 33rd Hawaii International Conference on System Sciences*. Volume 6. Washington, DC: IEEE Computer Society (2000): 6007.

Buckingham, David, ed. *Youth, Identity, and Digital Media*. Cambridge, MA: MIT Press, 2008.

Cooper, Alan. *The Inmates are Running the Asylum: Why High-tech Products Drive us Crazy and How to Restore the Sanity*. Indianapolis, IN: Sams Publishing, 2004.

Dernie, David. *Exhibition Design*. New York, NY: W. W. Norton & Company, 2006.

Fogg, B. J. *Persuasive Technology: Using Computers to Change What We Think and Do*. San Francisco, CA: Morgan Kauffman, 2003.

Forlizzi, Jodi, and Katja Battarbee. "Understanding Experience in Interactive Systems." *DIS '04: Proceedings of the 5th Conference on Designing Interactive Systems: Processes, Practices, Methods and Techniques*. New York, NY: ACM, 2004: 261–8.

Henderson, Samantha, and Michael Gilding. "I've never clicked this much with anyone in my life: Trust and hyperpersonal communication in online friendships." *New Media & Society* 6, no. 4 (2004): 487–506.

Kadende-Kaiser, Rose. "Interpreting language and cultural discourse: internet communication among Burundians in the diaspora." *Africa Today* 47, no. 2 (2000): 120–48.

Katz, James, and Mark Aakhus, eds. *Perpetual Contact: Mobile Communication, Private Talk, Public Performance*. Cambridge: Cambridge University Press, 2002.

Khaslavsky, Julie, and Nathan Shedroff. "Understanding the seductive experience." *Communications of the ACM* 42, no. 5 (1999): 45–9.

Kuniavsky, Mike. *Observing the User Experience: A Practitioner's Guide to User Research*. San Francisco, CA: Morgan Kaufmann, 2003.

Leena, Koivusilta, Tomi Lintonen, and Arja Rimpelä. "Intensity of mobile phone use and health compromising behaviours—how is information and communication technology connected to a health-rrelated lifestyle in adolescence?" *Journal of Adolescence* 28, no. 1 (2005): 35–47.
Leung, Linda. *Digital Experience Design: Ideas, Industries, Interaction.* Bristol: Intellect Books, 2008.
—*Mind the Gap: Refugees and Communication Technology Literacy.* Sydney: Australian Communications Consumer Action Network, 2011.
Leung, Linda, and Cat Finney Lamb. *Refugees and Communication Technology.* Sydney: UTS Shopfront, 2010.
Leung, Linda, Cat Finney Lamb, and Liz Emrys. *Technology's Refuge: The Use of Technology by Asylum Seekers and Refugees.* Sydney: UTS ePress, 2009.
Norman, Donald A. *The Design of Everyday Things.* New York, NY: Basic Books, 2002.
—*Emotional Design: Why We Love (or Hate) Everyday Things.* New York, NY: Basic Books, 2004.
Preece, Jenny. "Empathic communities: reaching out across the web." *Interactions* 5, no. 2 (1998): 32–43.
Shedroff, Nathan. *Experience Design 1.* Indianapolis, IN: Black Riders, 2001.
United Nations High Commissioner for Refugees (UNHCR). "About Refugees." [Accessed May 25, 2013 at http://www.unrefugees.org.au]
Wilska, Terhi-Anna. "Mobile phone use as part of young people's consumption styles." *Journal of Consumer Policy* 26, no. 4 (2003): 441–63.
Wyatt, Sally, Flis Henwood, Nod Miller, and Peter Senker. *Technology and In/equality: Questioning the Information Society.* London: Routledge, 2001.

Part Two: Objects and Environments

5 Narrativity of Object Interaction Experiences: A Framework for Designing Products as Narrative Experiences

Abbott, H. Porter. *The Cambridge Introduction to Narrative.* 2nd edition. Cambridge: Cambridge University Press, 2008.
Bal, Mieke. *Travelling Concepts in the Humanities: A Rough Guide.* Toronto; London: University of Toronto Press, 2002.
Baroni, Raphael. "Tellability." In Peter Hühn et al., eds. *The Living Handbook of Narratology.* Hamburg: Hamburg University Press, 2013. [Accessed June 13, 2014 at hup.sub.uni-hamburg.de/lhn/index.php?title=Tellability&oldid=2035]
Blythe, Mark A., and Peter C. Wright. "Pastiche scenarios: fiction as a resource for user centred design." *Interacting with Computers* 18, no. 5 (2006): 1139–64.
Bordwell, David. *Narration in the Fiction Film.* Madison, WI: University of Wisconsin Press, 1985.
Bruner, Jerome. "The narrative construction of reality." *Critical Inquiry* 18, no. 1 (1991): 1–21.
Desmet, Pieter, and Paul Hekkert. "Framework of product experience." *International Journal of Design* 1, no. 1 (2007): 57–66.
Dewey, John. *Art as Experience.* New York, NY: Perigee Books, 2005.
Dukíc, Goran. *Wristcutters: A Love Story.* Autonomous Films, 2007.
Forlizzi, Jodi. *Designing for Experience: An Approach to Human-centered Design.* Master of Design thesis, Department of Design, College of Fine Arts, Carnegie Mellon University, 1997.
Gell, Alfred. *Art and Agency: An Anthropological Theory.* Oxford: Oxford University Press, 1998.
Grimaldi, Silvia. "The Ta-Da Series: Presentation of a Technique and its Use in Generating a Series of Surprising Designs." In Mari Anne Karlsson, Pieter Desmet, and Jeroen van Erp, eds. *Proceedings from the 5th Conference on Design and Emotion 2006.* Göteborg: Chalmers University of Technology, 2006.
—"The Ta-Da Series: A Technique for Generating Surprising Designs Based on Opposites and Gut Reactions." In Pieter Desmet, Mari Anne Karlsson, and Jeroen van Erp, eds. *Design and Emotion Moves.* Newcastle upon Tyne: Cambridge Scholars Publishing, 2008: 165–89.

—"Cinematic Narratives of Product Interaction Experiences: Methods for Cross-media Fertilisation of the Design Process." In Jamie Brasset, Paul Hekkert, Geke Ludden, Matt Malpass, and Janet McDonnell, eds. *Out of Control: Proceedings of 8th International Design and Emotion Conference*. London: Central Saint Martin's College of Arts & Design, 2012.

—"Story of Use: Analysis of Film Narratives to Inform the Design of Object Interactions." In Eva Brandt, Pelle Ehn, Troels Degn Johansson, Maria Hellström Reimer, Thomas Markussen, and Anna Vallgårda, eds. *Nordes 2013: Experiments in Design Research Online Proceedings*. Copenhagen: The Royal Danish Academy of Fine Arts, 2013: 374–7.

Hassenzahl, Marc. *Experience Design: Technology for All the Right Reasons*. San Rafael, CA: Morgan & Claypool, 2010.

Herman, David. *Story Logic: Problems and Possibilities of Narrative*. Lincoln, NE: University of Nebraska Press, 2004.

Kim, Ji-woon. *A Tale of Two Sisters*. Cineclick Asia; Big Blue Film, 2008.

Leigh, Mike. *Vera Drake*. Momentum Pictures; Fine Line Features, 2004.

Löwgren, Jonas. "Toward an articulation of interaction aesthetics." *The New Review of Hypermedia and Multimedia* 15, no. 2 (2009): 129–46.

McKee, Robert. *Story: Substance, Structure, Style and the Principles of Screenwriting*. New York, NY: HarperCollins, 1999.

Ryan, Marie-Laure. "On the Theoretical Foundations of Transmedial Narratology." In Jan C. Meister, ed. *Narratology beyond Literary Criticism. Mediality, Disciplinarity*. Berlin: Walter de Gruyter, 2005: 1–23.

Sacks, Oliver. *The Man Who Mistook His Wife for a Hat and Other Clinical Tales*. New York, NY: Simon & Schuster, 1998.

Shainberg, Steven. *Secretary*. Lionsgate, 2002.

Stern, Daniel N. *The Present Moment in Psychotherapy and Everyday Life*. New York, NY: W. W. Norton & Company, 2004.

Wright, Peter, and John McCarthy. "Empathy and Experience in HCI." In *CHI '08: Proceedings of the SIGCHI Conference on Human Factors in Computing Systems*. New York, NY: ACM, 2008: 637–46.

Young, Kay, and Jeffrey L. Saver. "The neurology of narrative." *SubStance* 30, no.1/2 (2001): 72–84.

6 Centers of Experience: Bodies and Objects in Today's Museums

Belting, Hans. "Place of Reflection or Place of Sensation." In Peter Noever, ed. *The Discursive Museum*. Vienna: MAK, 2001.

Bennett, Tony. *The Birth of the Museum: History, Theory, Politics*. New York, NY: Routledge, 1995.

Bishop, Claire. *Artificial Hells: Participatory Art and the Politics of Spectatorship*. New York, NY: Verso, 2012.

Busch, Otto von. "Fashion Hacking." In Susan Yelavich and Barbara Adams, eds. *Design as Future-Making*. London: Berg, 2014 (forthcoming).

Cauman, Samuel. *The Living Museum*. New York, NY: New York University Press, 1958.

Deleuze, Gilles. *Negotiations 1972–1990*. New York, NY: Columbia University Press, 1997.

Dierking, Lynn, and John Falk. "Redefining the Museum Experience: The Interactive Experience Model." In Arlene Benefield, Stephen Bitgood, and Harris Shettel, eds. *Visitor Studies: Theory, Research, and Practice*. Jacksonville, AL: Center of Social Design, 1992: 173–6.

—*The Museum Experience*. Walnut Creek, CA: Left Coast Press, 2011.

Duncan, Carol. *Civilizing Rituals: Inside Public Art Museums*. New York, NY: Routledge, 1995.

Foucault, Michel. "Of other spaces." *Diacritics* 16, no. 1 (1986): 22–7.

Fried, Michael. *Art and Objecthood: Essays and Reviews*. Chicago, IL: University of Chicago Press, 1998.

Hantelmann, Dorothea von. *How to Do Things with Art: The Meaning of Art's Performativity*. Zürich: JRP Ringier and Presses du Réel, 2010.

Helguera, Pablo. *Education for Socially Engaged Art: A Materials and Techniques Handbook*. New York, NY: Jorge Pinto, 2011.

Klonk, Charlotte. *Spaces of Experience: Art Gallery Interiors from 1800 to 2000*. New Haven, CT: Yale University Press, 2009.

Kwinter, Sanford. "Playboys of the Western World." In Cynthia Davidson, ed. *Far From Equilibrium: Essays on Technology and Design Culture*. New York, NY: Actar, 2008: 22–35.
Lefebvre, Henri. *The Production of Space*. Malden, MA: Blackwell, 1992.
LeWitt, Sol. "Paragraphs on conceptual art." *Artforum* 5, no. 10 (1967): 79–83.
Lippard, Lucy. *Six Years: The Dematerialization of the Art Object from 1966 to 1972*. Berkeley, CA: University of California Press, 1973.
Mouffe, Chantal. "From antagonistic politics to an agonistic public space." *Artforum International* 48, no. 10 (2010): 326–84.
O'Doherty, Brian. *Inside the White Cube: The Ideology of the Gallery Space*. Berkeley, CA: University of California Press, 1999.
Pine, B. Joseph II, and James H. Gilmore. *The Experience Economy: Work is Theater and Every Business a Stage*. Cambridge, MA: Harvard Business School, 1999.
Price, Cedric, and Joan Littlewood. "The fun palace." *The Drama Review* 12, no. 3 (1968): 127–34.
Situationist International. "Preliminary Problems in Constructing a Situation." *Internationale Situationniste* no. 1 (1968).
Staniszewski, Mary Anne. *The Power of Display: A History of Exhibition Installations at the Museum of Modern Art*. Cambridge, MA: MIT, 1998.
Thompson, Nato, ed. *Living as Form: Socially Engaged Art from 1991–2011*. Cambridge, MA: MIT Press, 2012.

7 Space, Experience, Identity, and Meaning

Chan, Heinsen. "Crowne Plaza & Holiday Inn Express." Interview by Peter Benz. Tsuen Kwan O, March 22, 2013.
Cooper, Anthony Ashley (3rd Earl of Shaftesbury). "The Moralists: A Philosophical Rhapsody. A Recital, of Certain Conversations on Natural and Moral Subjects." In Philip Ayres, ed. *Characteristicks of Men, Manners, Opinions*. Volume 2. Oxford: Oxford University Press, 1999: 3–124.
Desmet, Pieter, and Hendrik Schifferstein, eds. *From Floating Wheelchairs to Mobile Car Parks: A Collection of 35 Experience-driven Design Projects*. The Hague: Eleven International, 2011.
Führ, Eduard. "Frankfurter Küche" und Spaghetti Carbonara: Funktionalität von Architektur und Kunst des Gebrauchens." [Accessed August 10, 2013 at http://www.tu-cott,bus.de/theoriederarchitektur/Lehrstuhl/deu/gebrauch.html]
Hogarth, William. *The Analysis of Beauty*. Pittsfield, MA: The Silver Lotus Shop, 1909.
Hume, David. *A Treatise of Human Nature*. Edited by Lewis A. Selby-Bigge and Peter H. Nidditch. 2nd edition. Oxford: Clarendon Press, 1978.
Interconti Hotel Group. "The World of IHG." Presented at the IHG Brand Briefing, Crowne Plaza Tsuen Kwan O, Hong Kong, November 24, 2012.
Loos, Adolf. "The Poor Little Rich Man." In *Spoken into the Void: Collected Essays 1897–1900*. Cambridge, MA: MIT Press, 1982.
McAteer, John. "The Third Earl of Shaftesbury (1671–1713)." In *Internet Encyclopedia of Philosophy* (2011). [Accessed September 13, 2013 at http://www.iep.utm.edu/shaftes/]
Machens, Cord. "Neues zur Entstehung der Arten für Charles Darwin (1809*) und A. von Humboldt (1859†). VI. Tektonische Versuche im Steinkohlenwald." In *Bauwelt*, 2010.
Pallasmaa, Juhani. "Geometry of Feeling: The Phenomenology of Architecture." In A. Krista Sykes, ed. *The Architecture Reader: Essential Writings from Vitruvius to the Present*. New York, NY: George Braziller, 2007: 242–5.
Poole, Adrian. "Identity of Meaning." In *Identity. Darwin College Lectures 21*. Cambridge; New York, NY: Cambridge University Press, 2010.

8 Four Themes to (Phenomenologically) Understand Contemporary Urban Spaces

Baudrillard, Jean. *Simulacra and Simulation*. Ann Arbor, MI: University of Michigan Press, 1994.

Boym, Svetlana. *The Future of Nostalgia*. New York, NY: Basic Books, 2001.

Butler, Judith. *Gender Trouble: Feminism and the Subversion of Identity*. New York, NY: Routledge, 2006.

Castello, Lineu. *Rethinking the Meaning of Place: Conceiving Place in Architecture-Urbanism*. Farnham: Ashgate, 2010.

Crawford, Margaret. "Introduction." In John Chase, Margaret Crawford, and John Kaliski, eds. *Everyday Urbanism*. Expanded edition. New York, NY: Monacelli Press, 2008.

De Certeau, M. *The Practice of Everyday Life*. Berkeley, CA; London: University of California Press, 1988.

Deleuze, Gilles, and Felix Guattari. *A Thousand Plateaus: Capitalism and Schizophrenia*. New edition. London; New York, NY: Continuum, 2004.

Dovey, Kim. *Becoming Places: Urbanism/Architecture/Identity/Power*. London: Routledge, 2010.

Franck, Karen A., and Quentin Stevens. *Loose Space: Possibility and Diversity in Urban Life*. London: Routledge, Taylor & Francis, 2007.

Gallagher, Winifred. *The Power of Place: How our Surroundings Shape our Thoughts, Emotions, and Actions*. New York, NY; London: Harper Perennial, 2007.

Gehl, Jan. *Life between Buildings: Using Public Space*. Washington, DC: Island Press, 2011.

Jameson, Fredric. *Postmodernism or The Cultural Logic of Late Capitalism*. London: Verso, 1991.

Josselson, Ruthellen. "Identity and Relatedness in the Life Cycle." In Harke A. Bosma, David J. de Levita, Tobi Graafsma, and Harold D. Grotevant, eds. *Identity and Development: An Interdisciplinary Approach*. London: Sage, 1994: 81–102.

Kaplan, Stephen. "The restorative benefits of nature: toward an integrative framework." *Journal of Environmental Psychology* 15 (1995): 169–82.

Korpela, Kalevi, Terry Hartig, Florian G. Kaiser, and Urs Fuhrer. "Restorative experience and self-regulation in favorite places." *Environment and Behavior* 33, no. 4 (2001): 572–89.

Lawson, Bryan. *The Language of Space*. Oxford: Architectural Press, 2001.

Leach, Neil. "Belonging: Towards a Theory of Identification with Space." In Jean Hillier and Emma Roorksby, eds. *Habitus: A Sense of Place*. 2nd edition. Farnham: Ashgate, 2005: 297–311.

Lefebvre, Henri. *Critique of Everyday Life. Volume 1: Introduction*. London: Verso, 1991.

McLeod, Mary. "Henry Lefebvre's Critique of Everyday Life: An Introduction." In Steve Harris, and Deborah Berke, eds. *Architecture of the Everyday*. New York, NY: Princeton Architectural Press, 1997: 9–29.

Massey, Doreen B. "A global sense of place." *Marxism Today* 38 (1991): 24–9.

—*For Space*. London: Sage, 2005.

Merleau-Ponty, Maurice. *Phenomenology of Perception*. London: Routledge Classics, 2002.

Norberg-Schulz, Christian. *Genius Loci: Towards a Phenomenology of Architecture*. New York, NY: Rizzoli, 1980.

Pallasmaa, Juhani. *The Eyes of the Skin: Architecture and the Senses*. New edition. Chichester: Wiley-Academy, 2005.

Petcou, Constantin. "Media-Polis/Media-City." In Neil Leach, ed. *The Hieroglyphics of Space: Reading and Experiencing the Modern Metropolis*. London: Routledge, 2002: 282–8.

Proshansky, Harold M., Abbe K. Fabian, and Robert Kaminoff. "Place-identity: physical world socialization of the self." *Journal of Environmental Psychology* 3, no. 1 (1983): 57–83.

Relph, Edward. *Place and Placelessness: Research in Planning and Design*. London: Pion, 1976.

Sack, Robert D. *Homo Geographicus: A Framework for Action, Awareness, and Moral Concern*. Baltimore, MD: Johns Hopkins University Press, 1997.

Smith, Jonathan A. *Interpretative Phenomenological Analysis: Theory, Method and Research*. Los Angeles, CA; London: Sage, 2009.

Soja, Edward W. *Thirdspace: Journeys to Los Angeles and Other Real-and-Imagined Places*. Cambridge, MA; Oxford: Blackwell, 1996.

Tschumi, Bernard. "The Architectural Paradox." In K. Michael Hays, ed. *Architecture Theory since 1968.* Cambridge, MA; London: MIT Press, 1998: 219.

Van Eyck, Aldo. "The Dogon People 2." In Charles Jencks and George Baird, eds. *Meaning in Architecture.* New York, NY: George Braziller, 1970: 218–28.

Virilio, Paul. *Polar Inertia.* London: Sage, 2001.

Vischer, Robert, Conrad Fiedler, Heinrich Wölfflin, Adolf Göller, Adolf Hildebrand, and August Schmarsow. *Empathy, Form and Space: Problems in German Aesthetics 1873–1893.* Chicago, IL: Getty Center for the History of Art, 1994.

Walmsley, D. J. *Urban Living: The Individual in the City.* London: Longman Scientific & Technical, 1988.

Wise, John M. "Ecstatic Assemblages of Visuality." In Hille Koskela and John M. Wise, eds. *New Visualities, New Technologies: The New Ecstasy of Communication.* Farnham; Burlington, VT: Ashgate, 2012: 1–5.

Wodiczko, Krzysztof. *Critical Vehicles: Writings, Projects, Interviews.* Cambridge, MA: MIT Press, 1999.

Part Three: Interactions and Performances

9 Co-Producing a Festival Experience: A Socio-Material Understanding of Experience Design

Akrich, Madeleine. "The De-scription of Technical Objects." In Wiebe E. Bijker and John Law, eds. *Shaping Technology/Building Society: Studies in Sociotechnical Change.* Cambridge, MA: MIT Press, 1992: 205–24.

Born, Georgina. "The social and the aesthetic: towards a post-bourdieuian theory of cultural production." *Cultural Sociology* 4, no. 2 (2010): 171–208.

Boswijk, Albert, Thomas Thijssen, and Ed Peelen. *The Experience Economy: A New Perspective.* Amsterdam: Pearson Education Benelux, 2007.

Callon, Michel. "Some Elements of a Sociology of Translation: Domestication of the Scallops and the Fishermen of St. Brieuc Bay." In John Law, ed. *Power, Action and Belief: A New Sociology of Knowledge?* London: Routledge, 1986: 196–223.

DeNora, Tia. *Music in Everyday Life.* Cambridge; New York, NY: Cambridge University Press, 2000.

Dewey, John. *Art as Experience.* New York, NY: Minton, Balch & Company, 1959.

Gomart, Emilie, and Antoine Hennion. "A Sociology of Attachment: Music Amateurs, Drug Users." In John Law and John Hassard, eds. *Actor Network Theory and After.* Oxford: Blackwell Publishers, 1999: 220–47.

Hennion, Antoine. "Music lovers: taste as performance." *Theory, Culture & Society* 18, no. 5 (2001): 1–22.

—"Those things that hold us together: taste and sociology." *Cultural Sociology* 1, no. 1 (2007): 97–114.

Humphreys, Ashlee, and Kent Grayson. "The intersecting roles of consumer and producer: a critical perspective on co-production, co-creation and prosumption." *Sociology Compass* 2, no. 3 (2008): 963–80.

Latour, Bruno. "Technology is Society Made Durable." In John Law, ed. *A Sociology of Monsters? Essays on Power, Technology and Domination.* London: Routledge, 1991: 103–31.

Norman, Donald A. *The Design of Everyday Things.* New York, NY: Doubleday, 1988.

Pine, B. Joseph II, and James H. Gilmore. *The Experience Economy: Work is Theater and Every Business a Stage.* Cambridge, MA: Harvard Business School, 1999.

Prahalad, C. K., and Venkat Ramaswamy. *The Future of Competition: Co-creating Unique Value with Customers.* Boston, MA: Harvard Business School Press, 2004.

Roskilde Festival. "Roskilde Dictionary". No date. [Accessed January 6, 2014 at http://roskilde-festival.dk/camping/practical/festival_for_beginners/roskilde_dictionary/]

Turner, Victor. "Liminality and Communitas." In Victor Turner, Roger D. Abrahams, and Alfred Harris, eds. *The Ritual Process: Structure and Anti-structure.* Chicago, IL: Aldine Publishing, 1969: 94–113.

10 CurioUs: The Logic of Performance

Anderson, Andrea. *The Community Builder's Approach to Theory of Change: A Practical Guide to Theory Development*. New York, NY: The Aspen Institute Roundtable on Community Change, 2011.

Findeiss, Amy, Eulani Labay, and Kelly Tierney. "CurioUs: Dynamic-led Aesthetics of Performance." In Helinä Melkas, and Jacob Buur, eds. *PIN-C '13: Proceedings of the Participatory Innovation Conference*. Lahti: Lappeenranta University of Technology, 2013: 92–5.

Lehrer, Rachel. "Performing in Public Space." Interview by Amy Findeiss, Eulani Labay, and Kelly Tierney. New York, NY: November 3, 2011.

Metropolitan Transportation Authority. "Facts and Figures," n.d.a [Accessed October 4, 2011 at http://www.mta.info/nyct/facts/ffsubway.htm]

—"Arts for Transit and Urban Design," n.d.b [Accessed October 4, 2011 at http://www.mta.info/mta/aft/muny]

Nichols, Matthew. "Interaction with Commuters and Repurposing of Space." Interview by Amy Findeiss. New York, NY: October 11, 2011.

Petersen, Marianne G., Ole S. Iversen, Peter G. Krogh, and Martin Ludvigsen. "Aesthetic Interaction: A Pragmatist's Aesthetics of Interactive Systems." In *DIS '04: Proceedings of the 5th Conference on Designing Interactive Systems: Processes, Practices, Methods, and Techniques*. New York, NY: ACM, 2004: 269–76.

11 Designing for a Better Patient Experience

Fox, Susannah. *Online Health Search 2006*. Washington, DC: The Pew Research Center: 2006.

Fox, Susannah and Sydney Jones. *The Social Life of Health Information*. Washington, DC: The Pew Research Center, 2009.

Horn, Robert E. "Information Design: The Emergence of a New Profession." In Robert Jacobson, ed. *Information Design*. Cambridge, MA: MIT Press, 2000: 15–34.

Lane, Marty M., and Gretchen C. Rinnert. "Interactive Tools and Online Communities that Support Media Literacy." In David Durling, Rabah Bousbaci, Lin-Lin Chen, et al., eds. *Proceedings from Design Research Society 2010: Design & Complexity*. Montreal: Université de Montréal, 2010.

Sarasohn-Kahn, Jane. *The Wisdom of Patients: Health Care Meets Online Social Media*. Oakland, CA: California HealthCare Foundation, 2008.

Stanford Hospital and Clinics. "In Stanford Hospital Unit, iPads Fill in for TVs as Patient Entertainment." In Stanford Hospital and Clinics (2010). [Accessed November 21, 2011 at http:// stanfordhospital.org/newsEvents/newsReleases/2010/ipads-release.html]

Snyderman, Nancy, prod. "More Kids Skipping School Vaccines." In *NBC Nightly News with Brian Williams*. November 28, 2011 [Television broadcast].

Thomas, Richard K. *Health Communication*. New York, NY: Springer Science + Business Media, 2006.

Wright, Kevin B., Lisa Sparks, and H. Dan O'Hair. *Health Communication in the 21st Century*. Malden, MA: Blackwell, 2012.

12 Designing Mobile User Experiences: A Framework for a Design Methodology

Amabile, Teresa, Constance N. Hadley, and Steven J. Kramer. "Creativity under the gun." *Harvard Business Review* 80, no. 8 (2002): 52–61.

Battarbee, Katja, and Ilpo Koskinen. "Co-experience: user experience as interaction." *CoDesign* 1, no. 1 (2005): 5–18.

Buxton, William. *Sketching User Experiences: Getting the Design Right and the Right Design*. San Francisco, CA: Morgan Kaufmann, 2007.

Cropley, Arthur. "In praise of convergent thinking." *Creativity Research Journal* 18, no. 3 (2006): 391–404.

DegreeDirectory. "What is Design Methodology?" [Accessed August 25, 2013 at http:// degreedirectory.org/ articles/What_is_Design_Methodology.html]

De Sá, Marco, and Luís Carriço. "Lessons from Early Stages Design of Mobile Applications." *MobileHCI '08: Proceedings of the 10th International Conference on Human Computer Interaction with Mobile Devices and Services*. New York, NY: ACM, 2008: 127–36.

Duh, Henry, Gerald Tan, and Vivian Chen. "Usability Evaluation for Mobile Device: A Comparison of Laboratory and Field Tests." *MobileHCI '06: Proceedings of the 8th International Conference on Human Computer Interaction with Mobile Devices and Services*. New York, NY: ACM, 2006: 181–6.

Durrant, Abigail, Michael Golembewski, David Kirk, Steve Benford, Duncan Rowland, and Derek McAuley. "Exploring a Digital Economy Design Space in Theme Parks." *DESIRE '11: Proceedings of the Second Conference on Creativity and Innovation in Design*. New York, NY: ACM, 2010: 273–84.

Edelson, Daniel C. "Design research: what we learn when we engage in design." *Journal of the Learning Sciences* 11, no.1 (2009): 105–21.

Glushko, Robert. "Seven Contexts for Service System Design." In Paul P. Maglio, Cheryl A. Kieliszewski, and James C. Spohrer, eds. *Handbook of Service Science*. New York, NY: Springer, 2010: 219–49.

Irvine, Ashley. "The Evolving Trend of Theme Park Apps." [Accessed on February 6, 2013 at http://www.themeparknewsdirect.com/2010/07/the- evolving-trend-of-theme-parkapps]

Jumisko-Pyykkö, Satu, Mandy Weitzel, and Dominic Strohmeier. "Designing for User Experience: What to Expect from Mobile 3D TV and Video?" *UXTV '08: Proceedings of the 1st International Conference on Designing Interactive User Experiences for TV and Video*. New York, NY: ACM, 2008: 183–92.

Østergaard, Claus. "A Foundation for Mobile User Experience in Theme Parks." *Proceedings of Academic Mindtrek 2013*. New York, NY: ACM, 2013: 30–8.

Pine, B. Joseph II, and James H. Gilmore. *The Experience Economy*. Updated edition. Boston, MA: Harvard Business Review Press, 2011.

Richardson, Ingrid, and Rowan Wilken. "Parerga of the Third Screen: Mobile Media, Place, and Presence." In Rowan Wilken, and Gerard Goggin, eds. *Mobile Technology and Place*. London: Routledge, 2012: 181–97.

Roto, Virpi. *Web Browsing on Mobile Phones: Characteristics of User Experience*. PhD disseration. Espoo: Helsinki University of Technology, 2006.

Sims, Niki H. *How to Run a Great Workshop: The Complete Guide to Designing and Running Brilliant Workshops and Meetings*. London: Pearson Business, 2006.

Stößel, Christian. "Familiarity as a Factor in Designing Finger Gestures for Elderly Users." *MobileHCI '09: Proceedings of the 11th International Conference on Human–Computer Interaction with Mobile Devices and Services*. New York, NY: ACM, 2009.

Strauss, Anselm C., and Juliet M. Corbin. *Basics of Qualitative Research: Grounded Theory Procedures and Techniques*. Thousand Oaks, CA: Sage Publications, 1990.

Taminen, Sakari, Antti Oulasvirta, Kalle Toiskallio, and Anu Kankainen. "Understanding mobile contexts." *Personal and Ubiquitous Computing* 8, no. 2 (2004): 135–43.

Wigelius, Heli, and Heli Väätäjä. "Dimensions of Context Affecting User Experience in Mobile Work." In Tom Gross, Jan Gulliksen, Paula Kotzé, Lars Oestreicher et al., eds. *Proceedings of INTERACT 2009: The 12th International Conference of the International Federation for Information Processing*. Berlin; Heidelberg: Springer, 2009.

Wilken, Rowan and Gerard Goggin. "Mobilizing Place: Conceptual Currents and Controversies." In Rowan Wilken and Gerard Goggin, eds. *Mobile Technology and Place*. London: Routledge, 2012: 3–25.

Wright, Peter, John McCarthy, and Lisa Meekison. "Making Sense of Experience." In Mark A. Blythe, Kees Overbeeke, Andrew F. Monk, and Peter C. Wright, eds. *In Funology: From Usability to Enjoyment*. Dordrecht: Kluwer Academic Publishers, 2004: 43–53.

13 Suspending Reality: A Disruptive Approach to Designing Transformative Experiences

Design Council. *Double Diamond Design Process*. London: Design Council, 2005. [Accessed at http:// www. designcouncil.org.uk/designprocess]

Dunne, Anthony, and Fiona Raby. "Critical Design F.A.Q." In Léa Gauthier, ed. *Design for Change*. Paris: Black Jack Editions, 2011.

Hassenzahl, Marc. *Experience Design: Technology for All the Right Reasons*. San Rafael, CA: Morgan & Claypool, 2010.

Koskinen, Ilpo, John Zimmerman, Thomas Binder, Johan Redström, and Stephan Wensveen. *Design Research Through Practice: Lab, Field and Showroom*. Waltham, MA: Morgan Kaufmann, 2011.

Mullaney, Tara. "Designing for Durable Relationships with Products." In Kei Sato, Pieter Desmet, Paul Hekkert, Geke Ludden, and Anijo Mathew, eds. *Proceedings from the 7th International Conference on Design & Emotion*. Chicago, IL: IIT, 2010.

Mullaney, Tara, Tufve Nyholm, and David Edvardsson. "Wellbeing in Healthcare Environments: A Human-Centered Design Research Approach to Improving the Cancer Patient Experience during Radiation Therapy." In Alaster Yoxall, ed. *Proceedings of the 1st European Conference on Design4Health*. Sheffield: Sheffield Hallam University, 2011: 255–65.

Nelson, Harold G., and Erik Stolterman. *The Design Way: Intentional Change in an Unpredictable World*. Englewood Cliffs, NJ: Educational Technology Publications, 2003.

Pine, B. Joseph II, and James H. Gilmore. "Welcome to the experience economy." *Harvard Business Review* 76 (1998): 97–105.

Schön, Donald A. *The Reflective Practitioner: How Professionals Think in Action*. New York, NY: Basic Books, 1983.

14 Understanding and Designing the Meal Experience and its Psychological Consequences

Adrià, Ferran, Juli Soler, and Albert Adrià. *A Day at elBulli*. London: Phaidon, 2008.

Aduriz, Andoni L. *Mugaritz: A Natural Science of Cooking*. London: Phaidon, 2012.

Baas, Matthijs, Carsten K. W. De Dreu, and Bernard A. Nijstad. "A meta-analysis of 25 years of mood-creativity research: Hedonic tone, activation, or regulatory focus?" *Psychological Bulletin* 134, no. 6 (2008): 779–806.

Bell, Rick, Herbert L. Meiselman, Barry J. Pierson, and William G. Reeve. "Effects of Adding an Italian Theme to a Restaurant on Perceived Ethnicity, Acceptability, and Selection of Foods." *Appetite* 22, no. 1 (1994): 11–24.

Bless, Herbert, and Klaus Fiedler. "Affective States and the Influence of Activated General Knowledge." *Personality and Social Psychology Bulletin* 21, no. 7 (1995): 766–78.

Blumenthal, Heston. *The Fat Duck Cookbook*. London: Bloomsbury, 2008.

Boutrolle, Isabelle, Julien Delarue, Delphine Arranz, Michel Rogeaux, and Egon P. Köster. "Central Location Test vs. Home Use Test: Contrasting Results Depending on Product Type." *Food Quality and Preference* 18, no. 3 (2007): 490–9.

Cardello, Armand V., Rick Bell, and F. Matthew Kramer. "Attitudes of Consumers Toward Military and Other Institutional Foods." *Food Quality and Preference* 7, no. 1 (1996): 7–20.

Castro, John M. de, and Elisabeth S. de Castro. "Spontaneous Meal Patterns of Humans: Influence of the Presence of Other People." *American Journal of Clinical Nutrition* 50 (1989): 237–47.

Danziger, Shai, Jonathan Levav, and Liora Avnaim-Pesso. "Extraneous Factors in Judicial Decisions." *Proceedings of the National Academy of Sciences of the United States of America* 108, no. 17 (2011): 6889–92.

Edwards, John S. A., Herbert L. Meiselman, Audrey Edwards, and Larry Lesher. "The Influence of Eating Location on the Acceptability of Identically Prepared Foods." *Food Quality and Preference* 14, no. 8 (2003): 647–52.

Falkenstein, Michael, Jörg Hoormann, Stephan Christ, and Joachim Hohnsbein. "ERP Components on Reaction Erors and their Functional Significance: A Tutorial." *Biological Psychology* 51 (2000): 87–107.

Fischler, Claude. "Commensality, Society and Culture." *Social Science Information* 50 (2011): 528–48.

Flammang, J. A. *The Taste for Civilization: Food, Politics, and Civil Society*. Urbana and Chicago, IL: University of Illinois Press, 2009.

Holm, Lotte, Marianne P. Ekström, Jukka Gronow, Unni Kjærnes, Thomas B. Lund, Johanna Mäkelä, and Mari Niva. "The Modernisation of Nordic Eating: Studying Changes and Stabilities in Eating Patterns." *Anthropology of Food* 7 (2012): 2–14.

Hurst, Rachel, and Jane Lawrence. "Raw, Medium, Well Done: A Typological Reading of Australian Eating Places." *Architectural Design* 75, no. 3 (2005): 11–19.

Jones, Martin. *Feast: Why Humans Share Food*. Oxford: Oxford University Press, 2007.

King, Silvia C., Herbert L. Meiselman, Annette W. Hottenstein, Therese M. Work, and Valerie Cronk. "The Effects of Contextual Variables on Food Acceptability: A Confirmatory Study." *Food Quality and Preference* 18, no. 1 (2007): 58–65.

King, Silvia C., Annette J. Weber, Herbert L. Meiselman, and Nan Lv. "The Effect of Meal Situation, Social Interaction, Physical Environment and Choice on Food Acceptability." *Food Quality and Preference* 15, no. 7–8 (2004): 645–53.

Kniffin, Kevin M., and Brian Wansink, B. "It's not just Lunch: Extra-pair Commensality can Trigger Sexual Jealousy." *PLoS ONE* 7, no. 7 (2012): DOI: 10.1371/journal.pone.0040445.

Kornblum, Sylvan, Thierry Hasbrouqc, and Allen Osman. "Dimensional Overlap: Cognitive Basis for Stimulus-response Compatibility—A Model and Taxonomy." *Psychological Review* 97, no. 2 (1990): 253–70.

Kramer, F. Matthew, Larry L. Lesher, and Herbert L. Meiselman. "Monotony and Choice: Repeated Serving of the Same Item to Soldiers Under Field Conditions." *Appetite* 36, no. 3 (2001): 239–40.

Leuthold, Hartmut, and Werner Sommer. "ERP Correlates of Error Processing in Spatial s-r Compatibility Tasks." In *Clinical Neurophysiology* 110, no. 2 (1999): 342–57.

Lyubomirsky, Sonja, Laura King, and Ed Diener. "The Benefits of Frequent Positive Affect: Does Happiness Lead to Success?" *Psychological Bulletin* 131, no. 6 (2005): 803–55.

Meiselman, Herbert L. "Experiencing Products within a Physical and Social Context." In Hendrik Schifferstein, and Paul Hekkert, eds. *Product Experience*. Oxford: Elsevier, 2008: 559–80.

—"The Future in Sensory/Consumer Research: Evolving to a Better Science." *Food Quality and Preference* 27, no. 2 (2013): 208–14.

Meiselman, Herbert L., Cees deGraaf, and Larry L. Lesher. "The Effects of Variety and Monotony on Food Acceptance and Intake at a Midday Meal." *Physiology & Behavior* 70, no. 1–2 (2000): 119–25.

Mitchell, Rachel L. C., and Louise H. Phillips. "The Psychological, Neurochemical and Functional Neuroanatomical Mediators of the Effects of Positive and Negative Mood on Executive Functions." *Neuropsychologia* 45, no. 4 (2007): 617–29.

NEMO Study Group. "Effect of a 12-mo Micronutrient Intervention on Learning and Memory in Well-nourished and Marginally Nourished School-aged Children: 2 Parallel, Randomized, Placebo-controlled Studies in Australia and Indonesia." *The American Journal of Clinical Nutrition* 86, no. 4 (2007): 1082–93.

Portwood, Madeleine M. "The Role of Dietary Fatty Acids in Children's Behaviour and Learning." *Nutrition and Health* 18, no.3 (2006): 233–47.

Rellecke Julian. *Automaticity in Emotional Face Processing*. PhD dissertation, Humboldt-University Berlin, 2012.

Rode, Elisabeth, Paul Rozin, and Paula Durlach "Experienced and Remembered Pleasure for Meals: Duration Neglect but Minimal Peak, End (Recency) or Primacy Effects." *Appetite* 49, no. 1 (2007): 18–29.

Rozin, Paul. "Towards a Psychology of Food and Rating: From Motivation to Module to Model to Marker, Morality, Meaning, and Metaphor." *Current Directions in Psychological Science* 5, no. 1 (1996): 18–24.

—"The Meaning of Food in our Lives: A Cross-cultural Perspective on Eating and Well-being." *Journal of Nutrition Education and Behavior* 37 (2005): S107–12.

Sanderson, Chris, and Martin Raymond, eds. *crEATe: Eating Design and Future Food*. Berlin: Gestalten Verlag, 2008.

Sobal, Jeffery, and Mary K. Nelson. "Commensal Eating Patterns: A Community Study." *Appetite* 41, no. 2 (2003): 181–90.

Sommer, Robert, and Jodie Steele. "Social Effects on Duration in Restaurants." *Appetite* 29, no. 1 (1997): 25–30.

Sommer, Werner, Birgit Stürmer, Olga Shmuilovich, Manuel Martin-Loeches, and Annekathrin Schacht. "How about lunch? Consequences of the Meal Context on Cognition and Emotion." *PLoS ONE* 8, no. 7 (2013). DOI: 10.1371/journal.pone.0070314.

Spence, Charles, Caroline Hobkinson, Alberto Gallace, and Betina Piqueras Fiszman. "A Touch of Gastronomy." *Flavour* 2, no. 14 (2013): DOI: 10.1371/journal.pone.0070314.

Steenbergen, Henk van, Guido P. H. Band, and Bernhard Hommel. "Reward Counteracts Conflict Adaptation: Evidence for a Role of Affect in Executive Control." *Psychological Science* 20, no. 12 (2009): 1473–7.

Steyer, Rolf, Peter Schwenkmezger, Peter Notz, and Michael Eid. *Der Mehrdimensionale Befindlichkeitsfragebogen (MDBF)*. Göttingen: Hogrefe, 1997.

Stürmer, Birgit, Roland Nigbur, Annekathrin Schacht, and Werner Sommer. "Reward and Punishment Effects on Error Processing and Conflict Control." *Frontiers in Psychology* 2 (2011): DOI: 10.3389/fpsyg.2011.00335.

Vogelzang, Marjie. *Eat Love*. Amsterdam: BIS Publishers, 2009.

Index

Page references in italics denote an illustration

Made in the USA
Las Vegas, NV
19 December 2020

14169763R00116